The Reinvention of Primitive Society

D1715815

The Invention of Primitive Society, Adam Kuper's decisive critique of ideas about the origins of society and religion that have been debated since Darwin, has been hugely influential in anthropology and post-colonial studies. This iconoclastic intellectual history showed that 'primitive society' was the imagined opposite to Western civilisation. By way of fascinating accounts of classic texts in anthropology, ancient history and law, the book revealed how wholly mistaken theories can become the basis for academic research and political programmes.

The publication of this expanded and radically revised new edition, now entitled *The Reinvention of Primitive Society*, coincides with a revival of the myth of primitive society by the 'indigenous peoples movement', which taps into a widespread popular belief about the noble savage, and reflects a romantic reaction against 'civilisation' and 'science'. In a new final chapter, Kuper challenges this most recent version of the myth of primitive society. Another new chapter traces conceptions of the barbarian, savage and primitive back through the centuries to ancient Greece. The remaining chapters have all been recast and updated to take new research into account.

The Reinvention of Primitive Society: Transformations of a Myth is essential reading for readers interested in anthropological theory and current post-colonial debates, and indeed for anyone who is curious about the ways in which we systematically misunderstand other peoples.

Adam Kuper is Professor of Anthropology at Brunel University UK, and a Fellow of the British Academy. He is the author of a number of books, including *The Chosen Primate: Human Nature and Cultural Diversity* (Harvard 1994), *Anthropologists and Anthropology: The Modern British School*, third edition (Routledge 1996) and *Culture: The Anthropologists' Account* (Harvard 1999). The founding president of the European Association of Social Anthropologists, he was for many years editor of *Current Anthropology*, and is co-editor of *The Social Science Encyclopedia*, third edition (Routledge 2003).

The cover illustration

A Polynesian from the island of Huahine, near Tahiti, Omai came to England in 1774 as a member of the crew of HMS *Adventure*, one of the ships that participated in Captain Cook's second Pacific voyage. He was presented to King George III, who made him an allowance and set him up in lodgings. He was feted in high society and painted by several leading artists, most famously in this portrait by Joshua Reynolds. A play based on his life was performed at the Theatre Royal in Convent Garden. He was returned home in 1776, in the course of Cook's third voyage, laden with gifts, including a suit of armour.

Omai's courtesy and elegance were widely admired. Dr Johnson told Boswell that when he dined with Omai and Lord Mulgrave one evening 'they sat with their backs to the light fronting me, so that I could not see distinctly; and there was so little of the savage in Omai, that I was afraid to speak to either, lest I should mistake one for the other'.

The Reinvention of Primitive Society

Transformations of a myth

Adam Kuper

Routledge
Taylor & Francis Group

LONDON AND NEW YORK

First edition published 1988 as
The Invention of Primitive Society: Transformations of an Illusion
Reprinted 1991, 1993, 1996, 1997

Second edition published 2005
by Routledge
2 Park Square, Milton Park, Abingdon, Oxon, OX14 4RN

Simultaneously published in the USA and Canada
by Routledge
270 Madison Ave, New York, NY 10016

Transferred to Digital Printing 2009

Routledge is an imprint of the Taylor & Francis Group, an informa business

© 2005 Adam Kuper

Typeset in Sabon by
HWA Text and Data Management Ltd, Tunbridge Wells
Printed and bound in Great Britain by
TJI Digital, Padstow, Cornwall

British Library Cataloguing in Publication Data
A catalogue record for this book is available from the
British Library

Library of Congress Cataloging in Publication Data
Kuper, Adam.
 The reinvention of primitive society : transformations of a myth /
  Adam Kuper. – 2nd ed.
  p. cm.
 Rev. ed. of: The invention of primitive society.
 Includes bibliographical references and index.
  1. Ethnology – History. 2. Primitive societies. I. Kuper, Adam.
  Invention of primitive society. II. Title.
GN308.K87 2005
305.8´009–dc22   2005001214

ISBN 10: 0-415-35760-8 (hbk)
ISBN 10: 0-415-35761-6 (pbk)

ISBN 13: 978-0-415-35760-9 (hbk)
ISBN 13: 978-0-415-35761-6 (pbk)

For Hannah, Jeremy and Simon

Contents

Figures and tables

Figures

Tables

Preface

This book is a history of the ways in which anthropologists have thought about primitive society. It is my second shot at telling the story, and I have had some second thoughts, though not about the enterprise itself. The study of primitive society was one of the projects that made anthropology into a science in the second half of the nineteenth century. It was a specialised pursuit within a much broader discourse, one that embraced studies of primitive mentality and speculations about the origin of language and religion. All these topics were in turn connected, inescapably, to the great Darwinian question of human origins. Nevertheless, the sociological thread, the writings on primitive society, can be separated out quite easily and treated as a subject in its own right.

A more difficult issue is where to begin the story. When I wrote *The Invention of Primitive Society*, I began in the 1860s and 1870s, with the first salvos of the Victorian debates. I now think that this was a mistake. There are profound continuities in western myth-making about faraway peoples and distant ancestors. The men who wrote about primitive society in the second half of the nineteenth century read Darwin, and might even have known him personally, but they were well aware that their debates could be traced back for two-and-a-half thousand years. I have therefore added a brief history of the words barbarian, savage and primitive in order to tease out some of the recurrent themes of this discourse.

The first time around, I made the further error of supposing that the idea of primitive society was on its last legs. 'My aim', I wrote in the final paragraph of *The Invention of Primitive Society*, 'has been to free us from some of our history. Anthropologists developed the theory of primitive society, but we may make amends if we render it obsolete at last, in all its protean forms.' This was a vain hope.

Primitive society has made a come-back. On the right, the moral of evolutionary history turns out to be indistinguishable from the doctrine of original sin. The old Adam is still with us. In one of the most potent modern myths, William Golding's *The Lord of the Flies*, shipwrecked English schoolboys revert to savagery and reinvent chieftaincy, hunting, ritual dances and sacrifice. On the left, meanwhile, primitive society has become a political ideal, at least for many Greens and anti-globalisation activists. For the indigenous peoples movement, the world of hunter-gatherers is a lost Eden. (One of its theorists, Hugh Brody, called his recent book *The Other Side of Eden*.) Obviously the revival of the idea of primitive society by a powerful social movement is part of the story I have tried to tell, and I have added a new chapter to discuss it.[1]

Once I was adding new material I took the opportunity to edit the rest of the book, in order to take recent scholarship into account, to clarify the argument, and to make it more readable. I had also undertaken a book on Darwinian anthropology in the interim, which had made me think again about Darwin's influence on the Victorian anthropologists.[2] The process of revision quickly got out of hand, and all the original chapters have been radically rewritten and recast. The title of the book has been changed to reflect these changes, and the subtitle has been altered as well, because I now feel that the idea of primitive society is best described as a myth. The end-product is in many ways a new book. I hope that it will be given a second chance. After all, the theory of primitive society comes back time and again.

Adam Kuper
London, December, 2004

Part I

The idea of primitive society

The lofty contempt which a civilised people entertains for barbarous neighbours has caused a remarkable negligence in observing them, and this carelessness has been aggravated at times by fear, by religious prejudice, and even by the use of these very terms – civilisation and barbarism – which convey to most persons the impression of a difference not merely in degree but in kind.

(Henry Sumner Maine, *Ancient Society* (1861), pp. 116–17)

Chapter 1

The myth of primitive society

Primitive society was initially regarded as a subject for lawyers. The founding father of British anthropology, E. B. Tylor, commented in 1865 that the investigation of questions such as the form of primitive marriage 'belongs properly to that interesting, but difficult and almost unworked subject, the Comparative Jurisprudence of the lower races, and no one not versed in Civil Law could do it justice'.[1] The pioneering studies were written by lawyers – Henry Maine, Johannes Bachofen, J. F. McLennan, Lewis Henry Morgan. The issues that they investigated – the development of marriage and the family, of private property and the state – were conceived of in legal terms. Their initial source, their common case-study, was provided by Roman law.

If one book is to be placed at the head of the Victorian studies of primitive society, it is perhaps Henry Maine's *Ancient Law*, published in 1861, two years after *The Origin of Species*. Most of Maine's specific ideas were soon discarded, but he restated a classic notion of the original human condition, and he made it seem directly relevant to the concerns of his contemporaries. He assumed that the first human beings were members of a corporate family group ruled by a despotic father. Gradually, the more powerful patriarchs attracted waifs and strays to join them. Local association became increasingly important. Ultimately, societies based on kinship were replaced by societies based upon territory. This transition from blood to soil, from status to contract, was the greatest revolution in human history.

In the very year in which *Ancient Law* was published, a Swiss professor of Roman Law, Johannes Bachofen, reread the Greek myths as sociological documents and came to the startling conclusion that the original family structure was not patriarchal but matriarchal. In 1865 a Scottish lawyer, J. F. McLennan, reacting to Maine's theories, reached a similar conclusion to Bachofen, but apparently in ignorance of his work. The publication of McLennan's *Primitive Marriage* in turn inspired an American lawyer, Lewis Henry Morgan, to develop the most influential of these new images of early social institutions. His best-known book, *Ancient Society*, appeared 16 years after *Ancient Law*. It echoed Maine's title and belonged to the same universe of discourse.

These were not conventional legal texts, but the law itself was not, in those days, a narrow field. It included the history of law, and readily made room for speculative histories of the origins of law in primitive society. Great philosophical questions were up for debate, debates that could draw on the latest theories about history and about human nature. The massive presence of Darwin brooded over all discussions of human development in Victorian England, but the lawyers were generally more at home with the ideas of Herbert Spencer and of the Utilitarians. Macaulay, Stubbs, Freeman and Froude confronted them with new theories about the ancient origins of the British constitution.[2] They were also responsive to the findings of German philology, mediated in Britain by Max Müller. And they exchanged ideas about human origins and human evolution in the new 'Anthropological' societies. The Société d'Anthropologie de Paris was established in 1859, and similar initiatives followed in London in 1863 and in Berlin in 1869 (each, of course, with its own journal).

As anthropology began to be professionalised in the late nineteenth century, E. B. Tylor and James George Frazer established themselves as the leading authorities in the subject in Britain. Together they adjudicated the disputes between Maine, McLennan and Morgan, and settled the broad characteristics of primeval human societies. Primitive society was originally an organic whole. It then split into two or more identical building blocks. (This idea went back to Spencer.) The component units of society were exogamous, corporate descent groups, generally termed clans or gentes, which held goods and women in common. By the 1880s it was generally agreed (despite Maine's continued dissent) that these groups were originally 'matriarchal', tracing descent in the female line only. Marriage took the form of regular exchanges of women between men of different descent groups. These social forms, no longer extant, were preserved in the languages (especially in kinship terminologies), and in the ceremonies of contemporary 'primitive' peoples.

It is striking how much agreement there soon was even on matters of detail. By the last decade of the nineteenth century, almost all the new specialists would have agreed with the following propositions:

1 The most primitive societies were based on blood relationships.
2 The basic units of society were 'clans' or 'gentes' – that is to say, descent groups which were formed by the descendants of a man, in the male line, or of a woman, in the female line.
3 Property was owned in common, and the women were held collectively by the men of the clan.
4 Marriages were prohibited between men and women belonging to the same clan. (There was, however, much debate as to whether or not there had been an even earlier period of 'primitive promiscuity'.)
5 Each clan was thought to be descended from an animal or vegetable god, which it revered. This was 'totemism'.
6 'Survivals' of these institutions could be identified in the ceremonies or in forms of language of contemporary primitive societies.
7 Finally, after a great revolution, perhaps the greatest in human history, the descent groups withered away, private property rights were established, the modern family was born, and a territorial state emerged.

The rapidity with which the anthropologists worked out the idea of primitive society is very striking. However, its persistence is perhaps yet more extraordinary. Conventional histories of anthropology run through a succession of quasi-philosophical theories, but all these theories addressed the same idea of primitive society. This prototype persisted for well over a hundred years, despite the fact that the systematic empirical investigation of surviving 'primitive' societies began to be undertaken on any scale only in the last decade of the nineteenth century.

None of this would be particularly remarkable if the notion of primitive society was substantially accurate. But it is not. The whole conception is fundamentally unsound. There is not even a sensible way in which one can specify what a 'primitive society' is. The term implies some historical point of reference. It presumably defines a type of society ancestral to more advanced forms, on the analogy of an evolutionary history of natural species. However, human societies cannot be traced back to a single point of origin. Nor is there any way of reconstituting prehistoric social forms, classifying them, and aligning them in a time series. There are no fossils of social organisation.

The Upper Palaeolithic baseline

Fully modern human beings evolved in Africa some 150,000 years ago. The first migrants came to the Middle East over 40,000 years ago and entered Europe about 35,000 years ago. Here they gradually displaced the Neanderthal population, which represented an earlier human variety, also ultimately of African origin.

These fully modern humans are associated with a great cultural revolution. Its first traces have been found in the Middle East. Around 30,000 years ago it reached Europe. In archaeological terms, the revolution marked the transition from the long Palaeolithic age to the Upper Palaeolithic. It was not a rapid revolution, and some arch-aeologists suggest that it gained momentum in Europe only some 25–20,000 years ago. In Africa the parallel shift from Middle Stone Age to Upper Stone Age societies occurred only some 20,000 years ago. Nevertheless, however slowly, very great changes took place in the human way of life. Richard Klein judges that the transition to the Upper Palaeolithic 'signals the most fundamental change in human behaviour that the archaeological record may ever reveal' since the first invention of stone tools 1.5 million years ago.[3] Lewis Binford emphasises particularly 'the elaboration of burial; art; personal ornaments; new materials, such as bone, antler, and soft stone; long distance movement and/or circulation of goods; and increased variation in site size, duration, and content'. This outpour-ing of innovations led Binford to conclude that a more profound revolution had taken place. Language had developed, language in the modern sense, a flexible and creative medium, and it was language that created the conditions for 'the appearance of culture'.[4]

Such fundamental changes must have had repercussions for the way in which communities were organised. It is, however, very difficult to say what Upper Palaeolithic societies were like. Clearly they were small-scale. Their economy was based on hunting and gathering. There was probably little social stratification. Fire was controlled and used for cooking, and there are signs of what may be domestic hearths, but no firm conclusions can be drawn about whether there were households, and if so who lived in them, or whether men and women had different tasks. People buried their dead, perhaps an indication of religious feelings. Some scholars speculate that cave art reflects beliefs in a spirit world. However, little else can be safely said about the cosmological ideas current during the Upper Palaeolithic. In any case, it cannot be assumed that all Upper Palaeolithic societies were alike. On the contrary, there were probably local variations in beliefs and in customs. After all, there were significant technological differences between neighbouring settlements, which led to the exchange of goods, sometimes over large distances.

In short, the archaeological evidence can tell us little about the nature of Upper Palaeolithic societies, or even about the extent to which they conformed to a common pattern. It is only with the development of writing, some 7,000 years ago, that a sociologically informed prehistory becomes possible. There is, however, an alternative strategy for the reconstruction of the remote past. Darwin himself compared variations between living species in order to make deductions about their common ancestors. Anthropologists have always been tempted, more simple-mindedly, to treat living populations as stand-ins for Stone Age societies. For the Victorian anthropologists, the people closest to the Stone Age were either American hunter-gatherers or the Australian Aborigines, but the most famous 'Stone Age' surrogates in modern anthropology are the !Kung Bushmen of the Kalahari desert. They owe their prominence to studies carried out in the 1960s and 1970s by Richard Lee and his associates. Their explicit goal was to find living equivalents to the first foraging peoples in the plains of Eastern Africa. But they dreamt that they were discovering the natural state of humanity. 'We cannot avoid the suspicion that many of us were led to live and work among hunters because of a feeling that the human condition was likely to be more clear drawn here than among other kinds of societies.'[5]

The !Kung researchers were participating in a new movement in American anthropology that paid particular attention to the ways in which small populations of hunter-gatherers adapted to natural environments. The !Kung had no tools beyond digging-sticks, ostrich eggshell water containers, skin clothes and bags, and simple bows and arrows, and they had to make a living in a semi-desert.[6] Nevertheless, they sustained themselves with surprisingly little labour. Adults worked on average the equivalent of two and a half days a week, and yet their diet was more than adequate by most established nutritional standards. This contradicted the old view that hunter-gatherers lived a marginal existence. Marshall Sahlins hailed the !Kung as the original affluent society,[7] which may verge on hyperbole, but it seemed reasonable to suppose that ancient hunter-gatherers, who lived in more clement environments, must have enjoyed an even greater prosperity than the !Kung.

The economy of the !Kung rested on a division of labour. Both men and women gathered plant food, although women spent more time on this activity than did the men. However, only the men hunted. Hunting was in some ways a paradoxical activity: risky, time-consuming, costly in terms of energy expended. It was also less reliable than gathering, and vegetable foods provided the bulk of the !Kung diet. For much of the year, only some 20 per cent of the food intake was supplied by the hunters. But meat was prized, and in peak seasons the hunt provided up to 90 per cent of the food for the camp, and over the year a !Kung would get between 30 and 40 per cent of his or her calories from meat.

Some theorists now argued that the development of hunting played a crucial role in human evolution. African apes seldom engage in any but the most casual, opportunistic hunting. In the case of humans, successful hunting requires technical sophistication, planning, and co-operation. It also seems to depend in practice on a division of labour. Men do the hunting. Women gather food close to the home base, where they can keep an eye on the children. A male–female pair would therefore be best placed to feed themselves and a woman's children, and this would favour the evolution of the family.[8]

The !Kung were soon being used as a template for the inter-pretation of archaeological materials on Upper Palaeolithic societies. However, Edwin Wilmsen, who had himself undertaken a long-term field study of the !Kung, launched what came to be called a revisionist thesis.[9] His central criticism was that the evolutionists tore the !Kung from their real historical context. Kalahari foragers had lived in intimate contact with pastoral groups for perhaps a thousand years. For two centuries they had formed part of a complex Southern African society that included Europeans and Bantu-speaking farmers. They could not be taken to represent (in a phrase of Lee's that Wilmsen threw back at him) 'foragers in a world of foragers'. The !Kung were an underclass in a modern state.

Ethnographers of other Bushmen groups in the Kalahari suggested a different line of criticism. They described the variety of adaptations that Bushmen had made to local ecological conditions, and drew attention to differences of language, religious belief, settlement patterns and kinship arrangements. This argument could be generalised. If the !Kung were not typical of all Bushmen, there was even less reason to suppose that they could serve as the ideal type of all hunter-gatherers, throughout history. The Hadza of Tanzania, the pygmies of the Ituri forest in the Congo, various Inuit groups,

Malayan Aborigines, Amazonian hunter-gatherers were equally plausible exemplars, not to mention the Victorian favourites, the Australian Aborigines. In 1972, Marshall Sahlins lumped them all together in his *Stone Age Economics*, on the grounds that they all practised the 'household mode of production', a modest domestic economy in which everyone was content to rub along with just enough to live on. Julian Steward and Elman Service suggested that all these people lived in patrilineal bands, but there was abundant evidence that the local organisation and kinship systems of hunter-gatherers were not uniform. Nor did they have any unique social institutions. Alan Barnard showed, for instance, that the kinship system of some Kalahari Bushmen peoples had more in common with that of the neighbouring pastoralist Khoi or Hottentots than they did with the kinship systems of other Kalahari Bushmen.[10]

In any case, the revisionist critique remained relevant, whichever society of contemporary foragers was chosen to stand in for a Stone Age population. There were no pristine hunter-gatherers, miraculously surviving with their Upper Palaeolithic institutions intact, available for study by even the most adventurous field workers. All hunter-gatherers had been living for generations, sometimes for many centuries, cheek by jowl with neighbours who practised pastoralism or agriculture. They were all disadvantaged citizens, or subjects, of modern states. Their ways of life were adapted to this situation.

It follows that even if one could define what is meant by primitive society, it could not be studied empirically. We do know that Upper Palaeolithic societies were small-scale populations of hunters and gatherers, but there is no way in which the archaeological evidence can establish whether they were organised into family groups, or practised monogamy or polygamy, or worshipped totems, or divided their work between men and women, or had chiefs (let alone whether the office was transmitted by inheritance). The ethnographies of living hunters and gatherers record a variety of social institutions and religious beliefs, but some plausible generalisations might be ventured. Marriage and the family are universal; exchange relationship are highly valued; only men hunt; there are no powerful leaders; there is little social differentiation except for that between men and women. However, there are substantial differences between these societies, and even their common features may not have been shared by Upper Palaeolithic peoples. After all, thousands of years of history have intervened, a history that has treated modern hunter-gatherers harshly, driving them into inhospitable refuges, obliging them to adapt to disruptive neighbours. When they were studied in the nineteenth and twentieth centuries their lives had been decisively changed by encounters with farmers, pastoralists, traders and missionaries.

The term primitive might be used to represent the starting point of a common history through which all populations pass, at different speeds. A collective and progressive history of humanity is plausible if it is restricted to technological development, and to the secular growth of the human population as a whole. As recently as ten thousand years ago, the total human population was perhaps eight million. Today there are over six billion people on the planet. Whatever else, that is a classical measure of evolutionary success. However, these observations cannot be translated into a history of transient societies with uncertain boundaries, or expanded to encompass the history of social institutions, since the archaeological record yields little sociological information.

The persistence of an illusion

Not to put too fine a point upon it, the history of the theory of primitive society is the history of an illusion. It is our phlogiston, our aether. The persistence of the model is peculiarly problematic since its basic assumptions were directly contradicted by ethnographic evidence and by the logic of evolutionary theory itself. The difficulties were clearly stated by leading scholars in the late nineteenth and early twentieth century (notably Maine, Westermarck, Boas and Malinowski). Notwithstanding, anthropologists have busied themselves for over a hundred years with the manipulation of a myth that was constructed by speculative lawyers in the late nineteenth century.

A common way of accounting for the persistence of a myth is to suppose that it has political functions. Certainly the idea of primitive society could and did feed a variety of ideological positions. Among its most celebrated protagonists were Engels, Freud, Durkheim and Kropotkin, men with very different political programmes. British and American commentators on primitive society were also reacting to a variety of political events. The Morant Bay rebellion in Jamaica and the Civil War in the United States revived earlier debates on slavery. Arguments about slavery in turn raised the great question whether human beings all had a common origin, or whether the races were separate species, with different ancestors. These issues divided Victorian anthropologists, and they formed two warring associations, the Ethnological Society of London and the Anthropological Society of London.[11] The development of the Indian Empire and the colonisation of Africa raised further fundamental questions, about the nature of government, and of civilisation itself, which were heatedly debated in anthropological circles. In Germany, speculations about national culture and the *Volksgeist* fed the common belief that societies were based either on blood or on soil, but these romantic ideas were contested by liberal anthropologists in Berlin. In short, while the idea of primitive society was relevant to a number of great political issues, it was not necessarily associated with any one political position. Moreover, as intellectuals began to come to terms with the challenge of Lyell and Darwin to the authorised Biblical account of history, a number of the anthropologists decided that religious questions were even more urgent.

In the end, however, it may be that something yet more fundamental than political and religious concerns made primitive societies seem so good to think about. Europeans in the second half of the nineteenth century believed that they were witnessing a revolutionary transition. Marx defined a capitalist society emerging from a feudal society; Weber was to write about the rationalisation, the bureaucratisation, the disenchantment of the old world; Tönnies about the move from community to association; Durkheim about the change from mechanical to organic forms of solidarity. Each conceived of the new world in contrast to 'traditional society', but behind this 'traditional society' they discerned a primitive or primeval society, which was the true antithesis of modernity. Modern society was defined above all by the territorial state, the monogamous family, and private property. Primitive society must therefore have been nomadic, ordered by blood ties, sexually promiscuous and communist. There had also been a progression in mentality. Primitive man was illogical and superstitious. Traditional societies were in thrall to religion. Modernity, however, was the age of science.

But if primitive society was good to think about, it produced a mythology rather than a science. This does not mean that there were no developments in the theory, but then mythologies are also not static. 'A myth no sooner comes into being than it is modified through a change of narrator', according to Claude Lévi-Strauss. 'Some elements drop out and are replaced by others, sequences change places, and the modified structure moves through a series of states, the variations of which nevertheless still belong to the same set.'

These transformations do not simply result in minor changes, differences that can be reduced to 'small positive or negative increments'. Rather the transformations are accomplished by systematic manipulations of the myth as a whole, and they yield 'clear-cut relationships such as contrariness, contradiction, inversion or symmetry'.[12]

There was nothing particularly primitive about this kind of thinking. 'The kind of logic in mythic thought is as rigorous as that of modern science', Lévi-Strauss insists, 'and the difference lies, not in the quality of the intellectual process, but in the nature of things to which it is applied.'[13] In *La Pensée Sauvage* he developed the theme that the 'savage' (or wild, undomesticated) imagination worked in ways that were comparable to sophisticated scientific thinking, and to the processes that produce great art. To the extent that he is correct, scientific theories may have a great deal in common with Amazonian myths, scientists may often think rather like artists, and perhaps we all think, at least at times, like Amazonian Indians.

And yet there is surely one great difference between the established ideal of scientific thought and what Lévi-Strauss calls 'the logic of the concrete'. Scientific theories should be progressive. Understanding should advance. One does not go backwards in science. But if an argument proceeds – to put it crudely – by turning a previous argument on its head, then at some stage someone will effect a further transformation by setting it back in its former position. A series of structural transformations is likely to end up where it began. And it does seem that successive models of primitive society represent straightforward, even mechanical, transformations of their predecessors. Indeed, this book is very largely an account of the transformations of an illusion within an increasingly hermetic discourse.

Enter Darwin

To reject the reality of primitive society is often taken for a denial of Darwinism. Nothing could be further from the truth. Darwinian theory directs attention to variation, to adaptation to local conditions, and so to diversification. One of the few things that can safely be said about early human societies is that they must have represented a variety of adaptations. Since ecological variations constrain social organisation, especially where technology is simple, there would have been considerable differences in social structure. Purely on theoretical grounds, a Darwinian should be reluctant to believe that the first societies all had the same form, let alone that they were driven by some inner dynamic to generate a common series of transformations. This was obvious to some of the Victorian anthropologists. It was on these grounds that Henry Maine, no Darwinian, rejected the idea that all societies had passed through the same stages.

> So far as I am aware, there is nothing in the recorded history of society to justify the belief that, during the vast chapter of its growth which is wholly unwritten, the same transformations of social constitution succeeded one another everywhere, uniformly if not simultaneously. A strong force lying deep in human nature, and never at rest, might no doubt in the long run produce an uniform result, in spite of the vast varieties accompanying the stern struggle for existence; but it is in the highest degree incredible that the action of this force would be uniform from beginning to end.[14]

The origin of man

'Origin of man now proved. – Metaphysic must flourish. – He who understands baboon would do more towards metaphysic than Locke.'[15] Darwin entered this famous syllogism in his 'Notebook on Man', which he opened in 1838. Its central theme was that all mental activities can be reduced to neural processes. Even love of the deity was a function of the organisation of the brain – 'oh, you Materialist!'[16] Huxley had demonstrated that the brains of humans were structurally similar to those of other primates, though they were larger and presumably more complex. 'As the various mental faculties gradually developed the brain would almost certainly become larger', Darwin concluded. 'No one, I presume, doubts that the large proportion which the size of man's brain bears to his body, compared to the same proportion in the gorilla or orang, is closely connected with his higher mental powers.'[17]

The specialisation of the brain was a consequence of natural selection. Savages lived in the same sort of conditions as other animals. Survival was extremely chancy. 'Savages are known to suffer severely from recurrent famines; they do not increase their food by artificial means; they rarely refrain from marriage, and generally marry whilst young. Consequently they must be subjected to occasional hard struggles for existence, and the favoured individuals will alone survive.'[18] These favoured individuals would also outbreed the rest. 'We can see, that in the rudest state of society, the individuals who were the most sagacious, who invented and used the best weapons or traps, and who were best able to defend themselves, would rear the greatest number of offspring. The tribes, which included the largest number of men thus endowed, would increase in number and supplant other tribes.'[19]

The development of the brain would also foster moral and social qualities (which Darwin reckoned to be of greater importance than mere cleverness). A moral sense was to be found among other animals, but its high development among human beings was the result of natural selection 'aided by inherited habit'.[20] Intelligence and moral principles developed together. And as societies advanced, they became increasingly adept at inculcating moral values. 'The more efficient causes of progress seem to consist of a good education during youth whilst the brain is impressible, and of a high standard of excellence, inculcated by the ablest and best men, embodied in the laws, customs and traditions of the nation, and enforced by public opinion.'[21] 'Thus the social and moral qualities would tend slowly to advance and be diffused throughout the world.'[22]

There was a paradox here. The 'moral qualities' developed and spread through natural selection. Yet although they paid off for the community, this was at some cost to the individual.

> It must not be forgotten that although a high standard of morality gives but a slight or no advantage to each individual man and his children over the other men of the same tribe, yet that an increase in the number of well-endowed men and an advancement in the standard of morality will certainly give an immense advantage to one tribe over another. A tribe including many members who, from possessing in a high degree the spirit of patriotism, fidelity, obedience, courage, and sympathy, were always ready to aid one another, and to sacrifice themselves for the common good, would be victorious over most other tribes: and this would be natural selection.[23]

But is it natural selection? It looks more like what is now dismissively described as 'group selection'. Darwin's doctrine was that natural selection worked on individuals. However, he thought that human beings had become a domesticated species, and in domesticated species the breeder imposes his own demands, selecting for qualities that might not work very well in nature. Darwin noted with concern that the gains of natural selection were being recklessly dissipated in the most advanced modern societies. Wealth and power were inherited, even if the heirs were unfit. People shielded their weaker relatives and even encouraged them to breed. Nor were the fittest individuals necessarily rewarded with the most offspring. Darwin complained that men now chose their wives on frivolous grounds, and that ambitious and successful men tended to postpone marriage and to have few children, while the poor bred like rabbits.

Darwin concluded that as technology advanced so natural selection became less decisive. On this point, he cited the views of Alfred Russel Wallace, co-author of the theory of natural selection:

> Mr Wallace ... argues that man, after he had partially acquired those intellectual and moral faculties which distinguish him from the lower animals, would have been but little liable to bodily modifications through natural selection or any other means ... He invents weapons, tools, and various stratagems to procure food and to defend himself. When he migrates into a colder climate he uses clothes, builds sheds, and makes fires; and by the aid of fire cooks food otherwise indigestible. He aids his fellow-men in many ways, and anticipates future events. Even at a remote time period he practised some division of labour.[24]

'Evolutionism' or Darwinisim?

In the two decades that followed the publication of *The Origin of Species* in 1859, a series of monographs appeared that dealt in a fresh and urgent manner with primitive society, the evolution of marriage and the family, and the rise of science at the expense of magic and religion. The authors of these books (who included, most notably, Maine, Tylor, Lubbock, McLennan and Morgan) developed a coherent new discourse. Referring to each other's work, and despite differences on many issues that seemed to them to be of critical importance, they generally agreed (although Maine had his doubts) that a direct progression could be established from primitive society through various intermediate stages to modern society.

When anthropology became established in universities in the twentieth century, and histories of the discipline began to be written, these pioneer anthropologists were conventionally grouped together as 'evolutionists'. However, J. W. Burrow has protested against the ritual invocation of Darwin's name to explain the nature of Victorian anthropology. By profession, the pioneer anthropologists were lawyers, classicists and theologians. They were more susceptible to the influence of historians and philosophers than to the findings of natural scientists, and were more impressed by the lessons of comparative philology than by Darwinian biology. 'Darwin was undoubtedly important', Burrow concluded, 'but it is a type of importance impossible to estimate at all precisely. He was certainly not the father of evolutionary anthropology, but possibly he was its wealthy uncle.'[25]

To be sure, a wealthy uncle is not to be despised. However, Darwinian theory offered a number of distinct leads, and it was possible to pick and choose among them. The thesis that human beings had evolved from African apes profoundly disturbed many contemporaries. 'My dear old friend', the aristocratic Captain Robert FitzRoy, formerly of HMS *Beagle*, wrote to his one-time travelling companion, Charles Darwin, 'I, at least, cannot find anything "ennobling" in the thought of being a descendant of even the *most* ancient Ape.'[26] Fitzroy was sufficiently concerned to turn up at the famous debate on Darwin's *Origin of Species* that was held in Oxford in June 1860. Bishop Wilberforce demanded to know whether Huxley was descended from an ape on his grandmother's side of the family, or on his grandfather's. 'The Lord has delivered him into my hands', Huxley whispered to his neighbour, and he replied: 'If I would rather have a miserable ape for a grandfather or a man highly endowed by nature and possessed of great means and influence, and yet who employs these faculties for the mere purpose of introducing ridicule into a grave scientific discussion – I unhesitatingly affirm my preference for the ape.' There was a commotion in the room, during which Fitzroy stood up, waved a copy of the bible, implored the audience to believe the holy word of God, and expressed his sorrow that he had given Darwin the opportunity to collect facts in support of such a shocking theory.[27] Darwin was luckily too ill to attend the Oxford meeting. (Tummy trouble.) However, he was hardly sanguine about the reception of his ideas. He hesitated for a decade before he nailed his colours to the mast. Nevertheless, by the time that he published *The Descent of Man* in 1871 the doctrine of common descent had been generally accepted by British biologists and anthropologists.

Yet even the most sympathetically inclined of the anthropologists treated the rest of Darwinian theory as an *a la carte* menu. After all, the principle of natural selection was disputed by biologists who were close to Darwin. Even the faithful Huxley was a sceptic. The anthropologists generally ignored the issue, although they liked to quote Spencer's motto about the 'struggle for survival'. 'Neither Maine, nor Tylor, nor McLennan made much use of the theory of natural selection', Burrow writes, 'and Spencer used it only as a garnish for a theory he had already developed'.[28]

The father-figure of British anthropology, E. B. Tylor, was an orthodox enough Darwinian 'whenever he has to pronounce on the physical problems relating to human descent', his biographer observed, but otherwise his Darwinism did not run deep. 'Though he occasionally used ... the rather high-sounding phrase "evolution" which Darwin had taken over from Herbert Spencer, perhaps without paying much heed to its philosophical implications, Tylor decidedly prefers to speak simply of the "development" of culture.'[29] The most widely read of the Victorian anthropologists, James George Frazer, showed no interest in Darwinian theory.[30] The Oxford anthropologist R. R. Marett conceded, in his textbook *Anthropology*, published in 1911, that 'Anthropology is the child of Darwin', but like Tylor he emphasised the theory of common descent and had next to nothing to say about natural selection. 'What is the truth that Darwinism supposes? Simply that all the forms of life in the world are related together; and that the relations manifested in time and space between the different lives are sufficiently uniform to be described under a general formula, or law of evolution.'[31] His Cambridge counterpart, Alfred Haddon, who began his career as a biologist, made just two brief references to Darwin in his *History of Anthropology*, published in 1934. He concluded, like Marett, that Darwin's main contribution was to establish the natural origin of the human species.

Moreover, Darwinism lost ground among the biologists in the last decade of the nineteenth century, even in England. Julian Huxley has called this the 'eclipse of Darwinism', and it lasted until the evolutionary synthesis of the 1930s and 1940s united Darwinian theory and Mendelian genetics.[32] A theory that had been launched in 1800 by a French biologist, Jean-Baptiste de Lamarck, now came back into vogue. According to Lamarck, all species had an innate will to progress, and as they progressed they became increasingly complex and efficient. Not only did whole species change and improve, but each individual might acquire new and better characteristics in its own lifetime, which it bequeathed to its descendants. This notion that traits acquired in one generation could be passed on to the next was shared by most biologists even in the late nineteenth and early twentieth centuries, including, sometimes at least, Darwin himself. Lamarck also believed that evolutionary changes were in truth revolutionary. Advances took the form of great leaps.

Lamarckism had its ups and downs. The great French biologist Cuvier had denounced Lamarckism soon after the death of its author (using the occasion of the formal eulogy, which he had to give in his role as perpetual secretary of the French Academy of Sciences). However, many leading biologists in France would describe themselves as Lamarckians until the end of the nineteenth century, and in Germany Ernst Haeckel was as much a Lamarckian as a Darwinian. A neo-Lamarckian movement flourished in the United States through the 1880s, where it acquired a strong theological bias. In Britain, Darwin's mentor, Charles Lyell, had published a thorough critique of Lamarck, and Darwin himself regarded the theory with scorn. 'Heaven forfend me', he once wrote piously, 'from Lamarck's nonsense of "tendency to progression", "adaptations from the slow willing of animals", etc.'[33] But Lyell's treatment was so fair that he converted the social philosopher Herbert Spencer to Lamarckism, and Spencer was in turn to influence a number of social thinkers, including several of the Victorian anthropologists.

Burrow is surely correct: the direct influence of Darwinian theory on the thinking of the first two generations of anthropologists was diffuse and often superficial. For Tylor, Morgan, Frazer and Marett, Darwin provided the assurance that the history of human beings was one, even if racial differentiation might be accorded greater or lesser importance. He also provided a biological explanation for the gradual progress of rationality – as human beings developed, their brains had become larger. But he did not upset the ideas about cultural progress that the Victorians inherited from the philosophers of the eighteenth century.[34] On the contrary, Darwin was confident that civilisation had progressed, and morality with it. We should look back and rejoice:

> there can hardly be a doubt that the inhabitants of ... nearly the whole civilised world, were once in a barbarous condition. To believe that man was aboriginally civilised and then suffered utter degradation in so many regions, is to take a pitiably low view of human nature. It is apparently a truer and more cheerful

view that progress has been much more general than retro-gression; that man has risen, though by slow and interrupted steps, from a lowly condition to the highest standard as yet attained by him in knowledge, morals, and religion.[35]

Chapter 2

Barbarian, savage, primitive

The myth of the anthropologists is itself a transformation of older philosophical myths. The discourse was given a fresh impetus in the 1860s and 1870s, but it continued a much longer conversation, an ancient debate from whose underlying presuppositions even Darwin did not altogether escape. These premises are incapsulated in three still potent English words that have been used to describe people beyond the pale of civilisation: barbarian, savage, and primitive.

Thucydides remarked in his *History of the Peloponnesian War* that Homer did not call his heroes Greeks. 'He does not even use the term barbarian,' he added, 'probably because the Hellenes had not yet been marked off from the rest of the world by one distinctive appellation.'[1] A sense of Greek unity was forged only when isolated city states drew together to face the threat posed by Persia under Darius and his son Xerxes in the early years of the fifth century BCE. The Greeks then adopted the description 'barbarian' for their common enemy. They pretended that *barbaroi* stammered like idiots, or babbled like babies, or grunted like animals – *bar bar*. Hence the name. Politer and more rarefied terms for foreigners, *heterophone*, 'other speech', and *allogloss*, 'other tongue', insisted equally on the primacy of Greek. The initial mark of the barbarian was a deficiency of language.

A twin birth, the new ideas of Greeks and barbarians were inextricably linked. 'Greek writing about barbarians is usually an exercise in self-definition,' Edith Hall writes in her study, *Inventing the Barbarian*, 'for the barbarian is often portrayed as the opposite of the ideal Greek'.[2] Athenians were the ideal Greeks, of course, and Persians the prototypical barbarians. Yet both polar types were easily generalised, differences obliterated. A traveller complained in Plato's *Statesman* that just because the Greeks defined Hellenes as one species, they lumped all other nations together as barbarians, regardless of differences in language. 'Because they have one name they are supposed to be of one species also.'

Yet once it was admitted that there were different types of barbarian, the variants might be invoked in order to represent the Greeks more subtly, by way of a more complex play of oppositions. The master of this strategy was Herodotus, a slightly older contemporary of Thucydides, and the author of the other great account of the Persian wars. Herodotus was half-barbarian himself, his mother a Carian from western Asia Minor. Plutarch would look back on him in *c*. AD 100 as *philobarbus*, barbarian lover,[3] and he provided generally sympathetic accounts of a number of barbarian peoples, to whom he attributed a range of customs. However, François Hartog demonstrates that Herodotus worked with two basic contrasts: Greek vs. Persian, and Scythian vs. Egyptian.[4] The oldest people, the soft Egyptians, lived in the hottest land to the south. The youngest people, the hard Scythians, lived in the frozen north, on the margins of the inhabited world. The Egyptians had their ancient wisdom, while the Scythians were ignorant. Even their seasons are inverted: when it is summer in the Egyptian south it is winter in the Scythian north, and vice versa.

The Scythians and Egyptians also each stood in a different relationship to the main adversaries of the Greeks, the archetypal barbarians, the Persians. The Egyptians submitted to Darius, the Persian king. The Scythians, like the Greeks, had defeated the Persian army. So Greeks and Scythians were united as freedom fighters against the Persians. However, the Scythians and the Egyptians were contrasted in turn with the Greeks. The Scythians were nomads, who carried their houses with them, while the Greeks insisted that they were autochthonous, natives of their homeland, and urban dwellers. The Egyptians lived in a different climate, on the banks of a unique river, and 'so they have made all their customs and laws of a kind which is for the most part the converse of those of all other men'.[5]

Above all, there was a political divide between the Greeks and the barbarians. The Greeks, or at least the Athenians, lived in the ideal state, the democratic *polis*. All Greece resisted tyranny. Barbarians were not democratic. They were either a leaderless rabble or the slaves of tyrannical rulers. The Scythians were homeless anarchists, without leaders. In contrast to the Scythians, the Egyptians were urban and sophisticated. However, they were ruled by an absolute king. The archetypal barbarians, the Persians, were the very model of royal tyranny. 'There is a link between barbarianism and royalty', Hartog concludes, 'among barbarians, the normal mode for the exercise of power tends to be royalty. And reciprocally, royalty is likely to have something barbarian about it.'[6]

This association of barbarians with tyranny proved to be an enduring characterisation of the anti-Greek. 'For barbarians, being more servile in character than Hellenes ... do not rebel against a despotic government', Aristotle wrote, a century after Herodotus and Thucydides. Indeed, 'among barbarians no distinction is made between women and slaves, because there is no natural ruler among them: they are a community of slaves, male and female. Wherefore the poets say, "It is meet that Hellenes should rule over barbarians;" as if they thought that the barbarian and the slave were by nature one.' Barbarian kingdoms were tyrannies 'because the people are by nature slaves.'[7] There were slaves in Athens, but they were always foreigners, and so could be classed as barbarians: and according to the logic of Aristotle, as barbarians it was their nature to be slaves.

Not only was the barbarian incapable of independence and devoid of civic values. He lacked the emotional self-control of a mature Greek man. Barbarians represented on the Athenian stage gabbled in strange languages, dressed in skins, ate raw meat, carried bows but not the spears that brave men used for close fighting, and were servile and emotional. Warriors behaved more like women than like self-reliant and restrained Greek men. In the *Persians* of Aeschylus, Xerxes appears as an effeminate tyrant.[8]

Dramatists might play with the image of the barbarian, and confront audiences with the paradoxical figures of the noble barbarian, and the barbarous Greek,[9] but in general the two stereotypes were fixed in their proper places, each at the furthest possible remove from the other. Even if it was admitted that Greeks had once been barbarians themselves, what mattered was that they had moved far beyond this point of departure. 'The old customs are exceedingly simple and barbarous', Aristotle wrote. 'For the Greeks at one time went about armed and bought their women from one another; and all the other ancient customs which still persist anywhere are altogether foolish ... And in general, men desire the good and not merely what their fathers had.'[10]

After the Greeks

Poles apart, as different as different can be, barbarians are the opposite of our imagined selves. There could be no barbarians before there were Greeks, or, later, Romans, or Christians, or Europeans.

They define us, as we define them. Any attempt to subvert this opposition implied that contemporary society was not, after all, so different from that of the barbarians. In his essay 'Of Cannibals', written in 1578, Michel de Montaigne reflected on what he had heard about the people of Brazil, and remarked that 'there is nothing barbarous and savage in that nation, from what I have been told, except that each man calls barbarism whatever is not his own practice; for indeed it seems we have no other test of truth and reason than the example and pattern of the opinions and customs of the country we live in.'[11]

This was, of course, intended ironically. Montaigne has been described as a relativist, yet he never doubted that there were absolute standards of truth and reason. His point was that neither the barbarian nor the Frenchman is truly rational. However, the Indians of Brazil enjoy pleasant and leisurely lives, admirable in their simplicity, and in accord with a natural philosophy. 'These nations, then, seem to me barbarous in this sense, that they have been fashioned very little by the human mind, and are still very close to their original naturalness. The laws of nature still rule them, very little corrupted by ours.'[12]

> I am sorry that Lycurgus and Plato did not know of them ... This is a nation, I should say to Plato, in which there is no sort of traffic, no knowledge of letters, no science of numbers, no name for a magistrate or for political superiority, no custom of servitude, no riches or poverty, no contracts, no successions, no partitions, no occupations but leisure ones, no care for any but common kinship, no clothes, no agriculture, no metal, no use of wine or wheat. The very words that signify lying, treachery, dissimulation, avarice, envy, belittling, pardon – unheard of. How far from this perfection would he find the republic that he imagined ...

It had to be admitted that the Brazilians did dreadful things, for instance killing and eating their prisoners, but within living memory Frenchmen were breaking their enemies on the rack, or burning them alive. Was this less terrible than eating one's enemies after their death? We may call others barbarians if we judge them by the standards of pure reason, Montaigne concluded, but not if we compare them to ourselves, 'who surpass them in every kind of barbarity'.[13]

Montaigne knew more than Plato about barbarians, and not only because he had studied the reports of explorers, about which he was sceptical. Christopher Columbus had returned to the Old World with seven kidnapped Indians who were widely exhibited, and in the sixteenth century Indian slaves and exhibits became commonplace in Europe. When Henry II and Catherine de Médici made a ceremonial entry into the city of Rouen in 1550, they were welcomed by pageants featuring gladiators and elephants, a mock sea battle, and parades of captives. There was also a full-scale reproduction of a Brazilian village with three hundred naked inhabitants, 50 of whom were genuine Indians, who had been brought to France by a local merchant. They gave displays of dance and warfare.[14] Montaigne claimed to have met some of these Brazilians in Rouen in 1562, and to have conversed with one of them. The interpreter was unreliable, but he managed to establish that the Indian had been a reluctant leader at home. Chosen for his valour, his privilege was to march into battle in front of his men. In times of peace, however, his only reward was 'that when he visited the villages dependent on him, they made paths for him through the underbrush by which he might pass quite comfortably'. 'All this is not too bad', Montaigne commented, 'but what's the use? They don't wear breeches.'[15]

Montaigne introduced his essay on cannibals with another set of examples, which were also designed to unsettle the conviction of his readers that they would know a barbarian if they saw one.

> When King Pyrrhus passed over into Italy, after he had reconnoitred the formation of the army that the Romans were sending to meet him, he said: 'I do not know what barbarians these are' (for so the Greeks called all foreign nations), 'but the formation of this army that I see is not all barbarous'. The Greeks said as much of the army that Flaminius brought into their country, and so did Philip, seeing from a knoll the order and distribution of the Roman camp, in his kingdom under Publius Sulpicius Galba. Thus we should beware of clinging to vulgar opinions, and judge things by reason's way, not by popular say.[16]

These instances came easily to an educated European of the sixteenth century, well versed in classical texts. However, Montaigne's anecdotes all tell how Greeks were forced to recognise one class of barbarians, the Romans, as their equals on the battlefield. These are surely Roman myths. According to Gibbon, the Romans at first 'submitted to the insult, and freely gave themselves the name of Barbarians'. But in time they 'claimed an exemption for Italy, and her subject provinces; and at length removed the disgraceful appellation to the savage or hostile nations beyond the pale of the empire.'[17] They called the northern coast of Africa Barbary ('justly', says Gibbon). Urban and urbane, civic-minded, disciplined, powerful, the Romans came to see themselves as standing side by side with the Greeks against the barbarians at the gates.

Respectful of Greek models, Roman intellectuals deployed the barbarian in fresh thought experiments. Aristotle had sketched a history of political development. The first society was the family, each family ruled by the eldest man. ('As Homer says: "Each one gives law to his children and to his wives."') In time, related families gathered in villages.

> When several villages are united in a single complete community, large enough to be nearly or quite self-sufficing, the state comes into existence, originating in the bare needs of life, and continuing in existence for the sake of a good life. And therefore, if the earlier forms of society are natural, so is the state, for it is the end of them, and the nature of a thing is its end.

'Hence it is evident that the state is a creation of nature, and that man is by nature a political animal.'[18]

Nature might be a guarantee of reason, and there is a long tradition of preferring nature, and natural habits, to artifice.[19] Yet natural dispositions might be transcended by a more sophisticated reason. In the second paragraph of *De Inventione*, published in 55 BCE, Cicero imagined a time when people wandered about in the fields like beasts, relying on physical strength and not using their reason. They had no notion of gods, or of public duty; no legitimate marriage; no law. Then a great man came along and persuaded a number of people to live together and to join in useful and honourable work. At first they were refractory, but his wisdom and eloquence made them gentle and civil. Yet language could be a two-edged sword. A tyrant could use rhetoric to bamboozle simple folk. In this myth, barbarians are still defined in relation to language: not simply to the Greek language itself, but to rational discourse more broadly conceived.

After the adoption of Christianity as the official religion of the Roman Empire, Christianity came to be identified with *Romanitas*. Before that, Roman commentators had condemned Christian rites as barbaric. Now it was the pagans who were defined as barbarians. 'As different is the Roman from the barbarian,' wrote the fifth century Latin poet Prudentius, 'so man is different from the animal, or the speaking person from the mute, and as they who follow the teachings of God differ from those who follow senseless cults and super-stitions.'[20]

For Prudentius, the first criterion that marked the Christian Roman off from the barbarian was, therefore, a deficiency of language. (The Tower of Babel was a monument of barbarism.) Yet Christians them-selves spoke many languages, and sometimes could not communicate with one another. 'If then I know not the meaning of the voice,' the evangelist Paul had warned (in 1 Corinthians, 14.11), 'I shall be to him that speaketh a barbarian, and he that speaketh will be a barbarian unto me.' But not all languages were equal. After citing Paul, and debating what the language of Christendom should be (Greek? Latin? Hebrew?), Thomas Aquinas insisted that spoken language was less serviceable than written language. It was a script that made possible the growth of knowledge and the development of legal instruments. Aquinas therefore praised Bede for introducing writing to Britain, so raising the people from a state of barbarism. The arguments of Aristotle and Aquinas on language and on slavery still resonated for Jesuits in Spanish America in the sixteenth century, when Catholic Europe debated whether Indians had souls, and whether they were condemned by their very nature to be slaves. The Jesuits agreed with Aquinas that it was above all the absence of a written language which distinguished the barbarian.[21]

Enter the savage

The barbarian was a fecund object of contemplation for more than two millennia, but the voyages of discovery of the late fifteenth century brought back news of a yet stranger figure: half beast, half man, according to some accounts. He was christened the savage. The French adjective *sauvage* meant wild, uncultivated and undomes-ticated. It was later used to describe violent and coarse people. Emerging into the consciousness of Europe with the first reports on the inhabitants of America, the savage merged with the monsters of the Middle Ages, who combined human features and animal traits, and even had attributes of devils.[22]

In what was perhaps his last play, *The Tempest*, written in 1610 or 1611, some thirty years after Montaigne's essay on cannibals,

Shakespeare introduced the figure of Caliban. His name is an acrostic of cannibal. Half man, half beast, the only native of the island, Caliban lives in a hole in the ground. Prospero describes him as:

> A devil, a born devil, on whose nature
> Nurture can never stick ...

Caliban is not only the antithesis of the civil person. He is contrasted to another creature, Ariel, half man half spirit, who lives in the air. Caliban can barely speak, Ariel sings enchantingly. Both are bound in the service of Prospero, the master of the island, yet while Prospero refers to Caliban as 'my slave', he calls Ariel 'my servant'.

Prospero had treated Caliban kindly at first, attempting to teach him, and even sharing his sleeping quarters. Then Caliban attempted to rape Prospero's daughter, Miranda, and was cast out. The gentle Miranda reproaches Caliban for not benefiting from her instruction:

> I pitied thee,
> Took pains to make thee speak, taught thee each hour
> One thing or other: when thou didst not – savage! -
> Know thine own meaning, but wouldst gabble like
> A thing most brutish, I endowed thy purposes
> With words that made them known ...

To which Caliban replies:

> You taught me language, and my profit on't
> Is, I know how to curse ...

The political tone of the *Tempest* appears to be very different from Montaigne's sceptical view of authority. The noblemen are judged according to their fidelity to the true king. Their drunken servants and sailors quarrel among themselves and are subdued only by force. The savages are beyond the pale of society. Caliban has to be beaten and tormented into submission. The good Ariel is a willing agent, although Prospero has to remind him (Ariel cannot bring himself to remember) that he had formerly been the slave of the wicked witch Sycorax, Caliban's mother. Because Ariel refused to carry out her evil wishes, Sycorax imprisoned him in a tree, where he remained until released by Prospero. Yet both Ariel and Caliban constantly plead for their freedom. Caliban tries to escape Prospero, only to bind himself in service to a drunken sailor, who gives him liquor. Ariel is finally freed by his grateful master to fly away into the world of nature. ('Where the bee sucks, there suck I ... Merrily, merrily, shall I live now, / Under the blossom that hangs on the bough.')

However, the play's endorsement of hierarchy and order is not unambiguous. The good counsellor, Gonzalo, looks over Prospero's island and imagines a Utopia that echoes Montaigne's account of Brazil:

> I'th'commonwealth I would by contraries
> Execute all things: for no kind of traffic
> Would I admit: no name of magistrate:
> Letters should not be known: riches, poverty,
> And use of service – none:
> No use of metal, corn, or wine, or oil:
> No occupation, all men idle, all:
> And women too, but innocent and pure:
> No sovereignty –

('Yet he would be king on't', a sceptical courtier remarks.)

Caliban and Ariel were slaves who might be freed by their master, but other dramatists represented the savage as a free man. A little more than half a century after Caliban, an Indian hero proclaims in John Dryden's play, *The Conquest of Granada*:

> I am as free as Nature first made man
> 'Ere the base Laws of Servitude began
> When wild in woods the noble Savage ran.

Why then had we lost this aboriginal freedom? In the seventeenth century, philosophers drew on Cicero and imagined an alternative to the biblical account of human origins, one that would explain why free men might sacrifice their liberty to follow a king. A human plan, an original social contract, took the place of a divine covenant. Instead of a fall from paradise, human beings had advanced from an aboriginal condition close to that of the beasts in a state of nature. They might have been free, but they were deprived of the comfort and security of a social existence. Guided by the light of reason, independent but vulnerable individuals therefore combined to form a society. Thomas Hobbes, a refugee from civil war and regicide in England, reflected on those ancient anarchic days. 'During the time men live without a common power to keep them all in awe, they are in that condition which is called war.' They lacked industry, agriculture, navigation, buildings. They had 'no knowledge of the face of the earth; no account of time; no arts; no letters; no society; and which is worst of all, continual fear, and danger of violent death; and the life of man, solitary, poor, nasty, brutish and short'.[23] For men in this desperate condition, society offered security. In the view of Hobbes, that provided a rational basis for the absolute power of the sovereign. However, the same myth could be used to show that legitimate authority must depend on the will of the subject. The contract had been broken, Rousseau was to argue, the people betrayed by leaders to whom they had confided their liberties and their goods.

These notions of a 'state of nature' and a 'social contract' were thought experiments, but Hobbes supposed that some savages still lived in this original condition. 'For the savage people in many places of America, except the government of small families, the concord whereof dependeth on natural lust, have no government at all, and live at this day in that brutish manner.'[24] On this point at least, John Locke agreed with him. 'Thus in the beginning, all the world was *America*.'[25] Ethnographic reports might therefore be incorporated into our own history. In 1724, Lafitau published his *Moeurs des sauvages américains comparées aux moeurs des premiers temps*, in which he compared his own, partly first-hand, information on the Indians of Brazil with the beliefs and customs of peoples separated from them by many centuries, and living on different continents. 'The Tahitian is in touch with the origin of the world,' Denis Diderot concluded a generation later, 'the European with its old age.'[26]

In the second half of the eighteenth century a genre of universal histories became fashionable. The medieval cosmology of the Great Chain of Being was set in motion, historicised. There had been an advance from an original state of savagery through barbarism to the highest human condition, which was now termed civilisation. In French, the terms *civilité, politesse,* and *police* (meaning law-abiding), go back to the sixteenth century. Throughout the seventeenth century peoples with these characteristics were contrasted with 'savages' and 'barbarians'. But it was only in the middle of the eighteenth century that the term *civilisation* was coined. It became current at the same time as the word *progress* acquired its modern sense, and the two neologisms were soon closely associated with each other.[27] Progress was characterised above all by the advance of reason, and reason was engaged in an epic struggle to overcome the resistance of traditional societies, with their superstitions, irrational prejudices, and blind loyalty to cynical rulers. The ultimate victory of civilisation was certain, for it could call to its aid science: the highest expression of reason, the true and efficient knowledge of the laws that inform nature and society alike.

When the word *civilisation* was coined, savage became its common antithesis. Savagery represented the original condition of humanity. Civilisation marked the climax of human progress. But what stages had intervened? In the Greek view, ancient peoples had lacked the fundamental civil institution, the city. Cicero suggested that the first human beings were solitary wanderers. They were then persuaded to follow a leader and form a society. Montesquieu identified a further revolution that marked the transition from savagery to barbarism. 'There is this difference between savage and barbarous nations', he wrote in his *Spirit of the Laws* in 1748, 'the former are dispersed clans, which for some particular reason, cannot be joined in a body; and the latter are commonly small nations, capable of being united. The savages are generally hunters; the barbarians are herdsmen and shepherds.'[28]

Jacques Turgot, a pioneer economist, and the leading financial administrator under Louis XV of France, published his *Sur le progrès successif de l'esprit humain* in 1750. This stressed the economic factor and the development of property rights, whose enjoyment Locke had put at the very heart of liberty. Turgot outlined a four stage model of economic and social progress, marked by an advance from hunting, first to pastoralism and later to agriculture, and then on to commerce and markets and the division of labour. In 1755, in his second *Discourse on Inequality*, Rousseau sketched a similar series of revolutions. At first, scattered individuals lived among the animals, with whom they were in competition. Gradually some men developed tools, domesticated other species, and began to form loose associations with one another. A great revolution brought about the establishment of families and introduced notions of property. Related families then combined to form communities, and language was invented. A second revolution came with the development of metallurgy, agriculture and the division of labour. It was accompanied by the growth of war, and led inexorably to the dictatorship of the strongest.

Turgot himself had taken a more optimistic view of progress. Political and moral arrangements improved as more advanced forms of economic life developed. There was also a parallel progression from theological to metaphysical and so to empirical reasoning. For a later generation, Auguste Comte propounded 'a great fundamental law ... that each of our leading conceptions – each branch of our knowledge – passes successively through three different theoretical conditions: the theological, or fictitious; the metaphysical, or abstract; and the scientific or positive.'[29]

The writers of the Scottish Enlightenment built diligently on these foundations. Turgot's four-stage model provided them with their framework. ('The four stages of society are hunting, pasturing, farming and commerce', to quote Adam Smith's concise summation.)[30] All history was one, all societies had a common point of origin. In Thomas Love Peacock's satirical novel *Crotchet Castle*, a Scotsman is teased – 'Pray, Mr. MacQuedy, how is it that all gentlemen of your nation begin everything they write with the "infancy of society"?' The answer was obvious. Our present circumstances could be understood once we had grasped our origins. Savages represented the starting point of history. Moreover, they could still be observed, in remote parts of Australia, the Americas, Africa and Australia. The Scots felt that this gave them an advantage over the ancient philosophers, who did not know anything about 'men in the earliest and rudest state'. Scholars could now draw on reports from America where there were still societies 'so extremely rude, as to be unacquainted with those arts which are the first essays of human ingenuity in its advance towards improvement'.[31] 'It is in their present condition,' Adam Ferguson wrote, 'that we are to behold, as in a mirror, the features of our own progenitors'.[32]

Darwin and the savages[33]

These were the ideas with which English explorers travelled in the early nineteenth century. In 1830, Robert FitzRoy, the aristocratic and conservative captain of HMS *Adventure,* came ashore on Tierra del Fuega and confided to his diary:

> Disagreeable, indeed painful, as is even the mental contemplation of a savage, and unwilling as we may be to consider ourselves even remotely descended from human beings in such a state, the reflection that Caesar found the Britons painted and clothed in skins, like these Fuegians, cannot fail to augment an interest excited by their childish ignorance of matters familiar to civilized man, and by their healthy, independent state of existence.[34]

A few years later, a young gentleman scientist whom FitzRoy had invited to sail with him on board HMS *Beagle*, was even more direct. 'The astonishment which I felt on first seeing a party of Fuegians on a wild and broken shore will never be forgotten by me', Charles Darwin wrote, 'for the reflection at once rushed into my mind – such were our ancestors.'[35]

During FitzRoy's first encounter with the Fuegians, there had been thefts from his ship. Fitzroy took hostages, promising to release them when the goods were returned. The ploy failed, and he was left with three Fuegians on his hands. A fourth man was bought from his uncle for a pearl button and named Jeremy (Jemmy) Button. FitzRoy decided to take the Fuegians back to England with him, where they would be educated, he decided, 'in English, and the plainer truths of Christianity, as the first objective; and the use of common tools, a slight acquaintance with husbandry, gardening and mechanism, as the second'.[36] In short, they were to be instructed in the elements of his civilisation: language, religion, and technology. One of the party (Fitzroy's favourite) died from smallpox, but under the guidance of the rector of Walthamstow the survivors were instructed in the Christian religion and in English language and customs. FitzRoy presented the Fuegians to the King and Queen. A fund was launched to finance missionary activity on their islands, and a missionary joined the *Beagle's* second voyage.

The *Beagle* returned the three surviving Fuegians to their homes, where it was hoped that they would serve as intermediaries for the missionary. Darwin befriended them on the voyage, but his first direct encounter with what he called 'untamed savage' Fuegians came on the morning of December 1832, and as he remarked in his diary and in letters home, it impressed him profoundly. Writing to his sister Caroline from the *Beagle*, Darwin listed 'the three most interesting spectacles I have beheld since leaving England – a Fuegian savage – Tropical Vegetation – & the ruins of Concepcion'.[37] 'Viewing such men, one can hardly make oneself believe that they are fellow creatures placed in the same world'.[38] Fuegian homes were rudimentary; they slept 'on the wet ground, coiled up like animals'; their food was miserable and scarce; they were at war with their neighbours over means of subsistence. 'Captain FitzRoy could never ascertain that the Fuegians have any distinct belief in a future life.' Their feelings for home and hearth were stunted. Their imaginations were not stimulated, their skills 'like the instinct of animals' were not 'improved by experience.'[39] 'Although essentially the same creature, how little must the mind of one of these beings resemble that of an educated man.' 'What a scale of improvement is comprehended between the faculties of a Fuegian savage & a Sir Isaac Newton.'[40] And yet Darwin noted that the Fuegians did well by some tests. 'There can be no reason for supposing the race of Fuegians are decreasing, we may therefore be sure that he enjoys a sufficient share of happiness (whatever its kind may be) to render life worth having. Nature, by making habit omnipotent, has fitted the Fuegian to the climate and productions of his country.'[41]

There was little to distinguish the young Charles Darwin's reflections from those of Captain FitzRoy. Both agreed that savages were very different indeed from Victorian Englishmen, but that they were nevertheless capable of rapid improvement. Darwin reflected that 'in contradiction of what has often been stated, 3 years has been sufficient to change savages into, as far as habits go, complete & voluntary Europeans'.[42] Indeed, he expressed concern that the Fuegians would not be able to readjust to the harsh island conditions. When the *Beagle* revisited the Fuegian camp, the Englishmen found that Jemmy Button had become much thinner. However, he assured the captain that he was 'hearty, sir, never better', and that he was contented and had no desire to alter his present way of life. 'I hope & have little doubt [Jemmy] will be as happy as if he had never left his country', Darwin wrote in his diary, 'which is much more than I formerly thought.'[43] FitzRoy was nevertheless encouraged to suppose that civilisation had left its imprint. He described the farewell signal fire that Jemmy lit as the *Beagle* sailed away, and commented that Jemmy's family 'were become considerably more humanized than any savages we had seen in Tierra del Fuego'. One day a shipwrecked seaman might be saved by Jemmy's children, 'prompted, as they can hardly fail to be, by the traditions they will have heard of men of other lands; and by an idea, however faint of their duty to God as well as their neighbour'.[44]

Darwin and FitzRoy agreed that the Fuegians stood low on the scale of development – on the very lowest rung, Darwin believed. Nevertheless, there was no intrinsic reason why individual Fuegians should not very quickly be 'civilized'. 'These Indians appear to have a facility for learning languages' Darwin noted, 'which will greatly contribute to civilization or demoralization: as these two steps seem to go hand in hand.'[45] Lack of intelligence did not seem to be the explanation for their backwardness. The Australians might be regarded as having superior accomplishments to the Fuegians, but

Darwin doubted that they were more intelligent. Remarkably, the one speculation Darwin made on the cause of the backwardness of these people was purely sociological in nature. The Fuegians bartered freely and shared everything – 'even a piece of cloth given to one is torn into shreds and distributed; and no one individual becomes richer than another'.[46] This insistence on exchange (which so tormented the Englishmen, who accused them of thieving) was based on the assumption of equality. And in Darwin's view, it was precisely this equality that held them back.

> The perfect equality among the individuals composing the Fuegian tribes, must for a long time retard their civilization. As we see those animals, whose instinct compels them to live in society and obey a chief, are most capable of improvement, so is it with the races of mankind. ... On the other hand, it is difficult to understand how a chief can arise till there is property of some sort by which he might manifest his superiority and increase his power.

Conversely, Darwin attributed the relative sophistication of the Tahitians to their hierarchical social order. 'If the state in which the Fuegians live should be fixed on as zero in the scale of governments, I am afraid the New Zealand would rank but a few degrees higher, while Tahiti, even as when first discovered, would occupy a respectable position.'[47]

Evolution and the invention of the primitive

The four-stage model of the Scottish Enlightenment remained influential for more than a century, but after mulling over his observations from the voyage of the *Beagle* for two decades, Darwin was to give Victorian England a rival view of history, which in retrospect has been called evolutionism. It gave birth to a new scientific conception: primitive man.

Words derived from the Latin *primitivus* had been commonly used in many European languages to denote something that was the first or earliest of its kind, or the original condition of an institution, or to describe the first inhabitants of a country. To call something primitive was not necessarily pejorative. The *OED* gives two examples from the seventeenth century diaries of John Evelyn. The 'primitive church' referred to the early Christian church, and Evelyn claimed that: 'The Church of England is certainly, of all the Christian professions on the earth, the most primitive, apostolical, and excellent'. Primitive could also connote a natural human condition, and Evelyn described the innocent virtue of a 'maiden of primitive life' who 'has for many years refus'd marriage, or to receive any assistance from the parish'.

More specialised usages developed in the sciences. In mathematics the description primitive applied to prime numbers or to axiomatic expressions. In biology the word came to be used for rudimentary structures, or for tissues or organs that were formed in the earliest stages of growth. Finally, in the second half of the nineteenth century, scientists began to talk of primitive man, and primitive society. Primitive people were savages, but seen now in a different perspective, as the point of departure of all human beings. They had an intimate place in our own history. We belonged to the same family. They were our living ancestors.

This was no longer a rather vague conceit, but a precise genealogical proposition. In 1862, Darwin wrote to a sympathiser, Charles Kingsley:

> That is a grand & almost awful question on the genealogy of man ... It is not so awful & difficult to me ... partly from familiarity & partly, I think, from having seen a good many Barbarians. I declare the thought, when I first saw in T. del Fuego a naked painted, shivering hideous savage, that my ancestors must have been somewhat similar beings, was at that time as revolting to me, nay more revolting than my present belief that an incomparably more remote ancestor was a hairy beast. Monkeys have downright good hearts, at least sometimes ...[48]

Once Darwin and Huxley had established that all humans were descended from primates, probably African, Darwin began to speculate on the links between primates and, for example, a man like Jemmy Button. He instructed himself to 'forget the use of language & judge only by what you see. Compare the Fuegians & Ourang outang & dare to say difference so great.'[49] Nor was there so great a difference between Jemmy and Darwin himself.

> The American aborigines, Negroes and Europeans are as different from each other in mind as any three races that can be named;

yet I was incessantly struck, whilst living with the Fuegians on
board the 'Beagle', with the many little traits of character,
showing how similar their minds were to ours; and so it was
with a full-blooded negro with whom I happened once to be
intimate.

Anthropology was the new science of this primitive humanity, and
anthropologists were beginning to collect more systematic evidence
on these issues. Darwin cited them in his support. 'He who will
read Mr Tylor's and Sir J. Lubbock's interesting works can hardly
fail to be deeply impressed with the close similarity between the
men of all races in tastes, dispositions and habits.'[50] But if the
primitive was our common ancestor, the link between the apes and
modern human beings, even our brother, Darwin did not hesitate to
describe him as a savage and a barbarian.

Part II

Ancient law, ancient society and totemism

'The educated world of Europe and America practically settles a standard by simply placing its own nations at one end of the social series and savage tribes at the other, arranging the rest of mankind between these limits according as they correspond more closely to savage or to cultured life.'

(Edward B. Tylor, *Primitive Culture* (1871) Volume 1, p. 26)

Chapter 3

Henry Maine's patriarchal theory

Born in 1822, raised in conditions of shabby gentility, Henry Maine went up to Cambridge in 1840 where he enjoyed a brilliant under-graduate career, distinguished by the award of the Chancellor's medal for English verse (for a poem on the birth of the Prince of Wales), and election to the elite Cambridge secret society, the Apostles.[1] On graduation he became a fellow of Trinity Hall, a Cambridge college noted for its lawyers, and began to specialise in Roman Law. At the age of twenty-five he became Regius Professor of Civil Law at Cambridge. This sounds rather grander than it was. His friend, James Fitzjames Stephen, described the professorship as an 'ill-paid sinecure', and Maine soon moved on to a Readership in Roman Law in the Middle Temple. In London, he became an active political journalist, and was one of the founders of *The Saturday Review*. A 'hard-headed Peelite ... with a taste for Burkean rhetoric',[2] he championed aristocratic forms of government and opposed the extension of the suffrage. And he became fascinated by the Indian question.

The Utilitarians and India

The future of India was perhaps the central political question in Britain in the late 1850s, and it raised great legal and philosophical issues.[3] In 1858, in the aftermath of the Sepoy Mutiny, Parliament stripped the East India Company of its remaining political powers and transferred the government of India to the crown. But there was no consensus on policy. Administrators of a Burkean persuasion were reluctant to undertake large reforms, and they were inclined to collaborate with local authorities. Meanwhile, a coalition of evangelicals, free traders, Empire builders, and philosophical radicals were pressing for radical change.

The Utilitarians were prominent in this 'anglicising' party. Their prophet, Jeremy Bentham, had long taken a special interest in Indian affairs. Together with his disciple John Austin, Bentham developed elaborate legal codes that were designed to promote both collective happiness and rational individual freedom. They failed to persuade any government to enact their codes, but Bentham died in the hope that they might one day become law in India. He knew that he could count on the support of one of the most powerful men in the India Office, James Mill. 'Mill will be the living executive,' Bentham declared, 'I shall be the dead legislative of British India.'[4]

Mill was certainly willing. His research on India's history had persuaded him that 'despotism and priestcraft taken together, the Hindus, in mind and body, were the most enslaved portion of the human race'.[5] It was Britain's clear duty to reform Indian institutions. The priority was a code of law. 'As I believe that India stands more in need of a code than any other country in the world,' Mill wrote, 'I believe also that there is no country on which that great benefit can more easily be conferred. A Code is almost the only blessing – perhaps it is the only blessing – which absolute governments are better fitted to confer on a nation than popular governments.'[6] Mill's protégé, Thomas Babington Macaulay, became legal member of the Viceroy's Council, and in 1835 he designed a penal code for India that was based on pure Benthamite principles. However, the reform movement lost its impetus. Mill died. It was only with the transfer of power to the crown that the old debates were revived, and this time greater attention was paid to the question of legal reform, and in particular to the reform of land tenure.

Back in London, Maine followed these developments closely. The Indian government at last enacted Macaulay's penal code, but Maine was not interested in penal codes, commenting dismissively that 'nobody cares about criminal law except theorists and habitual criminals'.[7] However, proposals for the codification of civil law were a different matter entirely. It was here that the law became political. Maine published a series of articles in *The Saturday Review* castigating the Benthamites. Any reform of the legal system and of land tenure should be undertaken with caution if the foundations of Indian society were not to be put at risk. His masterpiece, *Ancient Law*, was a weightier vehicle for these arguments.

Sources for a conservative critique

Maine taught Roman law, which was dominated in his day by German scholars, notably Savigny and Jhering.[8] Friedrich Karl von Savigny, a conservative Prussian nobleman, had achieved early fame with a pamphlet, published in 1814, attacking a proposal to codify civil law. Savigny protested that a legal system was a complex historical growth. Like a language, the law grows out of the historical experience of a nation. It expresses what came to be called a *Volksgeist*. Apparent inconsistencies may be necessary fudges. Any reform should be gradual and respectful of established tradition. The central theme of his life-work, the multi-volume *Die Geschichte des Römischen Rechts in Mittelalter,* begun in 1834 and only completed in 1850, was that the introduction of Roman law in medieval Germany had succeeded because it had not disturbed the spirit of national law. The *doctores juris* had only allowed innovations that fitted into the German tradition.

Nationalist critics, the so-called 'Germanists', disputed the value that Savigny attached to the reception of Roman law. There were also 'Romanists', notably Jhering, who developed a less nationalistic and altogether more pragmatic version of the thesis. The internal differences of the German scholars were not critical to Maine's enterprise, however. What interested him were the parallels between ancient Germany and modern India, and between the role of Rome in Germany and of Britain in India. Savigny's history addressed the very issue that engaged the government of India. How could a traditional society be changed by legal reform?

The school of Savigny also provided Maine with a large historical perspective. It could be proved that Britain should indeed be compared with Rome, and India with ancient Germany. The proof was philological. Linguists had demonstrated that the Germanic languages were related to classical Greek and Latin, and ultimately to Sanskrit. All were members of one Indo–European family of languages. Jacob Grimm, a student of Savigny, had identified regular consonant-shifts in Proto-Indo–European (Grimm's Law). He had also, even more famously, with his brother Wilhelm, collected Germanic folktales, and German scholars had established parallels between German folklore and the mythology of ancient Rome and Greece, and even India. Grimm believed that there was also a characteristic type of Indo–European folk community. This he identified with the old German *mark*, the ancient village unit, in which land was supposedly held and worked in common. These ideas became fashionable in Britain. Max Müller, professor of Sanskrit at Oxford, spread the gospel of Indo–European philology. An English student of Grimm, John Kemble, described how the Saxons brought the *mark*-community with them to England. For the rising generation of historians, Stubbs, Freeman and Green, the *mark* was the direct ancestor of Westminster government.[9]

Maine embraced the new historiography,[10] and it provided the intellectual framework of *Ancient Society*. While Stubbs and Freeman were writing their constitutional histories of Britain, which traced its institutions back to German roots, Maine's *Ancient Law* offered a prospective constitutional history of the India he hoped to see, an India that followed the example of Britain, as Britain, and Germany, had once been helped along by Rome. He was now armed with the intellectual weapons he required to mount an assault on Bentham's fortress.

Ancient Law

Maine rather unfairly associated Bentham with the traditional radical postulate that there had been an original state of nature. Free men then agreed to a social contract and elected a leader to govern them, but the leader betrayed his trust. The only solution was to start over again. The philosopher should imagine himself back in a state of nature, and apply his reason to working out a rational and just system of government.

Maine regarded this kind of thinking with scorn. Its source, which he termed 'the ancient counterpart of Benthamism,'[11] was the Greek theory of Natural Law. This theory assumed that certain legal principles were universal. Anyone, anywhere would have to recognise that they were just. The Romans appealed to the notion of a Natural Law when they had to judge cases that involved foreigners, who had different laws and customs; but they were cautious and pragmatic. However, modern radical philosophers apparently believed that justice had been established in an original state of nature, and that its original principles should be restored. 'Rousseau's belief was that a perfect social order could be evolved from the unassisted consideration of the natural state', Maine wrote, 'a social order wholly irrespective of the actual condition of the world and wholly unlike it.'[12] Nor was this speculation an innocent intellectual pursuit. Maine charged that the theory had 'helped most powerfully to bring about the grosser disappointments of which the first French revolution was fertile'. No good could come of a theory that 'gave birth, or intense stimulus, to the vices of mental habit all but universal at the time, disdain of positive law, impatience of experience, and the preference of a priori to all other reasoning.'[13]

The only antidote was the historical method. Instead of relying on 'the unassisted consideration of the natural state', the 'rudiments of the social state' must be reconstructed scientifically. The evidence was there, if only one knew where to look for it, in 'accounts by contemporary observers of civilisations less advanced than their own, the records which particular races have preserved concerning their primitive history, and ancient law'.[14] ('It will at least be acknowledged that, if the materials for this process are sufficient, and if the comparisons be accurately executed, the methods followed are as little objectionable as those which have led to such surprising results in comparative philology.')[15]

If an investigator used this historical method it could be proved that Rousseau's Eden was a fantasy. Yes, early society was the absolute contrary of modern society, but not because it was based on freedom, equality and brotherhood. On the contrary, the original ancient society was a patriarchal despotism in which the individual counted for nothing.

> Men are first seen distributed in perfectly insulated groups held together by obedience to the parent. Law is the parent's word … society in primitive times was not what it is assumed to be at present, a collection of individuals. In fact, and in the view of the men who composed it, it was an aggregation of families. The contrast may be most forcibly expressed by saying that the unit of an ancient society was the Family, of a modern society the Individual.[16]

Ancient sources confirmed that families were the original units of society. (Just read Homer, Maine suggested, or the Old Testament.) In his *History of British India*, published in 1817, James Mill had described the ancient Indian system:

> it was the usual arrangement in early stages of society, for the different members of a family to live together; and to possess the property in common. The father was rather the head of a number of partners, than the sole proprietor … The laws of

inheritance among the Hindus are almost entirely founded upon this patriarchal arrangement.[17]

In *The Saxons in England*, John Kemble had described in similar terms the 'great family unions ... some, in direct descent from the common ancestors ... others, more distantly connected ... some admitted into communion by marriage, others by adoption but all recognising a brotherhood, a kinsmanship'.[18]

However, kinship was reckoned in a very particular fashion in ancient law. Maine explained how it worked with reference to the Roman distinction between 'agnatic' and 'cognatic' relationships. '*Cognatic* relationship is simply the conception of kinship familiar to modern ideas; it is the relationship arising through common descent from the same pair of married persons, whether the decent be traced through males or females.'[19] *Agnatic* relationships were traced to a common ancestor exclusively through males. As the Roman maxim put it '"Mulier est finis familiae" – a woman is the terminus of the family. A female name closes the branch or twig of the genealogy in which it occurs. None of the descendants of a female are included in the primitive notion of family relationship.'[20]

Agnation is rooted in *Patria Potestas*, the power of the father. 'All persons are Agnatically connected together who are under the same Paternal Power, or who have been under it or who might have been under it ... In truth, in the primitive view, Relationship is exactly limited by Patria Potestas. Where the Potestas begins, Kinship begins; and therefore adoptive relatives are among the kindred. Where the Potestas ends, Kinship ends; so that a son emancipated by his father loses all rights of Agnation.'[21] On marriage, a woman came under the Patria Potestas of her husband.

Patria Potestas and agnation determined the nature of kinship, and kinship ties provided the basis for political relationships. 'The history of political ideas begins, in fact, with the assumption that kinship in blood is the sole possible ground of community in political functions.'[22] But in time, matters became more complicated. Outsiders were adopted into the family, under cover of a legal fiction. The theory of Patria Potestas was stretched to accommodate a very different reality. Society was no longer a family corporation whose members were related by blood in the male line. 'The composition of the state, uniformly assumed to be natural, was nevertheless known to be in great measure artificial.'[23] To make matters worse, the hereditary members of the inner core began to discriminate against individuals who became attached to them through weakness. As these second-class citizens came to constitute a majority, they rejected the principle of blood allegiance and cast about for a more equitable principle of association. The only alternative was 'the principle of local contiguity, now recognized everywhere as the condition of community in political functions.'[24] Blood ties were replaced by territorial loyalties.

And so political ideas changed. Patriarchal authority was challenged. Individuals began to assert their independence. In ancient society, all relationships were determined by birth position within the family. Maine called these relationships of status. In modern societies, individuals enjoyed the freedom to negotiate, and to enter into contractual relationships.

> The movement of the progressive societies has been uniform in one respect. Through all its course it has been distinguished by the gradual dissolution of family dependency and the growth of individual obligation in its place. The individual is steadily substituted for the Family, as the unit of which civil laws take account ... Nor is it difficult to see what is the tie between man and man which replaces by degrees those forms of reciprocity in rights and duties which have their origin in the Family. It is Contract. Starting, as from one terminus of history, from a condition of society in which all the relations of Persons are summed up in the relations of Family, we seem to have steadily moved towards a phase of social order in which all these relations arise from the free agreement of individuals.[25]

The argument was summed up in Maine's most famous generalisation: 'we may say that the movement of the progressive societies has hitherto been a movement *from Status to Contract*.'[26] The radicals had got hold of the wrong end of the stick. The social contract was a very modern invention.

The origin of law

When he turned to the history of law, Maine followed the same rhetorical strategy. He presented a version of Bentham's thesis, and then turned it upside down. In the first four chapters of *Ancient Law*, he set out to show that Bentham's theory flew in the face of history. Legislation and codification marked the peak of legal evolution, not its point of departure.

Bentham believed that law should be made by the political authority. Not precedent but legislation should form the basis of the legal system. Maine remarked that Bentham and Austin 'resolve every law into a *command* of the lawgiver, an *obligation* imposed thereby on the citizen, and a *sanction* threatened in the event of disobedience'. This was a fairly accurate description of the conditions of 'mature jurisprudence', but 'it is curious that the farther we penetrate into the primitive history of thought, the farther we find ourselves from a conception of law which at all resembles a compound of the elements which Bentham determined. It is certain that, in the infancy of mankind, no sort of legislature, not even a distinct author of law, is contemplated or conceived of.' On the contrary, in ancient times 'every man, living during the greater part of his life under patriarchal despotism, was practically controlled in all his actions by a regime not of law but of caprice'.[27]

Capricious patriarchal despots were gradually replaced by more sophisticated rulers, who claimed divine inspiration for their judgements. In time an aristocracy displaced the divinely-inspired leaders. In the west, this was a political oligarchy, in the east a priestly caste. The oligarchs did not claim divine inspiration. Their stock in trade was a monopoly of knowledge of custom, but this monopoly was eventually dissipated with the invention of writing. Customs were now set down in codes. The codification of the law was, of course, the great Benthamite moment, but Maine argued that the first codes simply restated custom. However, he complicated matters by suggesting that there was a moment when a system of customary law became ripe for codification. The Roman code, the Twelve Tables, had been compiled at a stage when usage was still wholesome, although further delay might have been fatal. In India, unfortunately, the masses had got their hands on the law and contaminated it with irrational superstitions.

But if codes simply ordered custom, the question remained whether, and if so how, rational and useful changes could be introduced in the law. Maine believed that there were a few progressive societies in which educated opinion had seen the necessity for improvements and introduced appropriate legal reforms. The Roman system was the best documented of these, and Roman legal history demonstrated that three mechanisms had operated successively to bring about legal change. These were legal fictions, equity, and legislation.

This may seem a curious trinity of instruments of reform. To grasp the logic of the argument it is necessary once again to see how

Maine was determined to upset the a priori theories of Bentham and Austin. They had given all the credit for legal progress to legislation. Maine argued that legislation had not been a significant factor until recent times. The Utilitarian theorists had emphasised the significance of equity, with its appeal to natural principles of law. Maine debunked the logic of equity, and played down its historical importance. On the other hand, Bentham and Austin heaped scorn on the use of 'irrational' legal fictions. According to Bentham, legal fictions were mystifications that despots relied on to retard progress. A legal fiction was 'a wilful falsehood, having for its object the stealing of legislative power, by and for hands which could not, or durst not, openly claim it, and but for the delusion thus produced could not exercise it'. 'Fiction of use to justice? Exactly as swindling is to trade.'[28]

Following Savigny and Jhering,[29] Maine argued that legal fictions were not originally instruments of reaction. On the contrary, they were mechanisms of progressive reform. Under the cover of fictions the elite could introduce reforms while maintaining the illusion, so cherished by the conservative majority, that nothing had really been altered. They 'satisfy the desire for improvement at the same time that they do not offend the superstitious disrelish for change'.[30] After a period of reform by way of legal fictions, the Romans had briefly adopted the principle of equity (at first only in their dealings with foreigners). Finally, as the laws became more and more unwieldy and complex, they were codified.

Chapters 6 to 9 of *Ancient Law* traced the development of the law of property. In ancient society, property was held in common under the control of the father, who was succeeded by his eldest son. Private property, contract and testaments were the product of a long historical development. The Roman invention of the will had created 'the institution which, next to Contract, has exercised the greatest influence in transforming human society'.[31] These reflections provided the guidelines for a generation of Indian officials who would warn against the disruption of ancient collective rights in land, and against the free market.[32]

The comparative method

It would be wrong to treat *Ancient Law* as a work of high scholarship. The history is very compressed and Maine drew heavily on Gibbon's review of the development of Roman law. 'Neither Maine himself, nor I suppose, anyone else in England, knew anything whatever about Roman Law at that time', according to his candid friend J. F. Stephen. 'I suppose he knew the Institutes, but I doubt if he ever knew much of the Pandects.' But, as Stephen admitted, Maine's use of legal history was a brilliant ploy. 'He was enabled to sniff at Bentham for knowing nothing about it, & writing in consequence about English law, in a merely revolutionary manner'. Stephen concluded that 'being a man of talent and originality, coming close to Genesis, Maine transfigured one of the driest of subjects into all sorts of beautiful things, without knowing or caring much of its details'.[33]

Maine insisted that he was following a scientific 'historical method', but he was frequently obliged to fudge the evidence. For example, early Roman sources unambiguously recognised individual rights, and described cognatic relationships. Maine protested that Roman lawyers had simply rewritten the past in order to disguise their innovations. The authentic origins of Roman law had to be reconstructed using the comparative method. The laws of the more backward members of the Indo–European family bore witness to the ancient practices of its more progressive members. India was a particularly rich source of information, for Hindu law seldom 'cast aside the shell in which it was originally reared'. While Roman sources might describe individual property rights, 'among the Hindoos, we do find a form of ownership which ought at once to rivet our attention from its exactly fitting in with the ideas which our studies in the Law of Persons would lead us to entertain respecting the original condition of property. The Village Community of India is at once an organised patriarchal society and an assemblage of co-proprietors.'[34]

Yet, however riveting, the Indian evidence was by no means unambiguous. Maine was obliged to be selective. For instance, he cited a rather murky passage from Elphinstone which seemed to endorse his claim that property had once been held in common. However, he ignored the testimony of George Campbell, whose *Modern India*, published by John Murray in 1852, must have been known to him. Commenting on Mill's account of the Indian village, Campbell admitted that some village communities 'comprised of a number of families, claiming to be of the same brotherhood or clan', but he insisted that 'they do by no means "enjoy to a great degree the community of goods", as Mill supposes. I never knew an instance in which the cultivation was carried on in common, or in which any of the private concerns of the villagers were in any way in common, and I very much doubt the existence of any such state of things.'[35] Maine found himself on still weaker ground when it came to contract. He disparaged the Roman sources but here Indian sources, however selectively used, were unhelpful. Maine was obliged to appeal to German sources, arguing that although the Romans had introduced their principles of contract to the German tribes, feudal laws otherwise differed little from primitive usages.

Maine in India

Ancient Law sent a straightforward message to the politicians. Indian society was based on communal ownership and the patriarchal family. The same had been true of ancient Germany. German societies had been civilised by the reception of Roman Law and by the development of private property and contract. India, however, had stagnated, a prey to obscurantism and despotism. The Indian Empire should now bring British legal principles to some of the most backward of the Indo–European peoples, just as the Roman lawyers had reformed German societies.

In 1861, shortly after the publication of *Ancient Law*, Maine was appointed legal member in the Viceroy's Council, effectively becoming the head of the Indian legal system. It is conceivable that he wrote *Ancient Law* in order to become legal member. He was certainly enough of a pragmatist to have done so. Lord Acton, who as a young Whig MP had put Maine's name forward for the position after his book appeared, later wrote in disillusion to Mary Gladstone that Maine's nature was 'to exercise power, and to find good reasons for adopted policy'.[36] He remained legal member from 1862 to 1869, longer than any other nineteenth-century incumbent of the office, and as his biographer remarked, he 'strove to make the major theses of his *Ancient Law* a self-fulfilling prophecy'.[37] He passed laws that extended freedom of contract, and promoted individual land rights. In speeches to the Council he cited his own theories, drawing parallels between the imposition of British law in India and the reception of Roman law by the Germans.[38] He told the graduating class of Calcutta University that 'their real affinities are with Europe and the Future, not with India and the Past'.[39]

Shortly after he returned from India, Maine was appointed to the newly created Chair of jurisprudence at Oxford, but although he was to be an academic for the rest of his life he retained political interests and ambitions. He made a bid to become Permanent Under-Secretary at the India Office, and was the first person to be appointed a life member of the Council of India. When he resigned his Oxford chair, in 1878, he received offers from the Indian government and the Foreign Secretary, and he later considered other official appointments. Nor did he lose his political interests. His penultimate book, *Popular Government*, published in 1885, was a tract against the Reform Bill and democracy. All this time, his academic career continued to prosper. In 1887, the year before his death, he was named to the Whewell Professorship of International Law at Cambridge.

Maine also remained the guru of Indian officials. Although, as Louis Dumont remarked, Maine 'hardly ever looked at the Indian village in itself, but only as a counterpart to Teutonic, Slavonic or other institutions,'[40] his theories dominated debates on law and land tenure in India for a generation. A new generation worked with his model and produced ethnographic reports that seemed to support his claims.

> A disproportionate number of the civilians who pioneered the anthropological revolution in India were pupils who had sat at his feet. And from the 1860s on, his best-selling books were required reading for the Indian Civil Service examination. Successful candidates paraded their master of Maine's *obiter dicta* in their answer-papers – and they went on parading their mastery in the letters, reports and memorandums they wrote in India. Familiarity with the master's theories was a precondition of promotion, as well as appointment.[41]

However, outside the circle of the Indian Civil Service, his legacy was by no means assured. Historians undermined his image of early Indo–European society. They showed that the people living in the *mark* were usually serfs, and that the *mark* could be understood only in its relationship to the feudal manor. Private property existed, and women might hold and transmit their own property.[42] His most famous scholarly contribution, his patriarchal theory, was almost universally abandoned by the anthropologists in the 1870s. And his thesis on classical antiquity was superseded by the work of a great classical historian, Fustel de Coulanges.

The Ancient City

Numa Denis Fustel de Coulanges published *La Cité Antique* (*The Ancient City*) in 1864, three years after the appearance of *Ancient Law*. Despite obvious similarities between the two books, Fustel knew nothing of Maine's work. At one level the parallels are easily explained, since the stages of development that both men tried to explain, from family to gens, phratry, tribe and city, were to be found in Aristotle and other sources. They were also both influenced by the school of 'Aryan' historiography, and engaged in the same sort of comparisons between Greek and Roman, Hindu and German practices. Yet there were also significant differences of approach. Like Maine, Fustel insisted on the otherness of the ancient world, but where Maine believed that ancient laws preserved the spirit of the earliest institutions, Fustel's premise was that rituals conserved past beliefs. Moreover, Fustel developed a very different theoretical proposition, which was that social institutions rest on religious foundations. 'The comparison of beliefs and laws shows that a primitive religion constituted the Greek and Roman family, established marriage and paternal authority, fixed the degrees of kinship, consecrated the right of property and the right of inheritance.'[43]

Born in 1830, educated at the École Normale Supérieure, Fustel was one of the leading historians of his generation. He was professor of history at the University of Strasbourg from 1860 until the German annexation of Alsace in 1870, and it was here that he wrote *La Cité Antique*. After the Franco–Prussian war he settled in Paris, where he taught at the Sorbonne and the École Normale, and he became a distinguished medievalist. (His six-volume *Histoire des institutions politiques de l'ancienne France* argued that French feudal institutions derived from Roman rather than German models. This may have provided some comfort to the French, still smarting from their defeat by the Prussian army at Sedan.)

In *The Ancient City*, Fustel argued that the first religions were cults of the dead. The dead were considered to be sacred, and their tombs became temples. Since it was believed that the deceased could eat and drink, the living were obliged to provide them with food and wine. If a man failed in his obligations to the dead, they would rise from their tombs to cause him trouble. Essentially, this religion was a cult of the family ancestors. Its rituals were originally celebrated within the home. There was a sacred fire at the domestic hearth, where the gods were fed. Meals were a communion in which the god participated together with deceased family members, who were also thought to haunt the hearth, and who served as intermediaries between the living and their god. The father was the priest. The congregation was the family. Ancestors and worshippers were concerned only with the rights and duties of family members, living and dead. Alongside ancestor worship there was a natural religion. Sprites also haunted the hearth. Eventually they grew into satyrs. Finally they were embodied in the figure of Pan.

But it was the domestic religion of the hearth and the ancestors that accounted for the form taken by the ancient family. 'The family is a religious association rather than a natural association', according to Fustel. 'No doubt the religion did not create the family, but it certainly provided the family with its regulations.'[44] Marriage was understood as the parting of a girl from her gods and her introduction to a strange hearth. Wedding ceremonies marked her rebirth as a member of her husband's family circle. Since daughters were incorporated into the religious cults of their husbands, kinship was traced only in the male line. 'Agnation is nothing other than the form of kinship originally established by the religion.'[45] Because a man's survival after death depended on the services of his descendants, the family had a religious obligation to perpetuate itself. Consequently, celibacy was not tolerated, and adoption was allowed in cases of infertility. Kinship therefore did not necessarily depend on blood ties. 'It was, in practice, the domestic religion that constituted kinship. Two men could call each other kin if they had the same gods and shared the same hearth.'[46] The father was the priest, and so the source of authority, but he had his religious obligations to his family and could not act tyrannically. 'Thanks to the domestic religion, the family was ... a small society with its chief and its government.'[47] The cult also gave rise to property relations, since there was an unbreakable bond between the family and its ancestral tombs, and so between the family and its land.

In time, more powerful families assimilated clients and a larger grouping emerged, the *gens*. The gens was still based on the foundations of the family cult and its system of private law. A considerable group could be organised on these principles, with a hereditary chief. Eventually, *gentes* coalesced to form what the Greeks termed a *phratry*. Each phratry built a new altar and sacred fire and initiated a new cult. Its communal meals were dedicated to a god who was similar to the divinities of the family hearth, though superior to them. In fact, the phratry constituted 'a little society that was modelled precisely on the family',[48] with its rule of patrilineal descent, chief priest, hereditary lands etc. Phratries in turn eventually united to form a tribe with its own religion, but organised still on the principles on which the family was based. For a very long period, ancient Greece and Italy would have been populated by such independent phratries and tribes, each with its own religious cult.

Eventually the tribes joined together to form cities, but family, phratry, tribe and city were all based on the same principles, and a federal constitution left the original groups with considerable independence. Shared beliefs were still the most fundamental bond. 'To the extent that people sensed that they had gods in common, they united in larger groupings.'[49] The foundation of a new town was accompanied by ceremonies that introduced the gods, set ritual boundaries, and consecrated it for eternity. The man who laid the foundations and performed the first religious ceremony became the father to the community. When the founder of the city died he became the common ancestor, revered by all and worshipped in communal meals in which all citizens participated. Later rulers were father figures. The society of the city was united by its cult, and its gods were particular to the city. 'The city was founded on a religion and constituted as a church.'[50] It was their religious beliefs that made people ready to obey rulers, and the roles of ruler and of judge were inseparable from that of priest. The laws were all religious precepts. The individual had no rights, his life and goods were at the disposal of the gods and so of the state. Deprivation of citizenship and exile were terrible punishments since they robbed a man of the consolations of religion. Strangers and slaves were not considered to be kin, and they were therefore outside the law and had no rights. In a war, two people and two sets of gods confronted each other.

A revolution of the aristocracy broke up the ancient political order. The aristocrats deprived the king of his political power. However, theirs was a conservative revolution, founded on social class and differences of birth, and the aristocrats appreciated the utility of the old religious beliefs. The king was therefore allowed to retain his sacerdotal functions. Nevertheless, the family religion was inevitably weakened, a process hastened by the development of inheritance laws that allowed the division of the family estate. Differences of social class developed, even within the extended family. The society divided into two opposed classes of aristocrats and plebeians. The law, which had been the exclusive domain of the priests, became public property. It was therefore no longer sacred and immutable. Political institutions lost their religious character.

Ultimately, Christianity became the religion of the Roman Empire, marking the end of the social transformation that had begun six or seven centuries earlier. Christianity was fitted for this role since it was a universal religion, not the cult of a specific city or nation. And it denied that state and church were one, so turning its back on the fundamental principle of the ancient order. In short, the history of the ancient order was the history of a particularistic religion, and it came to an end when a universal religion was introduced. 'We have written the history of a belief,' Fustel concludes. 'It established itself: human society was constituted. It modified itself: society underwent a series of revolutions. It disappeared: the society was transformed. Such was the law of ancient times.'[51]

Fustel was a more influential figure than Maine in the field of classical historiography,[52] at least outside Britain, but his works seem to have had little impact on the (mainly British) anthropologists who were concerned with primitive society. The one sociologist who paid serious attention to his ideas about the place of religion in ancient society was his former student, Émile Durkheim, but Durkheim ended by repudiating his master. 'M. Fustel de Coulanges has discovered that the primitive organization of societies was based on the family and that, furthermore, the formation of the primitive family had religion as its base', Durkheim wrote in his first great monograph, *The Division of Labour in Society*, published in 1893. But Fustel 'has taken the cause for the effect'. It is not religion that explains social arrangements. On the contrary, it is society 'which explains the power and nature of the religious idea'.[53] Turned upside down, Fustel's thesis was to have a significant influence on the sociology of primitive society.[54]

Matriarchy: the critique

Maine's influence soon waned within British anthropology. In 1861, the year in which *Ancient Law* appeared, a Swiss jurist, Johannes Bachofen, published a book entitled *Das Mutterrecht*. Himself a product of the German school of Roman historical legal studies, Bachofen took classical myths as his main source, in the manner of Grimm, but he came to a most startling conclusion. The most ancient societies were controlled not by patriarchs but by women.

Maine paid virtually no attention to Bachofen, and his ideas had little direct influence in Britain or America. Soon, however, the 'matriarchy' thesis was to be propounded in Britain by a formidable polemicist, John Ferguson McLennan. Born in Inverness in 1827, McLennan was the son of an insurance agent. He was educated at King's College, Aberdeen, and at Trinity College, Cambridge. Going down from Cambridge without a degree, he spent two years on Grub Street, writing for *The Leader* and other radical periodicals. In 1857 he was called to the bar in Edinburgh, and served as secretary of the Scottish Society for Promoting the Amendment of the Law. He contributed the entry on 'Law' to the *Encyclopaedia Britannica,* in which he sketched the conventional theory of political development, from the patriarchal family to the tribe to the state. Then, as Tylor remarked in his obituary, 'in 1865 he published a law-book which had the natural and immediate effect of losing him half his briefs. This was *Primitive Marriage,* the work by which he made his mark in the scientific study of man.'[55]

McLennan was to claim that he had read Bachofen's *Das Mutterrecht* for the first time only in 1866, and certainly the structure of his argument is very different.[56] A much more significant influence on *Primitive Marriage* is Malthus. In Chapter 3 of his *Essay on the Principle of Population* Malthus had speculated on the ways in which primitive communities had restricted their populations to a number which could be supported by their resources – a 'prodigious waste of human life occasioned by this perpetual struggle for room and food'. Denis Diderot had speculated in his *Supplément au voyage de Bougainville* about savage practices of population control, including cannibalism, castration, and infanticide. According to Malthus, however, population was controlled mainly by the great 'vices' of famine, epidemic and war, but he also referred gloomily to the sinful practices of abortion and infanticide.

British administrators discovered evidence of systematic female infanticide among some high-caste groups in North India, and in 1857 Cave-Browne published a detailed account, *Indian Infanticide: Its Origin, Progress and Suppression.* Primitive peoples lived in a state of war, McLennan believed, in a life and death struggle for scarce resources. One desperate recourse was to kill their daughters.

> Foremost among the results of this early struggle for food and security, must have been an effect upon the balance of the sexes. As braves and hunters were required and valued, it would be in the interest of every horde to rear, when possible, its healthy male children. It would be less in its interest to rear females, as

they would be less capable of self-support, and of contributing, by their exertions, to the common good. In this lies the only explanation which can be accepted of those systems of female infanticide still existing.[57]

McLennan proceeded logically from this premise. If the braves killed off the girls in their group, they would obviously have to look elsewhere for wives. Since a perpetual struggle was going on between different communities, they would have had to capture wives from enemy groups. Wives would nevertheless have remained in short supply. Men therefore shared the women they captured. (McLennan called this arrangement 'rude polyandry'.) Given rude polyandry, no man could be sure who his children were. Primitive people even denied that the father had a role in procreation. Consequently the first kinship systems would have been based on blood relationships traced through women only.

In time, the 'rude' forms of wife-sharing would have given way to a more refined arrangement. The sons of one mother, recognising a degree of solidarity, would agree to share their wives with one another but not with other members of their band. A child would now recognise that its father was one of a set of brothers. This would be a step in the direction of recognising paternity. Eventually, men insisted on exclusive rights in their wives. Paternity was now certain, at least in principle. While these advances were being booked on the domestic front, societies were also becoming more prosperous. Property ownership now became an issue. Men would naturally want to leave their property to the sons. Kinship ties between men would then become more important than ties traced through women: as 'the system of kinship through males arose, that through females would – and chiefly under the influence of property – die away.'[58] The final step was the emergence of the patriarchal family. Far from being the starting point of political evolution, as Maine supposed, it was end of the story. 'The order of social development', McLennan concluded, 'is then, that the tribe stands first; the gens or house next; and last of all the family.'[59]

Clearly, *Primitive Marriage* was a direct response to Maine's *Ancient Law*. Indeed, McLennan was out to undermine Maine. 'Maine is McLennan's chief antagonist', according to one commentator. 'Maine was also an ideal representation of everything to which McLennan was either antagonistic or to which he had aspired and had failed to achieve'.[60] McLennan was a lawyer without briefs, a poor hack, and a radical. Maine was a successful jurist, a prominent journalist, and an uncompromising reactionary.

McLennan also used a different method. Unlike Maine he did not limit himself to Indo–European comparisons. In the tradition of the philosophers of the Scottish Enlightenment, he assumed that social institutions had developed along a similar path all over the world.[61] Any account of 'primitive' behaviour might therefore be cited to support his speculations. It was not even necessary to find a primitive society in which men captured wives from enemy bands. It was enough to discover evidence that they had once engaged in such a practice. This was possible, because past practices left traces, fossils, what Tylor termed 'survivals'. McLennan believed that these took the form of symbolic performances – 'wherever we discover symbolical forms, we are justified in inferring that in the past life of the people employing them, there were corresponding realities'.[62] An example was the ritual pretence, which so often cropped up in marriage ceremonies, that the bride was being abducted. This referred back to a state of affairs in which men really had gone out and taken their wives by force.

Maine's defence

An American lawyer, Lewis Henry Morgan, developed a more elaborate and systematic version of McLennan's thesis. Leading British anthropologists were persuaded, but at first Maine tried to pretend that the new theory was irrelevant to his own thesis. He was writing about the history of Indo–European societies. His opponents may have based their arguments on observations, but 'on observation of the ideas and practices of the now savage races', observations that were in any case often unreliable. They deduced 'all later social order from the miscellaneous disorganised horde'.[63] However, there was no evidence that India had passed through a 'matriarchal' phase. All the Indo–Europeans were patriarchal. So also were the Semites and the 'Uralians' (the Turks, Hungarians and Finns). Therefore even if McLennan could show that the first savage societies were matriarchal, this would 'not concern us till the Kinship of the higher races can be distinctly shown to have grown out of the Kinship now known only to the lower, and even then they concern us only remotely'.[64]

Maine finally had to admit, however, that McLennan and Morgan had advanced a genuine alternative to his own thesis. Indeed, as he himself pointed out, they stood his theory of Patriarchal Society on its head. They derived 'the smaller from the larger group, not the larger from the smaller'.[65] The family now came at the end of the story instead of the beginning. Lawyer-like, Maine cast doubt on the reliability of reports on savage peoples, and drew attention to contradictions and lacunae in what McLennan and Morgan had to say. He also advanced a theoretical objection, a weighty one, since it had behind it the authority of Darwin himself. In *The Descent of Man*, published in 1871, Darwin had taken issue with McLennan, arguing that sexual jealousy was a fundamental emotion, one that human beings shared with the apes and other animals. The promiscuous hordes imagined by McLennan and Morgan were counter to man's sexual nature. Maine now suggested that that 'sexual jealousy, indulged through power, might serve as a definition of the Patriarchal Family'.[66]

None the less, by the time that Maine launched his counter-attack on McLennan and Morgan, in 1883, he was fighting a losing battle for the minds of the anthropologists at home. The comparative method of McLennan and Morgan, which drew on ethnographic materials from all over the world, was becoming fashionable. Tylor and Lubbock were its advocates, and Frazer a stylish exponent. The comparative method demonstrated the truth of the matriarchal thesis, and it became the orthodoxy of the next generation.

Chapter 4

Lewis Henry Morgan and *Ancient Society*

In the 1870s, a provincial American lawyer, Lewis Henry Morgan, produced what was to become one of the most influential versions of the theory of primitive society. Perhaps it was because of his very isolation, in Rochester, New York, that he was able to synthesise a stream of ideas that came from across the Atlantic, but he was not working altogether alone. Rochester had a lively intellectual culture,[1] and his good friend the Rev. McIlvaine, the Presbyterian minister, was a philologist and something of a Sanskrit scholar. It was McIlvaine who encouraged Morgan to develop his ideas, provided him with a crucial inspiration when he had reached an impasse, and secured the eventual publication of his first important theoretical work by the Smithsonian Institution. Morgan dedicated *Ancient Society* to his friend.

McIlvaine did his best to persuade Morgan to affirm his belief in the Christian faith, and he carefully monitored the implications of his theories. Indeed, he has been represented as a censor, who checked the free expression of Morgan's ideas for theological reasons. This interpretation derived some plausibility from McIlvaine's own claim:

> that whilst his great work on 'Ancient Society' was passing through the press, I called his attention to a passage which inadvertently might have found its place there, and which might be construed as an endorsement of these materialistic speculations in connection with evolution; and he immediately cancelled the whole page, although it had already been stereotyped.[2]

However, this view of McIlvaine's role altered as the context of the evolutionist debate in the United States was better appreciated.

McIlvaine's branch of the Presbyterian church participated in a markedly liberal movement within New England Calvinism in the second half of the nineteenth century.[3] Its leading members were committed to democratic ideals, repudiated slavery, flirted with Utilitarianism, and were prepared to accommodate the most advanced scientific theories. Not even the theory of evolution presented an insuperable problem. 'Evolution', one theologian explained, 'is God's way of doing things'.[4] The new chronology could also be taken on board. 'I cannot find sufficient data in the Scriptures for a revealed chronology', McIlvaine commented. 'Neither, as I read the first chapters of Genesis, does it appear that man was created in a high state of development, though certainly in a state of innocence.'[5]

In fact the northern Presbyterians welcomed Darwin's witness with reference to a very sensitive political issue. They were up in arms against their southern Presbyterian brethren, who justified slavery on the grounds that God had created several distinct human species, each with a particular destiny. During the Civil War an 'American school of anthropology' developed in the South which propagated this view. It drew the support even of Agassiz, a famous but eccentric Lamarckian biologist at Harvard.[6] According to the northern Presbyterians, this 'polygenist' thesis was a denial of the truth, to which both the Bible and the Declaration of Independence bore witness, that all men were created equal. Darwin insisted that the different races were simply varieties of one species, with a common origin, an aspect of his theory that was particularly emphasised by Asa Gray, Agassiz's rival at Harvard and the leader of the American Darwinians.

But on one crucial issue, Darwin's views were unacceptable to most Christians. He believed that the species were not fixed. Despite his initial caution, it also soon became evident that he agreed with Huxley that human beings had evolved from primate ancestors. These ideas were clearly irreconcilable with the Book of Genesis. However, a number of mainstream biologists remained convinced that the species were fixed, as Cuvier had argued. Agassiz taught that God had created particular species to fit into predetermined ecological relations. Adaptation was a sign of planning rather than of selection. Species were incarnations of a divine idea. 'Natural History must, in good time, become the analysis of the thoughts of the Creator of the Universe, as manifested in the animal and vegetable kingdoms.'[7] Morgan, a competent amateur biologist, wrote a study of the American beaver that won Agassiz's admiration, in which he affirmed his faith in Cuvier's fixed typology of species, and his belief in the separate creation of the human species.[8]

It was possible, however, to believe that the species were fixed without having to conclude that they were changeless. Agassiz and any number of good biologists ruled out 'transmutation', the change of one species into another. Nevertheless, they believed that a species might realise an inner potential, which gradually unfolded. Those who thought in this way commonly conceived of the development of species on the analogy of the evolution of the embryo. The tadpole might become a frog, but that did not amount to a change of species. The term 'evolution' itself was generally used in this embryological sense until the late 1870s.[9] Darwin did not use the word at all in *The Origin of Species* in 1859, nor did Morgan in in his *Systems of Consanguinity and Affinity* in 1871, although he introduced it six years later in *Ancient Society* as a synonym for progress.

All this fitted in very nicely with a common New England Calvinist belief that human history, since Christ, was a record of progress and moral improvement inspired by God, in which every group had its preordained role. This optimism was in stark contrast to the pessimism of Malthus, or the scepticism of Darwin. 'I believe in no fixed law of development', Darwin had written in *Origin*,[10] and when Christian intellectuals such as McIlvaine attacked his 'materialist' theory they meant in particular his view that natural history is contingent, unplanned, without a goal, the product simply of chance mutations and natural selection. McIlvaine made a similar objection to the thesis of Malthus, that it left no place for divine planning.[11] Progress was evidence of God's purpose, and in his speech at Morgan's funeral McIlvaine particularly praised Morgan's 'demonstration that progress is a fundamental law of human society, and one which has always prevailed – progress in thought and knowledge, in industry, in morality, in social organization, in institutions, and in all things tending to, or advancing, civilization and general well-being.'[12]

But these were only the broadest considerations that informed Morgan's thinking. He was more immediately concerned with issues in American ethnology, and, like Maine, he was particularly impressed with the approach that had been developed by students of the Indo–European languages.

The League of the Iroquois

Lewis Henry Morgan, the ninth of thirteen children, was born in 1818 in Aurora, New York. His father, a wealthy farmer, a state senator, and a devout Presbyterian, died when Morgan was a boy of eight. In 1838 he went to Union College, a school distinguished for its Whig politics, which found fashionable expression in the idealisation of the democratic civilisation of Athens.[13] In 1844 he began to practise law in Rochester, New York.

In Rochester, Morgan set up a fraternity. There was an Iroquois reservation nearby, and the fraternity took the name Iroquois and planned to organise itself on the lines of the Iroquois League. Morgan began to visit the nearby reservation and to collect ethnographic information. He campaigned against a move to deport the Iroquois to Kansas, and helped the tribe with a land claim.[14] Eventually he wrote up his ethnographic findings, discharging an undertaking that, so he thought, had now come to an end.

Although primarily a descriptive work, *The League of the Iroquois* set the Iroquois in a universal historical context, which Morgan took from Grote's vastly influential *History of Greece*.[15] Initially, Greeks belonged to separate, independent families. These then joined together to form a larger kinship corporation, the gens, which Grote described as at once a kinship and a political unit, democratic in nature, and with religious functions. In time gentes combined to form larger associations, the phratry and the tribe. There followed a period of monarchy and despotism, but Athens eventually pioneered a higher democratic form of government.

Morgan identified the Iroquois with Grote's earliest condition, in which government was based on 'family relationships'.

> These relations are older than the notions of society or government, and are consistent alike with the hunter, the pastoral and the civilized state. The several nations of the Iroquois, united, constituted one Family, dwelling together in one Long House; and those ties of family relationship were carried throughout their civil and social system, from individuals to tribes, from tribes to nations, and from the nations to the League itself, and bound them together in one common, indissoluble brotherhood.[16]

Morgan also incidentally described the unfamiliar Iroquois terminology for kin, which was 'unlike that of the civil or canon law; but was yet a clear and definite system. No distinction was made between the lineal and collateral lines, either in the ascending or descending series'.[17] He was later to argue that the kinship terminology reflected exotic forms of group marriage, but now he merely recorded the prosaic marriage arrangements of the Iroquois, remarking only on the apparent absence of affection between man and wife. Marriages were arranged by the mothers of the couple, who acted for larger family units.

The American Indian

'With the publication [of *The League of the Iroquois*] in January 1851', Morgan recorded, 'I laid aside the Indian subject to devote my time to my profession. My principal object in writing this work, which exhibits abundant evidence of hasty execution, was to free myself of the subject.'[18] He now concentrated on business, and prospered. In 1855 he became a director of the Iron Mountain Rail Road Company and he soon extended his interest to other railway projects. 'From the close of 1850 until the summer of 1857,' he recorded in his Journal, 'Indian affairs were laid entirely aside.'[19]

As he became rich, Morgan was able to devote more time to outside interests. He took up politics, serving as Republican congressman and then senator in the state assembly between 1861 and 1869, and he became chairman of the Indian affairs committee of the assembly. He also angled, unsuccessfully, for the federal post of Secretary of Indian Affairs. At the same time, he maintained his intellectual interests. With McIlvaine he founded the Pundit Club in Rochester, at which papers were read dealing with such matters as Lyell's geology, Sanskrit, and ethnology.[20]

In 1856 Morgan was elected to the Association for the Advancement of Science. This encouraged him to return at last to his Iroquois notes in order to prepare a paper for the following annual meeting. The paper he wrote, entitled 'Laws of descent of the Iroquois', dealt mainly with their system of classifying kin, which he considered a unique invention of the tribe. Soon, however, a fresh discovery was to change his mind. In the summer of 1858 Morgan found that the Ojibwa, who spoke a different language from the Iroquois, nevertheless had essentially the same system of classifying kin. 'Every term of relationship was radically different from the corresponding term in the Iroquois; but the classification of kindred was the same. It was manifest that the two systems were identical in their fundamental characteristics.'[21] This discovery suggested an extraordinary hypothesis.

> From this time I began to be sensible to the important uses which such a primary institution as this must have in its bearing upon the question of the genetic connection of the American Indian nation, not only, but also on the still more important question of their Asiatic origin.[22]

It was now, at the age of 40, that his most important research began.

To appreciate what Morgan had in mind, it is necessary first to consider the state of play in American ethnology at the time. This had just been thoroughly and critically reviewed by Samuel Haven, in his *Archaeology of the United States*, which was published by the Smithsonian Institution in 1856, precisely at the moment when Morgan's interest in American ethnology was quickened once again.

Haven conceded with some reluctance that 'The subject of American ethnology passes ... insensibly into the general question of the original unity or diversity of mankind.'[23] He reviewed in detail the linguistic studies of American languages, emphasising Gallatin's conclusion that the Indian languages shared a common and distinct character, probably resulting from a very long period of isolation. This unity existed despite wide variations in vocabulary: 'however differing in their words, the most striking uniformity in their grammatical forms and structure appears to exist in all the American languages'.[24] According to Gallatin, the most characteristic structural feature of the Indian languages was what Von Humboldt had called 'agglutination', i.e. glueing together; 'a tendency to accumulate a multitude of ideas in a single word', as Haven defined it.[25] Studies of physiology and archaeology also showed that American Indians were originally one people, with a long history. 'Their religious doctrines, their superstitions ... and their arts, accord with those of the most primitive age of mankind. With all their characteristics affinities are found in the early condition of Asiatic races.'[26] The evidence therefore supported the monogenist belief in the unity of the human race.

Haven's most striking data came from philology, and this was a field with which Morgan was familiar, if only from exchanges with McIlvaine. McIlvaine was a Sanskritist, but this meant that he was an Indo–European man. The models of Gallatin and other American linguists imitated those of the Indo–Europeanists, who had established relationships between languages formerly regarded as completely distinct, and demonstrated that the major European languages were distantly related to Sanskrit. Some speculated that their common point of origin was in India. The Semitic languages were similarly interrelated, and they too were of Asian origin. In the 1860s, scholars mooted the possibility that the Indo–European and Semitic language stocks were ultimately related to each other.

The Professor of Sanskrit at Oxford, Max Müller, suggested that there was a third stock, which he called 'Turanian'. It was divided into a European, northern branch (Turkish, Finnish, Mongolian, Basque, etc.) and a southern, tropical branch. This tropical language family included most if not all of the other languages in the world, including Tamil (the main Indian language which is not related to Sanskrit) and the languages of the American Indians. Southern Turanian seemed a very diverse group. Superficially at least, its members had few linguistic features in common. But Müller explained that the people who spoke Turanian languages were typically nomads. Consequently their languages were liable to rapid change and exhibited great dialectical variation. He instanced the terms for kin, explaining that these were stable in Aryan languages but not in Turanian. Yet although words themselves changed, underlying concepts might remain constant. At this level the Turanian languages 'share much in common, and show that before their divergency a certain nucleus of language was formed, in which some parts of language, the first to crystallise and the most difficult to be analysed, had become fixed and stationary. Numerals, pronouns, and some of the simplest applied verbal roots belong to this class of words.'[27] These languages had something else in common, Müller believed. They all exhibited von Humboldt's 'agglutinating' tendency.

Were these three linguistic stocks (all, probably, ultimately of Asian origin) independent? Were there any traces of an original language spoken by a once-united human race? Müller could find no philological basis for such a conclusion, but he proposed an alternative resolution of the issue. Using von Humboldt's typology, which classified languages according to grammatical principles that he termed 'isolation, agglutination and inflexion', Müller argued that language stocks could be ordered on a scale of progressive development. The most primitive languages were 'isolating'. Each word consisted of a single, stable root. At a more advanced level they were characterised by 'agglutination': roots were 'glued together' to form new words. The most developed languages went in for 'amalgamation', developing inflected forms in which the original roots, once simply glued together, merged to form quite new words.

There were difficulties with this scheme. Chinese, for instance, was classified as an 'isolating language' (i.e. each word consists of a single, stable root). Yet it was hard to believe that Chinese was exceptionally primitive. Müller tried to resolve this particular difficulty by providing Chinese with its own private evolutionary track. But for the rest, the southern Turanian languages could be classified as 'agglutinating', while the northern (or European) Turanian languages could be classified with the Semitic and Indo–European languages as 'amalgamating'. They had, however, once been 'agglutinating' themselves. The classification therefore cross-cut the established boundaries of language families and yielded a new classification, in which the languages of Europe, the Middle East and North India were associated together and opposed to most of the languages spoken in the tropics and in North America. But this did not contradict the idea that all human beings – and all languages – had a common origin. The languages of Europe were certainly more advanced, but they had once been 'agglutinating', and even 'isolating' themselves.

Müller linked this scheme of linguistic development with the four-stage model of the Scottish Enlightenment. Their economic stages were conventionally associated with a political development from anarchic communism to private property and the state. Müller now added a theory of linguistic progress. Some Indo–European scholars had tried to find philological clues to the early condition of the Indo–Europeans. Had they originally been nomads? At what stage might they have shifted from nomadism to agriculture? Müller's synthetic model opposed a category of primitive, anarchic, dispersed nomads, speaking agglutinating languages in a state of continual dialectical flux, and civilised, centralised, agricultural societies, with literate élites and, consequently, more stable and advanced languages characterised by 'amalgamation'. The beauty of this model was that it both divided and united humanity. Müller endorsed the division into 'higher' Aryan and Semitic and 'lower' southern Turanian people. At the same time, his model assumed that all language groups had a single origin. This was the paradigm to which Morgan referred most often in his *Systems of Consanguinity and Affinity of the Human Family.*

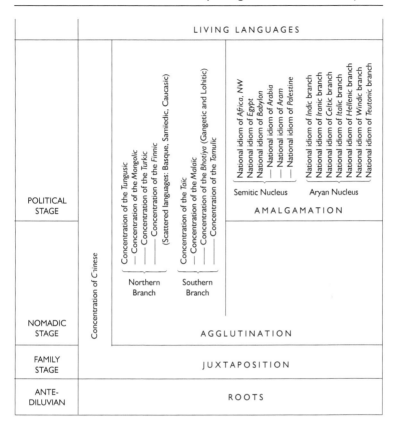

Figure 4.1 Müller's summary of linguistic progress (from Max Müller's contribution to C. C. J. Bunsen (1854), *Outlines of the Philosophy of University History Applied to Language and Religion,* 2 vols, London, Longman).

Asian origins

After stumbling upon the fact that the Ojibwa had substantially the same system of classifying relatives as the Iroquois, Morgan checked with Rigg's lexicon of the Dakota language and found that they lumped relatives together in the same 'classificatory' manner as the Iroquois and Ojibwa. How widely was the system distributed? In December 1858, Morgan sent schedules out to Indian areas to be filled in by missionaries and Indian agents, and the Smithsonian Institution arranged for copies to be posted to consular agents all over the world. The results were disappointing, perhaps not surprisingly, since the questionnaire ran to eight printed pages and its completion demanded considerable time and effort. A few satisfactory schedules were nevertheless returned, and Morgan carried out his enquiries in person in reservations in Kansas and Nebraska. By the middle of 1859 he was convinced that there was a uniform system of classifying relatives throughout North America. This he took as further evidence that the North American Indians had a common origin.

But if the Indians were ultimately one group, where had they come from? Morgan was inclined to accept the hypothesis of Schoolcraft and other specialists, supported by Haven, that they were ultimately of Asian origin. Obviously they were not 'Aryan', and so Morgan looked for connections among Müller's prototypical Asian Turanians, the Tamils. Accordingly, he invited an American missionary in South India, Dr Scudder, to prepare a schedule for Tamil and Telugu. McIlvaine testified that at this time Morgan:

> lived and worked often in a state of great mental excitement, and the answers he received, as they came in, sometimes nearly overpowered him. I well remember one occasion when he came into my study, saying, 'I shall find it, I shall find it among the Tamil people and Dravidian tribes of Southern India'. At that time I had no expectation of any such result; and I said to him, 'My friend, you have enough to do in working out your discovery in connection with the tribes of the American continent – let the peoples of the old world go'. He replied, 'I cannot do it – I must go on, for I am sure I shall find it all there'.[28]

When Scudder returned the Tamil–Telegu schedule, Morgan laid it side by side with the Seneca–Iroquois system and concluded that it had the same structure. He wrote to Scudder 'that we had now been able to put our hands upon decisive evidence of the Asiatic origin of the American Indian race'.[29] In *Systems of Consanguinity and Affinity of the Human Family* he expressed the same conclusion more grandiloquently: 'When the discoverers of the New World bestowed upon its inhabitants the name of *Indians*, under the impression that they had reached the Indies, they little suspected that children of the same original family, although upon a different continent, stood before them. By a singular coincidence error was truth.'[30]

Classificatory and descriptive systems of consanguinity

Morgan concluded that all the members of Müller's southern Turanian family had what he called 'classificatory' kinship terminologies. The Aryans, Semites and northern Turanians all had 'descriptive' systems. These two types of systems were quite distinct. Indeed, they were virtually inversions of each other.

In descriptive systems there are different terms for father and mother, husband and wife, brother and sister, and son and daughter. None of these terms is applied outside the nuclear family. Morgan argued that such systems mirror the reality of biological kinship, clearly marking the degrees of blood relationship. Classificatory systems, in contrast, did not reflect the natural degrees of kinship. (He initially called the two systems 'natural' and 'artificial'.) Classificatory kinship systems lumped relationships of different kinds together under one term. The same word might refer, for example, to father, father's brother, father's father's brother's son, and also perhaps to other relatives, confusing different kinds and degrees of biological relatedness. 'It thus confounds relationships, which, under the descriptive system, are distinct, and enlarges the signification both of the primary and secondary terms beyond their seemingly appropriate sense.'[31] The classificatory principle immediately suggested the mechanism of 'agglutination'. Indeed, the languages that applied one kin term to various degrees of relationships were precisely those which Müller regarded as 'agglutinating'.

But if classificatory systems did not properly describe biological relationships, they were by no means incoherent. If, for example, father's brother was 'father', then, quite properly, father's brother's wife was 'mother', father's brother's son 'brother', etc. Morgan concluded that 'a system has been created which must be regarded as a domestic institution in the highest sense of this expression. No other can properly characterize a structure the framework of which is so complete, and the details of which are so rigorously adjusted.'[32]

The classificatory systems were not all of the same kind. Morgan divided Müller's southern Turanian group into three types, the Malayan, the Turanian, and the Ganowanian (the American Indian group). In both the Turanian and Ganowanian systems, only one set of cousins were called 'brother' and 'sister'. These were the children of a person's father's brothers or mother's sisters. Other cousins (children of father's sisters or mother's brothers) were distinguished from siblings. The Malayan systems, in contrast, classed all cousins together with siblings, and all parents' siblings together with parents. This category included not only the peoples of the Pacific but a number of far-flung peoples, and even the Zulu, Morgan's only African group.

Morgan now wrote up his massive materials, tabulating and analysing 139 kinship schedules from all the over the world, listing over 260 kin-types for each. He believed that he had successfully completed a type of philological study. It demonstrated the unity and the ultimately Asian origin of the American Indian languages, and suggested the existence of two great linguistic stocks, one European and north-west Asian, and the other American or southern and tropical. Yet when he submitted the manuscript for publication, Joseph Henry, the director of the Smithsonian Institution, was reluctant to accept it, writing to Morgan that 'the first impression of one who has been engaged in physical research is that, in proportion to the conclusions arrived at, the quantity of your material is very large'.[33]

Henry sent Morgan's manuscript for consideration to two philologists and Sanskritists, Whitney at Yale, and McIlvaine himself. McIlvaine agreed that the analysis was incomplete. Morgan had demonstrated the inner coherence of classificatory systems, but their meaning remained a mystery. He remarked that at this stage:

> our friend had not perceived any material significance or explanation of the immense body of entirely new facts which he had discovered and collected. He could not at all account for them. In fact, he regarded this system, or these slightly different forms of one system, as invented and wholly artificial, so different was it from that which now prevails in civilized society, and which evidently follows the flow of the blood. During all these years, he had not the least conception of any process of thought in which it could have originated, or of anything which could have caused it so universally to prevail. He treated it as something which must throw great light upon pre-historic man, but what light he had not discovered.[34]

And yet, a year before the submission of the manuscript, McIlvaine had discussed with Morgan a plausible explanation of the classificatory systems. In a letter dated March 1864, he wrote:

I have just lighted upon certain references which throw some light upon the origin of your Tamilian or Indian system of relationships; at least on some parts of it. You remember we were talking about whether it did not point back to a state of promiscuous intercourse. You will find in Aristotle's politics Book II chapter 3 where he is refuting Plato's doctrine of a community of wives this sentence, 'Some tribes in upper Africa have their wives in common', and in a note in Bonn's translation of it the following references, 'For example the Masimanes (Herodotus IV, 172) and the Ayseuses (ib. IV, 180)'…

With respect to the Agathyrsi Herodotus says, 'They have their wives in common, that so they may all be brothers (kasignetoi) and being all akin, may be free from envy & mutual enmities'.

I am inclined to think that this state of society might, upon a full and minute investigation of the remains of antiquity, be found more extensively to have prevailed than is commonly supposed.[35]

The hypothesis was, then, that the mysterious 'classificatory' designation of kin was based on real parent–child relationships, as was the descriptive system. Both described a consanguineal reality, but the realities were differently ordered. In societies with 'classificatory' terminologies, wives were held in common. A child would therefore not know who its father was. Accordingly, all potential fathers were 'father', all their children 'brother' or 'sister', etc. Similarly, all the women who were actually or potentially the mates of a 'father' were termed 'mother'.

Morgan did not immediately develop this suggestion. It was only after Joseph Henry's rejection of his manuscript that he returned to the idea. According to one of his biographers, it was now that he studied, with some jealousy, McLennan's *Primitive Marriage*, which had just appeared.[36] McLennan began with a primitive band in which the men held their women in common. Then a form of marriage was instituted: one woman was shared by several male partners. At this stage, paternity was still uncertain and blood relationships could only be claimed through the mother. A more advanced form of polyandry was eventually adopted, in which brothers held one wife in common. It then became possible to trace kinship through men. With the growth of property, kinship in the male line became more and more important. Finally individual property was recognised.

This made men want to establish individual relationships of paternity, and stimulated the emergence of modern forms of marriage.

What Morgan seems to have done was to link the types of kinship terminologies he had discovered with the forms of marriage that McLennan described. A recent study by Thomas Trautmann concludes, however, that Morgan bought McLennan's book only in 1867, and that he was ignorant of McLennan's theory when he came up with his own. In response to repeated hints from McIlvaine, he had eventually constructed his own hypothetical series of marriage types.[37] This seems implausible. After all, Morgan and McIlvaine were doing their best to keep up with modern science, and the serious magazines would have brought them news of McLennan's ideas. Certainly the parallels are remarkable.

In February 1868, Morgan presented his new ideas to a meeting of the American Academy of Art and Sciences, under the title 'A conjectural solution to the origin of the classificatory system of relationship'. His audience included Agassiz and Asa Gray. Tense and disappointed, Morgan hurriedly left the room after giving his lecture. 'Agassiz does not know, nor could the other members present fully appreciate the remarkable character of the system', he wrote to a friend. 'I was afraid to show more lest they would not bear it.'[38] But in the event the Academy requested the text of his lecture for publication and elected him to its membership. This paper provided the basis for a new final chapter for *Systems*, which was now at last accepted for publication by the Smithsonian, although problems of format and expense delayed its appearance until 1871. It was the most expensive book which the Smithsonian had published up to that time.

Morgan did not mechanically fit the different systems of kin classifications to the types of marriage described by McLennan. Perhaps this would have been impossible, but in any case he introduced his own refinements into McLennan's model. McLennan had imagined that the first step in the direction of marriage would have been polyandry, in which several men shared one wife, as, apparently, was the practice in Tibet. Morgan, however, decided that the first form of marriage had been discovered by American missionaries in Hawaii. The 'Hawaiian custom' (which McIlvaine had indeed brought to his attention) was 'a compound form of polyginia and polyandria'. A set of brothers was married collectively to their own sisters. Nephews and nieces were therefore indistinguishable from sons and daughters.

All the children of my several brothers, myself a male, are my sons and daughters, Reason: I cohabit with all my brothers' wives, who are my own wives as well (using the terms husband and wife in the sense of the custom). As it would be impossible for me to distinguish my own children from those of my brothers, if I call any one my child, I must call them all my children. One is as likely to be mine as another.[39]

Similarly, a man's sisters were his wives, and so the children of any sister counted as his own. This form of classification, in which cousins were called brother or sister, had been identified by Morgan in his enquiries. He called it the Malayan system, and now he had an explanation for it. The classification of kin corresponded to what Morgan termed the 'Hawaiian custom', the marriage of brothers to their sisters.

This kind of 'marriage' was morally repugnant, as people gradually became aware. Pressure grew to reform. ('For it may be affirmed, as a general proposition, that the principal customs and institutions of mankind have originated in great reformatory movements.')[40] It was therefore decided to prohibit marriages between brothers and sisters. Group marriages continued, but a set of brothers would now marry someone else's set of sisters. Marriage would remain a combination of polyandry and polygamy, but while the children of a man's brother would still count as his children, the children of his sister would not. They would be distinguished as nephews and nieces. From the point of view of a woman, her sisters' children would be counted together with her own, but her brothers' children would be distinguished as nephews and nieces. And once again, Morgan had already discovered a system of kinship classification that made precisely these distinctions. It was found among the Iroquois and also among the Tamil or Dravidian peoples of South India.

Further stages in the development of the family were sketched more casually. Eventually, the development of private property made possible 'the true family in its modern acceptation'. Property was the very essence of civilisation. 'It is impossible to separate property, considered in the concrete, from civilization, or for civilization to exist without its presence, protection, and regulated inheritance. Of property in this sense, all barbarous nations are necessarily ignorant.'[41]

Everything was now properly accounted for. The structure was so neat that it just had to be true. 'It may be confidently affirmed

Table 4.1 The development of family types

I	Promiscuous intercourse
II	The intermarriage or cohabitation of brothers and sisters
III	The communal family (first stage of the family)
IV	The Hawaiian custom, giving
V	The Malayan form of the classificatory system of relationship
VI	The tribal organization, giving
VII	The Turanian and Ganowanian system of relationship
VIII	Marriage between single pairs, giving
IX	The barbarian family (second stage of the family)
X	Polygamy, giving
XI	The patriarchal family (third stage of the family)
XII	Polyandria
XIII	The rise of property with the settlement of lineal succession to estates, giving
XIV	The civilized family (fourth and ultimate state of the family), producing
XV	The overthrow of the classificatory system of relationship, and the substitution of the descriptive.

This table occurs in Morgan's 'A conjectural solution of the origin of the classificatory system of relationship' p. 463, and in *Systems of Consanguinity and Affinity*, p. 480.

that this great sequence of customs and institutions, although for the present hypothetical, will organize and explain the body of ascertained facts, with respect to the primitive history of mankind, in a manner so singularly and surprisingly adequate as to invest it with a strong probability of truth.'[42]

Morgan finally summed up the whole historical progression in Table 4.1.

Encountering the British anthropologists

Morgan visited Europe in 1871, taking delivery of his first copies of *Systems* in London. He met Max Müller, Maine, McLennan, Lubbock (whom he found playing cricket), Spencer, Huxley and even Darwin, whose sons visited him in turn in Rochester the following year.[43] 1871 was also the year in which Darwin published his *Descent of Man*. This book was, of course, of capital importance to all anthropologists. In it Darwin paid attention to McLennan's theory of matriarchy, and he raised the question of intellectual development, which was to become the central issue in anthropology in the following decades. Also in 1870–1871, Tylor and Lubbock each published his most import book: Tylor his *Primitive Culture*, and Lubbock his *Origin of Civilization*. Both profoundly affected Morgan's thinking.

Lubbock was responsible for making the new prehistory known in Britain. He had translated the crucial Scandinavian texts, which introduced a three-stage model of development through stone, copper (or bronze) and iron 'ages'. Following Nilsson, he had identified these archaeological phases with the classical Scottish 'stages of progress' through savagery (hunting and gathering), barbarism (nomadism and pastoralism, and then agriculture) and finally industrial civilisation. On the basis of this proven technological advance he and Tylor rejected the hypothesis that human beings had degenerated from a higher state. The fossils and survivals of human industry demonstrated, on the contrary, that progress was the general rule. Tylor was particularly interested in the development of religious ideas, but both he and Lubbock recognised the potential interest of the histories of marriage and the family that had been proposed by McLennan and Morgan. Lubbock discussed them at length, and in a friendly, though not uncritical, fashion. Morgan, in turn, took the Lubbock–Tylor model back to America, and in his most famous book, *Ancient Society*, which appeared in 1877, he turned it to his own ends.

Ancient society

'It can now be asserted upon convincing evidence that savagery preceded barbarism in all the tribes of mankind as barbarism is known to have preceded civilization,' Morgan wrote in the first chapter of *Ancient Society*. 'The history of the human race is one in source, one in experience, and in progress.'[44] The first part of the book, entitled 'Growth of intelligence through inventions and discoveries', summarised the schemas of Lubbock and Tylor that illustrated the development of technology, prosperity, morality, and social institutions. Morgan identified seven stages of development, or 'ethnical periods' (Table 4.2), through which different human groups progressed at different speeds, the Indo–Europeans or 'Aryans' taking the lead. 'The Aryan family represents the central stream of human progress, because it produced the highest type of mankind, and because it had proved its intrinsic superiority by gradually assuming the control of the earth.'[45]

The greater part of *Ancient Society* was devoted to the growth of 'ideas' of civil institutions: the 'growth of the idea of government'

Table 4.2 Morgan's 'ethnical periods'[46]

I	Lower status of savagery. From the infancy of the human race to the commencement of the next period
II	Middle status of savagery. From the acquisition of a fish subsistence and a knowledge of the use of fire, to etc.
III	Upper status of savagery. From the invention of the bow and arrow, to etc.
IV	Lower status of barbarism. From the invention of the art of pottery, to etc.
V	Middle status of barbarism. From the domestication of animals on the eastern hemisphere, and in the western from the cultivation of maize and plants by irrigation, with the use of adobe-brick and stone, to etc.
VI	Upper status of barbarism. From the invention of the process of smelting iron from ore, with the use of iron tools, to etc.
VII	Status of civilization

(Part II), of the family (Part III) and of property (Part IV). While movement from one phase to another might be triggered by a technical advance, the lines of social development are predetermined and inevitable. The development of human institutions expressed God's thoughts. The content of these divine ideas was, however, already familiar enough. First came the community based on kinship, its goods held in common, and then much later a territorial state and private property. But as both Tylor and Lubbock remarked in their reviews,[47] Morgan followed McLennan rather than Maine in arguing that the family was a late development. The gens was the original form of kinship, and it was the most enduring of human institutions.

The central theme of *Ancient Society* is the development of the gens through five stages, each of which Morgan illustrated with a case study of a particular people: the Australians, the Iroquois, the Aztec, the Greeks and the Romans. Every one of these cases had a special relevance for Morgan.

The Australian case represented the most primitive extant system. It was only a step away from the initial condition in which men married their own sisters. Paternity was not recognised, and only ties through the mother were used to build relationships of kinship. The Australians had, however, introduced an improvement: they forbade brothers and sisters to marry each other. A group of brothers held their wives in common, and sisters were still married off as a job lot, but men now exchanged their sisters with other men. A child could now be identified as the offspring of one of the set of brothers married to its mother, and the way was open for tracing descent through males. This argument had been made in more abstract terms in *Systems of Consanguinity and Affinity*, but Morgan could now draw on material that had been specially collected for him in Australia by the Rev. Lorimer Fison.

Once past the stage of the promiscuous band, more elaborate forms of organisation developed. Several gentes, corporations of kinsfolk, began to join in leagues or federations. This stage was illustrated by Morgan's own Iroquois material.

The following level of development was represented by the Aztecs. Here Morgan had to draw on published accounts, but he found that they completely misrepresented the true situation. The Spanish chroniclers had 'adopted the erroneous theory that the Aztec government was a monarchy, analogous in essential respects to existing monarchies in Europe'.[48] Morgan refused to believe this, on a priori grounds. The Aztecs were clearly only at the level of 'the middle status of barbarism', and so they could not have monarchies. Accordingly, he reinterpreted the Aztec materials. The Spanish chroniclers could be relied on when it came to ' the acts of the Spaniards, and to the acts and personal characteristics of the Indians ... But in whatever relates to Indian society and government, their social relations, and plan of life, they are nearly worthless, because they learned nothing and know nothing of either. We are at full liberty to reject them in these respects and commence anew; using any facts they may contain which harmonize with what is known of Indian society.'[49] Using this convenient formula, Morgan was able to recast the Aztec state as a more advanced version of the Iroquois federation. Once again he inspired an ethnographer, in this case Adolphe Bandelier, who produced data which apparently supported his argument.

The next stage was represented by the Greek gens. 'The similarities between the Grecian and Iroquois gens will at once be recognized',[50] Morgan wrote, which was not surprising, since he had based his description of the Iroquois gens on Grote's model of the Greek gens. (Indeed, he admitted that all the characteristics of the gentile system had been defined by Grote.) But Morgan now differed from Grote on two counts. First, Grote had erred in placing the family early on in Greek development – even making it anterior to the gens. Morgan had no doubt that he was mistaken, and did not hesitate to pit his theories against the conclusions of one of the leading classical scholars of the day. Second, he disputed Grote's view that the Greek state had begun as a monarchy. Once more he resorted to a *priori* argument, phrased in a particularly enlightening form:

> The true statement, as it seems to an American, is precisely the reverse of Mr. Grote's; namely, that the primitive Grecian government was essentially democratical, reposing on gentes, phratries and tribes, organized as self-governing bodies, and on the principles of liberty, equality and fraternity. This is borne out by all we know of the gentile organization, which has been shown to rest on principles essentially democratical.[51]

Finally, Morgan discussed the Romans. He had to admit that their political development had ended in dictatorship, but he refused to accept that this was an inevitable outcome of the gentile system. On the contrary, the Roman Empire 'was artificial, illogical, approaching a monstrosity; but capable of wonderful achievements ... The patchwork in its composition was the product of the superior craft of the wealthy classes.'[52] Data on less artificial, illogical, monstrous and elitist societies amply demonstrated that a democratic order, which builds upon the gentile tradition, is natural to humanity.

> As a plan of government, the gentile organization was unequal to the wants of civilized man: but it is something to be said in its remembrance that it developed from the germ the principal governmental institutions of modern civilized states ... out of the ancient council of chiefs came the modern senate; out of the ancient assembly of the people came the modern representative assembly ... out of the ancient general military commander came the modern chief magistrate, whether a feudal or constitutional king, an emperor or a president, the latter being the natural and logical results.[53]

If the Roman Empire was an unfortunate deviation, the constitution of the United States represented the authentic culmination of the long development of the ancient order of the gens.

Part III of *Ancient Society* described the development of the 'idea of the family'. Morgan recapitulated the sequence of family forms described in *Systems of Consanguinity and Affinity*, but now he linked them to stages of gentile organisation. Finally, he briefly reviewed the growth of property, which kept pace with the development of the family and the political system, although Morgan insisted that the increase in prosperity was a sign of progress rather than a cause. Ultimately, political, economic and social progress were a manifestation of God's purpose. The heroic achievements of our primitive ancestors 'were part of the plan of the Supreme Intelligence to develop a barbarian out of a savage, and a civilized man out of this barbarian'.[54]

Marx, Engels and the legacy of Morgan

In later chapters I shall be returning to Morgan's theory, since his work dominated the field of kinship studies for many years. But another tradition also stems from Morgan's writing, for he was adopted into the Marxist canon by Marx and Engels. Reinterpreted by Engels, Morgan became the most important ancestral figure for Soviet and Chinese ethnology.

Marx himself published little on either non-European or 'pre-feudal' societies. His best-known contribution on these subjects was his model of an 'Asiatic mode of production'. This was a primitive state organisation that was concerned only with war, taxation and public works. It was superimposed upon otherwise independent village communities. These village communities held land in common and redistributed their agricultural surplus internally, except for a portion that was appropriated by the state. This model presented later Marxists with grave theoretical problems, in part because it was not evident whether Marx thought of such systems as a geographically-specific Asian development, and in part because it was not clear in what direction societies of this type might be expected to evolve.[55]

Towards the end of his life, Marx took an interest in the new anthropology. He wrote extensive notes on the work of Morgan, Maine and Lubbock, evidently with a view to using them later in a book.[56] After Marx's death, Engels used these notes as a starting-point for his own book, *The Origin of the Family, Private Property and State*, which was published in 1884.

What particularly excited Engels was Morgan's 'rediscovery of the primitive matriarchal gens as the earlier stage of the patriarchal gens of civilized peoples'. This discovery 'has the same importance for anthropology as Darwin's theory of evolution has for biology and Marx's theory of surplus value for political economy'.[57] It proved that the family was not a natural institution but the product of economic conditions. In its modern form, the family was just a way of organising private property. The civilised monogamous family was not (as Morgan in fact firmly believed) the ultimate realisation of man's best instincts. It was a form of exploitation, comparable to the exploitation of one class by another. 'Within the family [the husband] is the bourgeois, and the wife represents the proletariat.' The family 'is based on the supremacy of the man, the express purpose being to produce children of undisputed paternity; such paternity is demanded because these children are later to come into their father's property as his natural heirs'.[58] If the family was artificial, so too was the state. Morgan revealed that before the state existed, political systems had been based upon kinship. Engels concluded that the state emerged only as a consequence of private property and class conflict. Get rid of that, and the state will wither away.

These ideas have a recognisable point of origin in Morgan's work, but Engels himself conceded that he had 'moved a considerable distance' from Morgan on some matters.[59] More recently, some feminist anthropologists found inspiration in Engels's discussion of the monogamous family, but by this stage the contribution of Morgan himself can hardly be discerned any longer.

Morgan's transformations

Morgan collected original ethnographic material by fieldwork and through sending out questionnaires. He also inspired others to do fieldwork on his behalf, notably Bandelier in Mexico and Fison in Australia. In the next generation the Bureau of American Ethnology was set up in the Smithsonian Institution essentially to carry out Morgan's programme of ethnological research. He even invented a whole new category of data, kinship terminologies, and persuaded generations of anthropologists that they were the key to defining systems of kinship and marriage.

Contemporaries were impressed by his empirical work, but Morgan's deductive method came under attack. McLennan argued that kinship terms could not be used to reconstruct forms of marriage and the family. The classificatory system 'is a system of mutual salutations merely'.[60] He also poured scorn on the notion that primitive people would not even have recognised their own mothers (and he pointed out that Darwin had expressed puzzlement on this score, in the second edition of *The Descent of Man*). On the contrary, recognition of the tie to the mother was very primitive, and formed the basis of the original condition of matriarchy.

Morgan's interpretative framework was less contentious, but then it was less original. He was very much the *bricoleur* of Lévi-Strauss's *pensée sauvage*, the handyman with an idea in his head of what he wants to make, and who finds the materials by sifting through whatever is to hand. He took the gens from Grote, group marriage from McLennan, schemas of technical and intellectual development from Lubbock and Tylor, philology from Müller. To be sure, he had his own convictions. He believed that the American constitution was the logical culmination of human political development. Not all the other anthropologists would have agreed on this point. More fundamentally, he was out to show that human history made moral sense, that it was a history of progress, and that it united all branches of the species. But if he could borrow ideas so promiscuously from Grote and Müller and McLennan and Tylor, it was because they all shared the larger elements of this faith, as did his friend and collaborator, the Rev. McIlvaine.

Chapter 5

The question of totemism

A broadly agreed picture of primitive society had been established by the 1870s, one that was to endure with no substantial changes for another generation. Kinship in blood was the original basis for social relationships, and the earliest societies were little more than coalitions of kinship groups. Marriages united whole groups of men and women. Descent was traced only in the female line. Gradually, this primeval system was reformed. Fatherhood began to be recognised. Relationships traced through males became more significant. Eventually the old regime was overthrown in a great revolution. A state was formed based upon territory, private property was recognised, and what Morgan called 'the true family in its modern acceptation' became the norm. Societies all over the world were destined to pass through the same stages, although some had apparently got themselves stuck in a condition of savagery or barbarism.

These apparently abstruse speculations about the origins of the family and property were relevant to classic philosophical debates about law and government. They were also of genuine interest to colonial administrators. However, religious issues probably engaged more British people, and more intensely, than discussions of the franchise or the government of India. For many, the most important thing about the Empire was that it provided an opportunity to bring Christianity to the heathens. 'Never was Britain more religious than in the Victorian age,' Theodore Hoppen writes. 'Contemporaries agonised over those who did not float upon the flood of faith.'[1] But faith was challenged by science. Owen Chadwick remarks that the churches were full of 'worshippers who had never heard of Tylor, were indifferent to Darwin, mildly regretted what they heard of Huxley'.[2] Nevertheless, readers of the serious papers were well aware that Darwin had put in question the very foundations of the Book of Genesis, that Huxley had announced that he was an 'agnostic', and that according to Tylor all religion was based on primitive logical errors and ambiguities of language.

Mr Tylor's science

Born into a well-to-do Quaker industrial family, Tylor did not attend a university. On a youthful tour abroad, riding on a tram in Havana, he met a fellow Quaker, Henry Christy, a wealthy antiquarian and an early convert to Darwinism. The two men went on to Mexico, where they were fascinated by the complex pre-Conquest Mexican civilisation. How had it arisen? Was it the result of diffusion from the Old World, or was it an independent development? Did it provide evidence for human progress, or, on the contrary, for degeneration?

The leading theorist in Britain concerned with these questions was Tylor's contemporary, Sir John Lubbock.[3] As a country neighbour of the Darwins, and a lifelong friend, Lubbock could count himself almost a birthright Darwinian. When the storm broke over him with the publication of *The Origin of Species*, Darwin had written to Lubbock (then only twenty-six years old), 'I settled some time ago that I should think more of Huxley's and your opinion – than of that of any other man in England'.[4] Darwin's mentor, Lyell, had published *The Geological Evidences of the Antiquity of Man* in 1863, and archaeologists began to relate their finds to the geological strata he identified. A relative chronology of ancient settlements and technologies began to be established. In *Prehistoric Times*, published in 1865, Lubbock distinguished an Old Stone Age, which he called the Palaeolithic, and a New Stone Age, which he called the Neolithic. If the artefacts of past societies were placed in chronological order, it became apparent that there had been world-wide progress. There might have been phases of decline, but there was no evidence that there had been degeneration from a higher condition.

Tylor adopted these arguments from the new archaeology. He also took up linguistics, read the German Indo–Europeanists on language and on myth, made a start on Sanskrit and Russian, and even dabbled in Greenlandish and Fijian.[5] In his *Researches into the Early History of Mankind and the Development of Civilization*, published in 1865, he put together a composite picture of linguistic, mythological and technical development. Taken together, they demonstrated the intellectual progress of humanity.

However, Tylor skirted the problem of religion, rather as Darwin had put off dealing with the question of the origin of the human species itself when writing *The Origin of Species*. Yet it was obvious what had to be the next questions on the scientific agenda. Darwin gave his account of human origins at last in *The Descent of Man* in 1871. In the same year, Tylor published his *Primitive Culture*. The first volume was essentially a revamp of his earlier *Researches*. The second volume was devoted to the origin of religion.

Tylor's theory was that the earliest religions arose from a mistake. People everywhere have dreams and visions, but primitive people confuse dreams with real experiences. When they dream of the dead they imagine that the dead must be living somewhere else, in another state, the state that they themselves entered in dreams, trances and fevers. Reflecting on these experiences, 'the ancient savage philosophers probably made their first step by the obvious inference that every man has two things belonging to him, namely, a life and a phantom.'[6] They then generalised this conclusion to embrace non-humans.

> Among races within the limits of savagery, the general doctrine of souls is found worked out with remarkable breadth and consistency. The souls of animals are recognized by a natural extension from the theory of human souls; the souls of trees and plants follow in some vague partial way; and the souls of inanimate objects expand the general category to its extremest boundary.[7]

In short, the first religion was based on 'the theory which endows the phenomena of nature with personal life'. Tylor called this primitive pantheism 'animism'. It was not merely of antiquarian interest. Vestiges of the primitive cult – what Tylor called 'survivals' – could be traced in the ceremonies of the most advanced religions. His main example was sacrifice. Rites of sacrifice were widespread, if not universal, and they tended to take similar forms everywhere. However, the reasons given for sacrifice changed as priests became more sophisticated. The justifications laid out in the Old Testament were anachronistic. To understand the primordial purpose of sacrifice, it was necessary to place it in its original context, which was animism. In animistic religions, offerings were made to the spirits of the dead after they appeared in dreams. The practice was then extended, and sacrifices were made to 'other spiritual beings, genii, fairies, gods'. These sacrifices took the form of burnt offerings, because spirits demanded not the flesh but the spirits of animals or plants: 'the object of sacrificing to the gods is that they are to consume or enjoy the souls of the things sacrificed'.[8]

In 1871, the year of *Primitive Culture*, not yet 40 years old, Tylor was elected a Fellow of the Royal Society. In 1875 Oxford awarded him an honorary degree. In 1881 he published the first general text-book in English on the subject, his *Anthropology*, which held the field for a generation. In 1884 Oxford created a Readership in Anthropology for him, and in 1896 he was made a Professor by personal title. Even Max Müller now spoke of anthropology as 'Mr Tylor's science', although perhaps not altogether approvingly.

The elements of this science were, however, familiar enough. Tylor's ideas about technological progress were drawn from Lubbock, his notions about the development of language and mythology from Müller, and his conception of sacrifice owed much to the German biblical scholar Wellhausen. Even Tylor's trademark theory of intellectual and religious development followed that of the French positivist Auguste Comte. Indeed, what he named 'animism' is hardly to be distinguished from what Comte termed 'fetichism'. A later generation credited Tylor with one large new idea, which was that technology, language, myth and belief form a single entity. Tylor called it 'culture or civilization', and defined it as 'that complex whole which includes knowledge, belief, art, morals, law, custom and any other capabilities and habits acquired by man as a member of society'.[9] It was a big idea, but French and German scholars had been writing in similar terms for the better part of a century about what the French termed 'civilisation' and the Germans called 'culture'.[10]

His friend Andrew Lang conceded Tylor's lack of originality, but he suggested that 'his merit lay in his patient, sagacious, well "documented", and, at last, convincing method of exposition'.[11] In other words, Tylor was a synthesiser, sifting and assessing theories and ethnographic reports. He did come up with a new idea about the origin of religion, though few of his contemporaries were entirely persuaded that all religions began in dreams, but perhaps his most enduring contribution was to place the evolution of religion on the agenda of British anthropology. The challenge now was to relate the early forms of religion to the earliest forms of society. The solution was produced by John McLennan. He called it 'totemism'.

The invention of totemism

It has been remarked that totemism, 'like radar, whiskey and marmalade, was a Scottish discovery or invention, for it was first defined by the Edinburgh lawyer John Ferguson McLennan, and Frazer, Robertson Smith and Andrew Lang were among the first to discuss it'.[12] McLennan was the least scholarly but perhaps the most original of these Scots. It fell to him for the second time to launch a theory, one that was to have an even greater impact than his theory of primitive marriage. He set it out in 1869, in an essay in *The Fortnightly Review*, which had published Tylor's original essay on 'The religion of savages' three years earlier.

McLennan started from Tylor's thesis that primitive peoples worshipped fetishes, which they believed to be animated by anthropomorphic spirits. These animistic beliefs gave rise to a new religion, which McLennan called 'totemism'. 'Fetishism resembles Totemism', he wrote with splendid effrontery, and in fact it turned out that totemism 'is Fetishism *plus* certain peculiarities. These peculiarities are, (1) the appropriation of a special Fetish to the tribe, (2) its hereditary transmission through mothers, and (3) its connection with the *jus connubii*.'[13] Primitive peoples believed that they were of the same species as their totem. Indeed, they were descended (in the female line, of course) from the original totemic animal. Marriage had to be with a person outside the descent group. In short, totemism was nature worship, or animism, or fetishism, but given a sociological anchor in McLennan's primordial society.

Citing a brief comment by Sir George Grey, and allowing himself generous interpretative licence, McLennan deduced that exogamous matrilineal groups existed in Australia, and that each group had its own totem.[14] A similar system prevailed, or had once prevailed, throughout Oceania. American reports confirmed that there the totems of the Indians were associated with matriarchal, exogamous groups. A rapid review of world ethnography revealed elements of a totemic system among the tribes of Siberia, Peru, Fiji, and even in classical India. The Greeks also had their natural spirits. Even the serpent story in Genesis may have had a totemic significance. And totemism planted the seeds not only of religion but also of science. When the names of animals were given to constellations of stars, this was a legacy of totemism. Beliefs about the descent of human beings from animals might be regarded as a first, faint hint of the theory of evolution.

Robertson Smith and *The Religion of the Semites*

In 1866 a group of intellectuals formed the Edinburgh Evening Club. McLennan was a founder member. Another was the theologian W. Robertson Smith, who became his friend.[15] In 1870 Smith was appointed to the chair of Hebrew and Old Testament at the Free Church College at Aberdeen. Here he began to propagate the new critical approach to the Bible, which he had learned in Germany from Julius Wellhausen, and which was to lead him to heresy – and also to the adoption of his friend's theory of totemism. A decade after the publication of McLennan's original article, his theory became a central issue in a theological *cause célèbre*.

In 1876, the first volume of a new edition of *Encyclopaedia Britannica* appeared. It carried articles by Robertson Smith on 'Angel' and 'Bible' in which he presented some of the central features of Wellhausen's theory.[16] The Bible was a compilation of sources of various dates, and it included mythological as well as historical elements. Two years later, Robertson Smith was called to answer charges of heresy before the General Assembly of the Free Church of Scotland. He was eventually cautioned, in May 1880.

That April, however, Robertson Smith travelled to Italy to visit McLennan, who had moved abroad for health reasons. In June he published an essay entitled 'Animal tribes in the Old Testament', in which he argued that ancient Semitic societies were totemic. Pre-Islamic Arabic sources indicated that tribal groupings were often named after animals, and sometimes after the moon and sun. Since sun and moon were evidently worshipped as gods, animals presumably once had a similar status. Moon worshippers believed that they were descended from their god. The same might well have been true where tribes were named after animals. And just as McLennan's theory predicted, ancient Semitic tribes were matriarchal and exogamous. The evidence was there in the names of some sub-tribes, which might 'denote the offspring of one mother'.[17] The very existence of the Queen of Sheba was proof of early matriarchy. The rest of McLennan's theory was also confirmed. The Greek geographer Strabo had reported traces of polyandry in Arabia. There were indications that female infanticide may have been practised. Some Arab marriage rituals could be interpreted as survivals of marriage by capture. 'These facts appear sufficient to prove that Arabia did pass through a stage in which family relations and the marriage law satisfied the conditions of the totem system'.[18] Totemic elements also survived in ancient Israel, if in an attenuated form. Robertson Smith suggested that the heathen practices against which the Hebrew prophets inveighed were totemic in origin, and that the second commandment itself was directed against nature worship.

This demonstration seems peculiarly thin. Robertson Smith himself admitted 'that we have very little direct information connecting these facts with animal worship', but he believed that there were good reasons for this. Greek sources are unreliable when it came to barbarian religions, and Islamic authors censored heathen ideas – 'we must remember the nature of the records'.[19] But however convincing, or unconvincing, this was a provocative argument, coming as it did from a man who had just been warned to mind his step by the church authorities. The General Assembly did not mince words in its reaction to the paper:

> First, concerning marriage and the marriage laws in Israel, the views expressed are so gross and so fitted to pollute the moral sentiments of the community that they cannot be considered except within the closed doors of any court of this Church. Secondly, concerning animal worship in Israel, the views expressed by the Professor are not only contrary to the facts recorded and the statements made in Holy Scripture, but they are gross and sensual – fitted to pollute and debase public sentiment.[20]

Robertson Smith was removed from his professorship in May 1881, but he was not cast into the outer darkness. He became co-editor of the famous ninth edition of the *Encyclopaedia Britannica* (and was reputed to have read every entry). In 1883 he was appointed Reader in Arabic at Cambridge and in 1889 he became Professor. He continued to develop his ideas on early Semitic religion and social organisation, notably in his entry on 'Sacrifice' in the *Britannica*, in his book *Kinship and Marriage in Early Arabia* (1885), and finally in his masterpiece, *Lectures on the Religion of the Semites* (1889).

Kinship and Marriage in Early Arabia is far more fully argued than Robertson Smith's essay on 'Animal worship', but it advances essentially the same ideas about primitive Semitic society. Notwithstanding obvious indications to the contrary, the strongly 'patriarchal' societies of ancient Arabia had been preceded by 'matriarchal' communities. The direct evidence was (hardly surprisingly) slight.

However, Robertson Smith now argued that comparisons could be used to fill the gaps in the data. 'In enquiring whether the Arabs were once divided into totem-stocks, we cannot expect to meet with any evidence more direct than the occurrence of such relics of the system as are found in other races which have passed through but ultimately emerged from the totem stage.'[21] On this evidence, ancient Arabia must have been full of totemic societies. But did they practise a totemic religion?

In his *Lectures on The Religion of the Semites*, Robertson Smith took up Tylor's discussion of sacrifice, which was 'the typical form of all complete acts of worship in the antique religions'.[22] According to the priestly code, sacrifices were acts of atonement. However, Smith's mentor Wellhausen had rejected this interpretation as anachronistic. Textual criticism revealed that the code was a post-Exilic document, which superimposed a late-priestly theology on earlier ritual practices. Originally, sacrifices were not even performed in the Temple. They were associated with what Wellhausen called a natural religion, which was situated within the life of the family. Following Tylor and Wellhausen, Robertson Smith also formulated a methodological rule: the rite was a more reliable source of information on ancient religion than the doctrine, since the rite was more stable. The 'ritual was fixed and the myth was variable, the ritual was obligatory and faith in the myth was at the discretion of the worshipper'.[23]

The only reliable way to understand sacrifice was to situate it in its original social setting. Primitive people believed they were physically descended from founding gods, which were their totems. Gods and their worshippers were kin who 'make up a single community, and ... the place of the god in the community is interpreted on the analogy of human relationships.'[24] In ancient Israel there was a more sophisticated doctrine. The divine father was conceived of in spiritual terms. Everywhere, however, gods and their worshippers were thought of as blood relatives. This was also the origin of morality, for 'the indissoluble bond that united men to their god is the same bond of blood-fellowship which in early society is the one binding link between man and man, and the one sacred principle of moral obligation'.[25]

The totemic gods were natural species, generally plants or animals. They were associated with shrines or sanctuaries, which followers had to visit. At certain times, a yet more intimate contact with the gods was required. This was achieved through sacrifice. Sacrifices 'are essentially acts of communion between the god and his worshippers'. 'The god and his worshippers are wont to eat and drink together, and by this token their fellowship is declared and sealed.'[26]

Sacrifices took one of two main forms. A vegetable sacrifice was thought of as a tribute or gift (which was Tylor's conception). However, since pastoralism preceded agriculture, animal sacrifices came before vegetable sacrifices, and animal sacrifices had a more primitive rationale. The original sacrificial object was the totemic animal itself. Normally, a totem animal could not be killed or eaten. It was 'unclean'. But by the same token it was sacred. Robertson Smith pronounced the evidence 'unambiguous'. 'When an unclean animal is sacrificed it is also a sacred animal.'[27] He concluded that among the Semites 'the fundamental idea of sacrifices is not that of a sacred tribute, but of communion between the god and his worshippers by joint participation in the living flesh and blood of a sacred victim'.[28]

The argument was clearly leading up to a climax in which something would have to be said about the sacrifices of gods themselves in Semitic religions, perhaps during communal meals. Smith took the step in this passage:

> That the God-man dies for His people and that his Death is their life, is an idea which was in some degree foreshadowed by the oldest mystical sacrifices. It was foreshadowed, indeed, in a very crude and materialistic form, and without any of those ethical ideas which the Christian doctrine of the Atonement derives from a profound sense of sin and divine justice. And yet the voluntary death of the divine victim, which we have seen to be a conception not foreign to ancient ritual, contained the germ of the deepest thought in the Christian doctrine: the thought that the Redeemer gives Himself for his people.[29]

Frazer cited this passage in his obituary essay on Smith and remarked that it was dropped in a later, revised edition of the *Lectures*.[30] Yet even if it was left implicit, the theological implications would have been evident to any contemporary scholar.

Frazer and *The Golden Bough*

James George Frazer was a shy young classicist, and when the charismatic Robertson Smith arrived at his Cambridge college, Trinity, they became allies. Frazer later recalled that 'one evening, I think in January 1884, when I had gone, contrary to my custom, to combination room after dinner he came and sat beside me and entered into conversation'.

> I think that one subject of our talk that evening was the Arabs in Spain and that, though I knew next to nothing about the subject, I attempted some sort of argument with him, but was immediately beaten down, in the kindest and gentlest way, by his learning, and yielded myself captive at once. I never afterwards, so far as I can remember, attempted to dispute the mastership which he thenceforward exercised over me by his extraordinary fusion of genius and learning. From that time we went for walks together sometimes in the afternoons, and sometimes he asked me to his rooms.[31]

Robertson Smith commissioned Frazer to write on 'Taboo' and 'Totemism' for the *Encyclopaedia Britannica*. His entry on totemism was far too long to be included unabridged, although Robertson Smith wrote to the publishers to urge 'that Totemism is a subject of growing importance, daily mentioned in magazines and papers, but of which there is no good account anywhere.' The entry simply had to be published. 'There is no article in the volume for which I am more solicitous. I have taken much personal pains with it, guiding Frazer carefully in his treatment; and he has put about seven months' hard work on it to make it the standard article on the subject.'[32] In the event, a shortened version of Frazer's entry was published in the *Encyclopedia*, but the full text was issued in book form in 1887. As Robertson Smith had predicted, it was to be the authoritative source on the topic, at least for the next decade. Baldwin Spencer recorded that when he went into the field, 'my anthropological reading was practically confined to two works, Sir Edward Tylor's "Primitive Culture" and Sir James Frazer's little red book on "Totemism".'[33]

Frazer provided a genuinely encyclopaedic review of the available literature. He identified totemism in many culture areas, although without making definite claims for its original universality, and he distinguished three types of totem: clan totems, sex totems and individual totems. Clan totems were by far the most important, and clan totemism was at once a religious system and a social system. Its social form was a system of exogamous clans that traced descent in the female line. The religious aspect 'consists of the relations of mutual respect and protection between a man and his totem', usually symbolised by a taboo on killing and eating the totem. These religious and social aspects had drifted apart in the course of time, but originally they were inseparable – 'the further we go back, the more we should find that the clansman regards himself and his totem as beings of the same species'.[34] According to the most primitive doctrine, the totem was the ancestor of the clan. Frazer did not, however, commit himself to a theory of totemism. 'No satisfactory explanation of the origin of totemism has yet been given.'[35]

In his most famous book, *The Golden Bough*, first published in 1890, Frazer took up Robertson Smith's central preoccupation, the sacrifice of the god. He linked it with the theory of a German folklorist, Wilhelm Mannhardt, who had explained German peasant cults of sacred trees as survivals of ancient fertility rituals.[36] Frazer combined these elements and constructed an ethnological detective story. It began with the ritual murder of 'the King of the Wood', the priest of the sanctuary of Nemi, near Rome. This sacred king was the embodiment of a tree spirit, and it turned out that he was not simply murdered, but rather sacrificed to ensure the fertility of nature. Clues were drawn from a vast range of ethnographic sources, all tending to show that primitive people identified their well-being with the fate of nature spirits, whose priest-kings were sacrificed in fertility rituals. 'The result, then, of our inquiry is to make it probable that ... the King of the Wood lived and died as an incarnation of the Supreme Aryan god, whose life was in the mistletoe or Golden Bough.'[37]

Initial sales of *The Golden Bough* were disappointing, but it was well reviewed, and it became widely influential. For many educated readers it offered an irresistible combination of classical scholarship, exoticism and daring rationalism. Frazer's reputation grew, and he began to distance himself from totemism and also from Robertson Smith. In the preface to the second edition of *The Golden Bough*, which appeared in 1900, he announced that 'the worship of trees and cereals', the central theme of his book, 'is neither identical with nor derived from a system of totemism'. And he positively disavowed the theories of Robertson Smith. 'I never assented to my friend's theory, and, so far as I can remember, he never gave me a hint that he assented to mine.'[38]

Successive editions of *Totemism* and *The Golden Bough* appeared, and Frazer compulsively added more and more ethnographic illustrations. He set great store by this accumulation of data, which

he considered to be at least as important as his theoretical contribution. 'Hypotheses are necessary but often temporary bridges
built to connect isolated facts,' he remarked in the Preface to the
second edition of *The Golden Bough*. 'If my light bridges should
sooner or later break down ... I hope that my book may still have its
utility and its interest as a repertory of facts.' He fostered what
amounted to an international intelligence service, sending out
questionnaires on topics which interested him, and helping his
protegés to publish their results. His network extended into Africa
and Asia, but he believed, with other experts, that the ultimate test
of anthropological theories would come from the central and
northern territories of Australia. After all, the naked black hunters
and gatherers of Australia were as close as could be to the Victorian
image of primitive humanity. The pioneer ethnographer Lorimer
Fison wrote in a letter to Lewis Henry Morgan in 1879: 'To use
your own words, in the Australian field we are "working at the very
foundations of that great Science of Anthropology which is sure to
come".'[39] Twenty years later, Frazer wrote to Spencer: 'The
anthropological work still to be done in Australia is ... of more
importance for the early history of man than anything that can now
be done in the world.'[40]

Yet remarkably little information was available on the Australian
Aborigines, and Morgan and Frazer set out to find educated men
who could collect the material they required. Both the major
Australian studies of the late nineteenth century were made by
partnerships in which a foreign scholar, without previous first-hand
experience of Australia, but directly inspired by metropolitan
theorists, joined up with a local man who had direct contact with
Aborigines. The first partnership, between Fison and Howitt, was
dedicated to Morgan's programme. They therefore collected
information about group marriage. Frazer would later call this aspect
of things 'totemism as a social system'. In the next generation,
directed by Frazer himself, Spencer and Gillen studied Australian
totemism as a religious system.

Fison and Howitt

The Rev. Lorimer Fison had been recruited by Morgan to fill in his
kinship questionnaire while working as a missionary in Fiji. In 1871
he went to Australia, and collected an Australian terminology with
the help of a fellow missionary.[41] He sent his findings to Morgan,

who immediately presented them to the Academy of Arts and Sciences, claiming they proved that the Australians employed the same system of kin classification as the American Indians and the Tamils. Moreover the original two intermarrying divisions could still be found throughout Australia. Men called women of the other division 'wife', and these women called them 'husband'. This was just a step above primitive promiscuity. In 1872 Fison advertised in a Melbourne journal for a local expert who would help him to make a systematic study of Australian kinship. A response came from Alfred William Howitt, a magistrate in the interior, and a well-known amateur geologist, who had led a relief party 11 years earlier to rescue the lost explorers Burke and Wills. In the 1860s he had begun to read the new literature on evolution, and he was primed for Fison's invitation.

The two men were soon in constant correspondence with Morgan,[42] and they also exchanged letters with Tylor and other authorities. In 1880, after a decade of this three-cornered collaboration, they published a monograph, *Kamilaroi and Kurnai*. This slim book effectively established the tradition of Australian ethnography, but it was distinguished particularly by its theoretical ambition. Specifically, it was designed to advance the cause of Morgan against McLennan.

McLennan and Morgan disagreed about the form that marriage took in the most primitive societies. According to Morgan, a set of brothers from one clan married a set of sisters from another. Traces of this ancient system of 'group marriage' could be found in kinship terminologies. McLennan, however, denied that the kin terms had any sociological significance. And where Morgan imagined that primitive communities practised a systematic exchange of wives, McLennan insisted that women had to be taken by force from foreign bands. What he termed exogamy was an act of war.

On all these points, Fison was determined to support Morgan. The subtitle of *Kamilaroi and Kurnai* was 'Group-marriage and relationship, and marriage by elopement', and Fison wrote:

> The chief object of this memoir is to trace the formation of the exogamous intermarrying divisions which have been found among so many savage and barbaric tribes of the present day, and to show that what the Hon. Lewis H. Morgan calls the Punaluan family, with the Turanian system of kinship [terminology], logically results from them. The Australian classes are

especially valuable for this purpose, because they give us what seem to be the earliest stages of development.[43]

'Class' was the term upon which Fison had settled for 'the exogamous intermarrying tribal divisions which have been observed in so many other parts of the world'.[44] He deduced that the Australians had begun with two exogamous and matrilineal marriage classes. These later subdivided, producing a four-class system, which cut the range of potential spouses in half. However, 'marriage must still be without the class, and descent is still reckoned in the female line'.[45] But he did not go so far as to claim that the Australians still actually practised group marriage.[46] Undeniably, 'certain modifications as to the extent of the matrimonial privilege have been introduced. Here, as elsewhere, present usage is in advance of the ancient rules. But those rules underlie it, and are felt through it, and the underlying strata crop up in many places'.[47]

Fison's thinking was notably abstract and deductive, and in a letter to Morgan he even suggested that the laws of the 'Turanian system' could be demonstrated from the Australian materials by steps 'as conclusive as any one of Euclid's demonstrations, if we can only establish three preliminary propositions': namely that marriages united men and women from different classes, that the kinship terminology identified these classes, and that the classes were exogamous.[48] He had a go at such a Euclidean demonstration in an appendix to the book. 'John Smith and John Brown, two first cousins, marry one another's sisters. Each has a son John and a daughter Jane. These first cousins marry, and have issue, a son and a daughter to each marriage. The same Christian names are continued.' ('The surnames represent the two intermarrying phratriae, or gentes'. See Figure 5.1.)[49]

This elegant model was complicated by two extraneous features. First, the marriage classes were cross-cut by groups which had animal totems. Fison had to admit that his information on the workings of these totemic groups was patchy, but he thought it likely that they were also exogamous. Second, it turned out that local communities did not coincide with marriage classes. This difficulty was dealt with in later publications, where, after first suggesting the term 'local clan', Howitt and Fison settled on the term 'horde'. A child lives with the horde in which it was born, normally his father's. These hordes were particularly important since they signalled the future development of a patriarchal society and the state.[50] But whatever

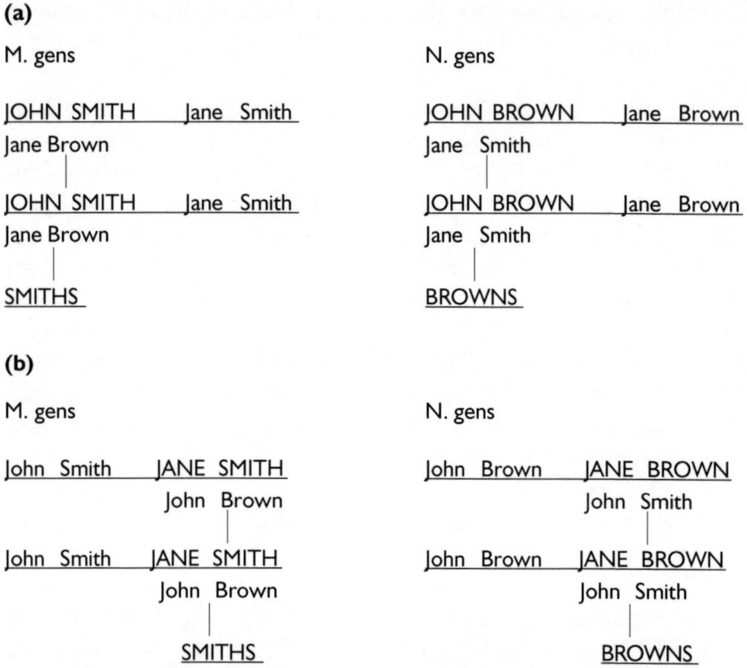

(a)

M. gens   N. gens

JOHN SMITH   Jane Smith   JOHN BROWN   Jane Brown
Jane Brown   Jane Smith
   | |
JOHN SMITH   Jane Smith   JOHN BROWN   Jane Brown
Jane Brown   Jane Smith
   | |
SMITHS   BROWNS

(b)

M. gens   N. gens

John Smith   JANE SMITH   John Brown   JANE BROWN
         John Brown   John Smith
            | |
John Smith   JANE SMITH   John Brown   JANE BROWN
         John Brown   John Smith
            | |
         SMITHS   BROWNS

Figure 5.1 Fison's model of the Australian 'class' system. (a) Descent through
males (Turanian system). (b) Descent through females (Gonowanian
system). From Fisson and Howitt, *Kamilaroi and Kurnai*, p.96.

the role of the totemic groups and hordes might be, 'Australian
exogamy' was 'the plain outcome of the class divisions'.[51]

McLennan had criticised the way in which Morgan used kinship
classifications as evidence of bygone systems of group marriage.
According to McLennan, kin terms were mere salutations, which were
of no historical significance. Fison was determined to show that the
division of relatives into marriage classes among the Australian
aborigines was mirrored in the kinship terminology (although he also
claimed to detect traces of the even more ancient 'Malayan' system).
This demonstration was no easy task. Fison admitted that 'when asked
to define the relationship in which he stands to other persons, [an
Australian aborigine] frequently takes into consideration matters other
than relationship, and so gives words which are not specific terms of
kinship. After years of inquiry into this matter, the humiliating
confession must be made that I am hopelessly puzzled.' Nevertheless,
he claimed, 'enough can be made out from the terms of kinship in

present use to show that relationship is based upon the same ideas with those which form the foundation of the system called by Mr Morgan the Turanian. Most certainly ... the terms of that system are the logical outcome of the Australian classes.'[52]

Fison's own data on the Kamilaroi suggested that there were traces of group marriage, but Howitt's more substantial ethnography of the Kurnai found nothing of the sort. Howitt made it clear that Kurnai marriage was an individual matter. Moreover, the social groups were based on locality rather than kinship. He suggested that this was because the Kurnai were exceptionally advanced, although Fison preferred to believe that they simply had a very odd history. *The Kurnai are the descendants of an isolated division of a tribe which formerly consisted of two exogamous intermarrying divisions,*' he explained, in italics, *'and their regulations as to marriage and descent are such as would arise from an endeavour to follow the regulations of such divisions under circumstances of peculiar difficulty.'* [53] In any case, Howitt and Fison agreed that the Kurnai diverged from the Australian pattern. It was therefore Fison's abstract model that provided the paradigmatic account of how the most primitive of social systems operated.

Tylor on exogamy

Back in the metropolis, Tylor and Frazer were beginning to collate the results of the first generation of ethnographers. In 1889, Tylor read a paper to a meeting of the Anthropological Institute. It was entitled 'On a method of investigating the development of institutions; applied to laws of marriage and descent'. His methodological innovations were certainly remarkable enough. McLennan and Frazer, and Tylor himself in *Primitive Culture*, relied on the accumulation of apt illustrations. Maine and Morgan worked with case studies. Tylor, however, now prepared a sample of exotic cultures and tried to measure statistical associations between cultural traits. He was directly influenced by Darwin's cousin, Francis Galton, a pioneer statistician, who as president of the Anthropological Institute took the chair when Tylor delivered the paper. (He rather unkindly pointed out one of its weaknesses, the fact that Tylor had not controlled for historical relationships between the cases in his sample.) Yet whatever the importance of this methodological innovation, it was not imitated for many years, and Tylor himself did not take it further. The substantive argument of the paper was, however, immediately influential.

Up to this point, Tylor had paid little attention to theories of primitive social structure. Now he weighed in to decide the main issues in contention between McLennan and Morgan. He began by listing indirect pieces of evidence which combined to suggest that societies had indeed passed 'from the maternal to the paternal systems', as had been proposed by Bachofen, McLennan, and Morgan.[54] Although he detected traces of McLennan's marriage by capture, he reasoned that it would not make much sense to capture wives in a matriarchal system. More probably, the custom signalled the passage to a patriarchal society. On the main issue, Tylor came down on the side of Morgan. It was now evident 'that exogamy was hardly to do with the capture of wives in war between alien nations, but rather with the regulation of marriages within groups or clans or tribes who have connubium', which was the word he used to mean the peaceful exchange of women in marriage. Finally, he accepted that the classificatory terminology mirrored the system of marriage exchanges. Fison and Howitt had demonstrated that clan exogamy and classificatory kinship terminologies were 'in fact two sides of one institution'.[55]

Twenty-one of the societies in Tylor's sample practised a distinctive form of exogamy in which 'the children of two brothers may not marry, nor the children of two sisters, but the child of the brother may marry the child of the sister.' He called this 'cross-cousin marriage', and argued that it was 'the direct result of the simplest form of exogamy, where a population is divided into two classes or sections, with the law that a man who belongs to Class A can only take a wife of class B'. He reasoned that this arrangement broke down if there were more than two clans involved, and concluded 'that the dual form of exogamy may be considered the original form'. Fison had already made precisely the same point, but Tylor claimed that he reached the conclusion independently, and had only later recalled coming across something similar in Fison's book.[56]

Tylor now added a novel and powerful sociological hypothesis to explain the development of exogamy, which he termed 'a political question of the first importance'. Whether descent was traced through women or through men:

> when tribes begin to adjoin and press on one another and quarrel, then the difference between marrying-in and marrying-out becomes patent. Endogamy is a policy of isolation, cutting off a horde or village, even from the parent-stock whence it separated

... Among tribes of low culture there is but one means known of keeping up permanent alliance, and that means is inter-marriage. Exogamy enabling a growing tribe to keep itself compact by constant unions between its spreading clans, enables it to overmatch any number of small intermarrying groups, isolated and helpless. Again and again in the world's history, savage tribes must have had plainly before their minds the simple practical alternative between marrying-out and being killed out.[57]

The echoes of Malthus and Darwin are loud and clear. Tylor had returned to McLennan's starting point, the struggle for survival, but he went off in a diametrically different direction. McLennan had imagined a war of all against all, complete with ghastly atrocities, infanticide and rapine. Tylor was a Quaker, and perhaps for this reason he preferred to imagine that the struggle for survival could be peacefully contained by a system of alliances.

Totemism as a religious system: Spencer and Gillen

The evidence from Australia had settled the questions of group marriage and exogamy. It was time to put the new theories about the origin of religion to the test of Australian ethnography. Providentially, an associate of Tylor was ready and willing to take this on.

Baldwin Spencer went out to Australia in 1887, at the age of twenty-seven, to take the chair of biology in Melbourne University. He had attended Tylor's lectures and collaborated with him on the removal of the Pitt Rivers collection to Oxford. He carried to Australia a letter from Tylor which suggested that 'I might be able to do some work of value if ever I chanced to come into contact with savage peoples'.[58] But first, in July 1894, he made what Elliot Smith was to call his most important discovery, Frank Gillen, the postmaster of Alice Springs. Gillen was already collecting materials on the Aranda tribe, 'with whom he was on the most friendly terms and by whom he was completely trusted',[59] although his grasp of the language was rather patchy, and he used pidgen English to question informants.[60] The two men organised expeditions to the centre and north of the country, and they eventually published two classic Australian ethnographies, *The Native Tribes of Central Australia* (1899) and *The Native Tribes of the Northern Territory* (1914).

The partnership between Spencer and Gillen was structurally

rather similar to that between Fison and Howitt. Once again a metropolitan intellectual was paired with a local expert. However, Spencer was a trained naturalist, while Gillen was a man of very little education, and Gillen's field research was completely subordinated to Spencer's ideas. 'Do please let me have a list of questions by each mail', he would write to Spencer. 'I must have the guidance of your scientifically trained mind to work or I shall accomplish very little.'[61] Spencer confirmed this mode of operation in a letter to Frazer. 'I send him up endless questions and things to find out, and by mutual agreement he reads no one else's work so as to keep him quite unprejudiced in the way of theories.'[62] Without guidance, a fieldworker might simply miss what was of importance. That was how Spencer explained Howitt's failure to report on the religious aspects of totemism. 'In those days,' as he wrote to Frazer, 'with no work such as yours and Tylor's to guide him there was little to show him what to look for in this line, and therefore there will be little reference in his book to customs associated with totemism other than in regard to its relationship to marriage.'[63] He himself depended on Frazer's encouragement. 'The knowledge that there is some one like you', he wrote to Frazer, 'who can piece together the odd fragments of information which isolated workers can acquire is a great stimulant.'[64]

For his part, Frazer assured Spencer that the data he and Gillen were collecting would be of more permanent value than any metropolitan theorising. Indeed, it was essential to separate the facts from what were, at best, provisional hypotheses. 'Descriptive and comparative ethnology should be kept most rigidly apart; to try to combine both is to spoil both.'[65] It was the business of the fieldworker to document and check, and, if necessary, to refute the speculations of the metropolis, and to correct misapprehensions based on unreliable reports. Spencer advised Frazer more than once that 'Australian anthropology is badly in want of a committee of expurgation'.[66] And Frazer recorded that Howitt's very last message to the metropolis, dictated from his deathbed, was addressed to those who made use of ethnographic information, 'impressing on them the importance of caution in accepting information drawn from the Australian tribes in their present state of decay.'[66]

There was, then, something of a chain of command, which ran from Frazer through Spencer to Gillen. Frazer set the questions, and Spencer obediently directed Gillen to the study of totemic beliefs and practices. They added little to Fison and Howitt's group-marriage thesis, although they did confirm that totems were distributed by locality rather than according to descent-group membership, and they showed that there was no relationship between the marriage classes and the totemic groups. On the other hand, they investigated anything relevant to totemism as a religious system in unprecedented detail.

Their sharply focused research yielded authoritative answers to some of the central questions of contemporary anthropology. Few of the old dogmas about totemism as a religious system were confirmed. The Australians did not believe that totems had souls. Totems were not worshipped. At least in Central Australia, there were no restrictions on eating the totem. On the contrary, members of the totem group took a leading part in killing and eating the totemic animals in the *intichiuma* ceremony. This was a fertility rite in which totemic animals or plants were killed to increase the number of the species. However, although McLennan's theory of totemism did not fit these Australian facts, the *intichiuma* ceremony did appear to support Robertson Smith's claim that the central rite in the original totemic religion was the sacrifice of the totem. In their account of the Aranda, Spencer and Gillen accordingly gave pride of place to the *intichiuma*, although they did not suggest that it was of central significance for the Aranda themselves.

Frazer's faith in Robertson Smith's theory was briefly rekindled. The discovery of the Aranda *intichiuma* seemed to prove that his mentor had guessed right after all. 'Thus from being little more than an ingenious hypothesis the totem sacrament has become, at least in my opinion, a well-authenticated fact.'[67] Frazer's enthusiasm soon cooled, however. Spencer would not agree that the totem was being worshipped. He even rejected Frazer's more modest suggestion that there was at least an element of 'conciliation' of the totem.[68] Frazer began to question whether totemic rituals should be considered religious at all. Perhaps they did not imply a belief in the divinity of the totem, and were no more than crude magical exercises. If that was the case then they would have little bearing on the history of religion.

That was Tylor's view. In an essay published in 1899 (the year in which Spencer and Gillen's monograph appeared), he concluded that totemism 'has been exaggerated out of proportion to its real theological magnitude. The importance belonging to totem-animals as friends or enemies of man is insignificant in comparison with that of ghosts or demons, to say nothing of higher deities.' It was high time to separate what was known about group marriage from speculations about the religion of the earliest societies. 'Exogamy can and does exist without totemism, and for all we know was originally independent of it'.[69]

A decade after, in 1910, Frazer published a typically exhaustive review of the field. Where Tylor had dealt with exogamy and totemism in two lectures, Frazer's *Totemism and Exogamy: A Treatise on Certain Early Forms of Superstition and Society* filled four large volumes. He painstakingly reviewed the theories and materials that had been produced, but his conclusions in the fourth volume by and large echoed Tylor's. In totemism a man 'identified himself and his fellow-clansmen with his totem'. This does not, however, amount to a religion. Frazer now judged that 'it is a serious, though apparently a common, mistake to speak of a totem as a god, and to say that it is worshipped by the clan'. Nor had totemism ever been universal. Robertson Smith was mistaken. There were no traces of totemism in ancient Semitic religions. Rather, 'totemism is an institution peculiar to the dark-complexioned and least civilised races of mankind'.[70] Totemism was not even a single, indissoluble complex. There was often, but not always, a taboo on eating and killing the totem. Members of the same totemic clan were often, but not always, prohibited from marrying each other. Moreover, some peoples in Melanesia and Australia practised both exogamy and totemism but without connecting the two institutions; and in some ethnographic areas one of the customs might be found without the other. There was, then, a 'radical distinction of totemism and exogamy'.[71]

When it came to explaining totemic beliefs, Frazer was dismissive of all current ideas, including his own of the day before yesterday, that totemism was to be understood as an organised system of co-operative magic. Totemism was in fact predicated upon an error. Ignorant about the biology of conception, savages assumed that a child was quickened in the womb by the spirit of a natural object. This produced the doctrine of individual totems, which he now thought must have been the original form of totemism.

Frazer also followed Tylor in endorsing Morgan's model of primitive social organisation, specifically in the form that Fison had described for Australia. Originally there was a two-class marriage system. Through a process of segmentation, a four-class and then an eight-class system developed. The class system imposed a classification of kin. Father's brothers' children and mother's sisters' children were members of a man's own exogamous class, and were called brother and sister. His mother's brothers' children and father's sisters' children were members of the other class. They were 'cousins', and marriage with them was entirely proper. This classificatory system of kinship terminology 'simply defines the relations of all the men and women of the community to each other according to the generation and the exogamous class to which they belong'.[72] Frazer concluded that these systems were deliberately designed to rule out more and more relatives as marriage partners. The driving force was a fundamental dread of incest.

Also in 1910, an American student of Boas, Alexander Golden-weiser, published a yet more critical summary of the situation, in which he dismantled even more conclusively the elaborate structure which had dominated anthropological theory for a generation.[73] Little remained standing of the theory that totemism was the original religion. Perhaps this suited both Tylor and Frazer. Tylor saw no reason to concede that totemism should share the limelight with animism. Frazer himself was engaged in developing his own reputation, and wanted to distance himself from Robertson Smith. On the other hand, neither Tylor nor Frazer had a special investment in the theory of exogamy, and they were content to underwrite the claims of their Australian clients. Power within the intellectual establishment was a crucial part of the story, for when an outsider formulated a devastating critique of the established theory of the evolution of the family he was largely ignored.

Westermarck and the family

Edward Westermarck, a Swedish Finn, was drawn into anthropology as a result of reading Darwin's *Descent of Man*.[74] His starting-point was an interest in the origins of sexual shame and morality. Reading Darwin, he came across the theory that early humans (and primitive people today) lived a life of sexual promiscuity. Darwin himself was sceptical, but Westermarck was inclined to believe it, and he followed up Darwin's sources, Morgan, McLennan and Lubbock. However, he began to develop doubts about their methods. He was not convinced that they could tell which customs were really 'survivals' of early practices. Westermarck pursued his researches in the Reading Room of the British Museum and sent out questionnaires to missionaries and other tropical residents. When he finally published his findings in 1891, at the age of thirty, he was a master of the field.

Westermarck was a strict Darwinian. His encyclopaedic *History of Human Marriage* was free of any Lamarckian vestiges. Perhaps the first orthodox application of modern evolutionary theory in anthropology, it was enthusiastically endorsed by Alfred Wallace (who shares the credit with Darwin for the formulation of the principle of natural selection).[75] A sign of this orthodoxy was that Westermarck included the primates in his argument. Indeed, primatology provided the best evidence that the family was universal, since it could be observed even among 'the man-like apes'. The gorilla and chimpanzee 'lives in families, the male parent being in the habit of building the nest and protecting the family ... Passing from the highest monkeys to the savage and barbarous races of man, we meet the same phenomenon.' Everywhere 'it is to the mother that the immediate care of the children chiefly belongs, while the father is the protector and guardian of the family ... the simplest paternal duties are ... universally recognized'.[76]

If the family was universal, the reason was to be found in natural selection. The husband or father protects mother and children. This was a great advantage, given the small number of offspring produced by primates and humans, the extended period of gestation, and the length of time during which the infant is unable to fend for itself. The male protector need not always be the biological father, but each female requires a male partner who will also protect her offspring. Where this protection is provided, more children will survive.

Writing to Westermarck, Tylor admitted that he was largely persuaded by his arguments,[77] but he was now entering the long twilight of his dotage, and he published nothing further on the matter. Westermarck's ideas were largely ignored by Rivers, who was the central figure in the study of social organisation in Britain in the next generation. The one young scholar who did pick up his argument was another exotic immigrant to London, the Pole Bronislaw Malinowski.

Malinowski on the family in Australia[78]

Like many of his generation of anthropologists, Malinowski began as a natural scientist. After taking a first degree in physics in Cracow he studied in Germany under Wundt, a pioneer in the field of experimental psychology and a polymath with an interest in ethnology. In 1910, at the age of twenty-six, he moved to the London

School of Economics to work with Westermarck. Here he completed a study, begun in Germany, on the problem of the family among the Australian aborigines. His monograph, *The Family among the Australian Aborigines*, was published in 1913.

Malinowski followed Westermarck in insisting that it was not the rules and pious formulae that counted, but the practice. He also argued that context was crucial. The operation of any institution is modified by other institutions with which it is associated. Consequently the family will have specific and perhaps unique features in any particular society. An institution is also informed by the perceptions, emotions and ideas of the people who use it. It was true that Aborigines denied that a man had any role in making his wife pregnant, yet if one read the reports on Aborigine life with an eye for how things worked it was apparent that men took responsibility for the children of their wives, and that they were emotionally engaged with them. The unit of mother, children and mother's husband camped together and took most of their meals with one another. In practice, then, the family existed in Australia, where it co-existed with 'group' kinship relationships.

Freud's *Totem and Taboo*

But if totemism had been discredited in Britain, Durkheim in France and Freud in Austria were fascinated by Frazer's compilation of facts. And Frazer's reluctance to engage in grand theory left the field wide open for new speculations. Freud had read *Totemism and Exogamy*. Durkheim had steeped himself in the works of the British school and the new Australian ethnography. Both men set themselves to explain the connection between the taboo on the totem and the rule of exogamy within the clan. In 1912 Durkheim published his *Elementary Forms of the Religious Life*, which was subtitled *The System of Totemism in Australia*. The following year Freud's *Totem and Taboo* appeared. The fame and influence of these books were to rival, perhaps surpass, Frazer's *The Golden Bough* itself.

Freud produced the most imaginative version of totemism, and it was also perhaps the most influential in the intellectual world at large in the long run. His starting-point was a speculation of Andrew Lang, which had been followed up by his cousin, J. Atkinson. Published in 1903, Atkinson's *Primal Law* was part of the speculative flood of books on human social origins that had followed the pioneering work of McLennan and Morgan, but it was among the very few that began from Darwin's reconstruction of the early human band.

Darwin had reviewed the evidence for the social organisation of various primate species in *The Descent of Man*. He emphasised the importance of sexual jealousy and rivalry, and concluded that early man probably 'lived in small communities, each with a single wife, or if powerful with several, whom he jealously guarded against all other men'. Alternatively, a powerful male might have lived alone with several mates and their offspring, like the gorilla. When a young male matured he would be engaged in a contest by the dominant male. Either the older male would be killed, or the young male would be chased away. Darwin thought that this had beneficial biological consequences. 'The young males, being thus expelled and wandering about, would, when at last successful in finding a partner, prevent too close interbreeding within the limits of the same family.'[79]

Atkinson speculated that mothers would eventually refuse to allow their sons to be expelled from home. First the youngest son would be allowed to stay, then others. The old male would have had to introduce a formal prohibition on incest to protect his sexual monopoly. All in all, Atkinson told a good-natured English fairy story about sensible reform. Freud's vision, however, was more revolutionary and more violent. The young males had risen up against the patriarch, murdered him and taken his women. This act of parricide was the more heinous since the father was also revered as a god. A guilty memory of the terrible crime would haunt mankind. Totemic sacrifices were acts of appeasement. The totem itself stands for the murdered god. Taboos were instituted to prevent the crime ever being repeated. The first law of totemic religions was the taboo on incest.

Freud believed in the inheritance of acquired traits. Descendants of the original parricides – men everywhere – could not shed the guilt of their ancestors. They had a horror of incest, which was universally tabooed. But Freud also believed that as the individual grew up he relived the experience of the race. Ontogeny recapitulated phylogeny. Therefore every boy had to deal with a guilty desire to murder his father and marry his mother. This was the 'Oedipus complex'. Neurotics (who were very like both primitives and children) failed to resolve their ambivalent feelings for their parents. They protected themselves from their conflicting urges by obsessive practices: private taboos.

Durkheim and the anthropologists[80]

Most accounts of Emile Durkheim's sociology treat his last major study, *The Elementary Forms of the Religious Life*, published in 1912, as his masterpiece, and the capstone of the arch of his theory. This was not, however, Durkheim's view. His nephew, Marcel Mauss, reported that on his deathbed Durkheim had made a supreme effort to begin writing his planned book on morality, which he had looked forward to as the 'goal of his existence, the very core of his spirit'.[81] Durkheim also set great store by his uncompleted work on the family. He had written only part of it (in Bordeaux between 1890 and 1892), but these pages were so precious that Durkheim would not be parted from them, even when he travelled. According to Mauss, he had 'wished to devote the rest of his life to this comparative natural history of the family and marriage up to the present'.[82] He took personal responsibility for the sections on the family and marriage in the *Année Sociologique* when it began to appear under his editorship, in 1898. Towards the end of his life he had even considered cutting the planned book on morality, and making it into an introduction to the book on the family.

In fact these three projects – the studies of religion, morality and the family – were closely united in Durkheim's mind. Durkheim's fundamental concern had always been to provide a scientific basis for morality. He viewed this as a matter of urgent political necessity. He was a secular republican and he was also a Jew, and a Jew from Alsace at that, a member of a newly enfranchised and vulnerable minority. Nineteenth-century France was a divided society that experienced a series of wrenching oscillations between revolution and reaction. The secular Republic was not secure in the aftermath of the defeat of the French army by Prussia. In 1894, a Jewish army officer, Captain Dreyfus, was convicted of treason and sentenced to life imprisonment. The novelist Emile Zola published an open letter in a national newspaper, which claimed that the trial was an anti-semitic plot, launching a controversy that lasted for 12 years and divided France between secular republicans, on the one side, and right-wing nationalists and Catholic reactionaries on the other.

Conservative writers believed that the sources of morality were the church and the family. Durkheim countered that modern European societies were undergoing fundamental changes, and that religion and the family system would have to change as well. But many serious students believed that there was something *natural* about family organisation. Frédéric Le Play, for example, a writer much appreciated by Napoleon III, had argued that the family was in some sense prior to, and independent of, society, and that it was a primordial source of moral values.[83] The French ethnologist Charles Letourneau had insisted that the primitive family forms were more natural than, and morally preferable to, our own.[84] Westermarck had argued that the human families were similar to those of chimpanzees and gorillas. Durkheim's aim was to show that the new organic societies and their institutions were no less moral or less natural than the ancient clan systems.

Durkheim turned to ethnology above all because it illustrated the range of human institutions. Things had been very different in the past. They might therefore be very different again in the future. The present institutional arrangements are not facts of nature, they are human constructs. The appeal to ethnology also made sense in terms of Durkheim's evolutionism, which owed much to Spencer and nothing to Darwin, who in any case had little influence in France at the time, even among natural scientists.[85] Spencer believed that all societies shared a common point of origin. Moreover, the original institutional forms were never lost, but were simply recombined in various, more complex, new forms. (This was a form of social Lamarckism. Spencer was himself a believer in the inheritance of acquired characteristics, and Durkheim – and Freud – shared the Lamarckian assumptions, which were common currency in Europe at the time.) Durkheim concluded that institutions could be most easily understood in their simplest, original form. All these considerations reinforced the appeal of anthropological materials, but there were also good tactical reasons for Durkheim's interest in ethnology. The Durkheimians were seeking an academic niche, and they eagerly appropriated what was, in France, an unclaimed field of scholarship.[86]

Durkheim on the family

In his early lectures, and in *The Division of Labour*, which appeared in 1893, Durkheim accepted the orthodox Anglo–American account of the evolution of the family from an original horde by way of matriarchy and patriarchy. However, he situated this model in a sociological context. Spencer had taught that evolution was a process in which everything started from a simple cell and became progressively more complex. The original society must therefore have been unicellular, as it were, and internally undifferentiated. By segmentation it gave rise to more complex social forms. The original horde split into two, yielding a society made up of two clans (or moieties). Durkheim identified this stage with the Australian society described by Fison and Howitt. According to Morgan, the Iroquois had eight clan units. Obviously they were a yet more advanced system, having segmented not once but three times. 'The horde which had ceased to be independent, and become an element in a more extended group, we call the clan', Durkheim wrote, adopting the jargon of the British anthropologists. But when it came to the structure, he used Spencer's language. 'Peoples formed by an association of clans we call segmentary clan-based societies.'[87] These segmentary clans were bound together by what Durkheim called 'mechanical solidarity'. Every group was the same, every person submerged his individuality in the group. These clans were usually recruited through kinship ties, but they could just as well be based on locality.

Modern societies were very different. Individuals mattered more. The economy was based on a complex division of labour. The society hung together because individuals recognised that they depended on the specialised contributions of other individuals. In *The Division of Labour* Durkheim argued that the family was withering away in these modern societies. Its moral, disciplinary and organisational functions would be taken over by trade unions and professional associations. Ties of descent, which had regulated communal property relationships, were losing their old importance. At the same time, the personal tie between husband and wife became relatively more significant. The nuclear family was the most important modern kinship institution. Nevertheless, traces of earlier family forms survived. 'The modern family contains within it, as if in miniature, the whole historical development of the family.'[88] Durkheim concluded that nostalgia for 'traditional' family forms was irrational. 'The family of today is not more or less perfect than that of old: it is different, because the circumstances are different. It is more complex, because the environment in which it exists is more complex: that is all.'[89]

The origin of the incest taboo

In 1895 Durkheim realised that Robertson Smith's theory of totemism offered a powerful, fresh perspective on these questions. Above all, the theory of totemism promised to relativise both the family and religion at a single stroke. He began to work out the implications of this theory in a long essay, 'La prohibition de l'inceste et ses origines'. It was given pride of place in the first issue of the *Année sociologique*, which appeared in 1898.

Durkheim began by restating the old idea of totemism. Clan members believed that they shared some kind of common substance with each other and with their clan totem. Totemic clans were originally exogamous and matrilineal. When local patrilineal clans developed, they copied the rule of exogamy. Australian 'marriage-classes' resulted from the combination of exogamous uterine clans and exogamous patrilineal local units. But the anthropologists had misunderstood the true nature of exogamy. They thought that it reflected a horror of sexual relations between close kin, and that it implied a general prohibition of marriages between blood relatives. However, some very close blood relatives might be marriageable – mother's brother's children, for instance. Moreover, marriages were frequently banned between certain non-relatives.

Durkheim looked instead for the causes of exogamy within totemism itself. The incest taboo was the consequence of religious beliefs. It was the product of another, greater taboo, the primal taboo on blood. Women are ritually segregated at puberty, menstruation and childbirth. This is because their blood is dangerous. These taboos on women were connected with the taboo on shedding the blood of a clansman, and with the taboos on killing or eating the totem. The key to the whole intellectual complex was the belief that the clansmen shared a common substance with the totem. 'Thus the totemic being is immanent in the clan; it is incarnated in each individual, and it resides in the blood. It is itself the blood.'[90] Because blood was sacred, it was taboo.

The argument was elaborated in *The Elementary Forms of the Religious Life* (1912), but Durkheim now parted company with his old teacher, Fustel, and insisted that religion was a reflection of society.[91] Religion was not really 'about' gods. Nor, for that matter, was the family really 'about' consanguinity. The simplest societies were composed of undifferentiated and repetitive clans, which might be based on kinship but could equally be based on territorial ties. Each clan was a distinctive unit. It therefore required a badge of identity, an emblem. The emblem was the origin of the totem. The religious features of totemism – the rituals, the prohibitions, the beliefs – followed from the identification of the social unit, the clan, with an emblem, the totem. When the members of the group came together at certain seasons, they did so under the common banner, the totem. The totem became a sacred object, and so the focus of ritual. The effect was 'to raise man above himself and to make him lead a life superior to that which he would lead, if he followed only his own individual whims: beliefs express this life in representations; rites organize it and regulate its working.'[92] And the subordination of individual 'whims' to the interests of the group was what Durkheim meant by morality. Religion and the family are the sources of morality, as the conservatives argued. However, as the nature of the society changes so do the religion, the family, and the moral code.

The fate of totemism

The theory of totemism may be traced back to McLennan's essay of 1869, although the subject only attracted wide attention a decade later, when Robertson Smith linked totemism to the religion of the ancient Semites. The theory was debated for a generation, but interest was clearly fizzling out by the time that the Austrian journal *Anthropos* published a disillusioned symposium on the subject in the early years of the First World War. The initiative came from Goldenweiser, who had published a critique of totemism in 1910. In 1912 he wrote to the editor of *Anthropos* to say that the publication of 'Durkheim's brilliant but unconvincing treatise on religion brings home the fact that ... the problem of totemism remains as replete with vagueness and mutual misunderstanding as ever.'[93] *Anthropos* duly launched a symposium on totemism, and although Europe was in the middle of the Great War, contributions were received from Thurnwald and Graebner in Berlin and Schmidt in Vienna; from Rivers and Radcliffe-Brown in Britain; and from Boas, Goldenweiser and Swanton in the United States. They generally agreed that 'totemism as a social system' should be treated separately from the totemic religion, but few contributors expressed much enthusiasm for totemism in either form, and certainly not for Durkheim's grand synthesis. His ideas were influential in France for rather longer, despite the powerful critique of Arnold van Gennep, *L'État actuel du problème totémique*, which appeared in 1920.

Yet although anthropologists abandoned totemism, it was to be their most enduring contribution to the way in which European intellectuals thought about primitive society in the early twentieth century. Durkheim taught sociologists about totemism, Freud instructed psychoanalysts. *The Golden Bough* inspired a whole school of classical scholarship. It furnished one of the themes of T. S. Eliot's *The Waste Land*, and even in the late twentieth century it could inspire a best-selling novel and a film, Jean Auel's *Clan of the Cave Bear*. Anthropology had apparently delivered a full-blown myth of the origin of the family, marriage and religion. These great bourgeois institutions had been spawned by primitive superstition. Totemism could therefore serve as a foundation story for rationalism. At the same time, it conjured up a world in which the human spirit was at one with nature, in which a poetic, mythical language was commonplace, and in which sexual instincts were uninhibited. It was the anthropologists' Garden of Eden.

Part III

Evolution and diffusion

Boas, Rivers and Radcliffe-Brown

> Scientifically the study of primitive societies does not require justification. They *exist* and as part of reality Science is bound to take note of them.
>
> (Robert Lowie, *Primitive Society*, 1929, p. 2)

Chapter 6

The Boasians and the critique of evolutionism

At the beginning of the twentieth century, the increasingly dominant Anglo–American anthropology was challenged by a distinctive German ethnological tradition. The Anglo–American school was 'evolutionist'. All societies passed through the same stages, driven by an internal dynamic of change. The Germans preferred particularist histories of ethnic groups. Changes came through contacts between peoples as they rubbed up against each other, borrowing ideas and reacting against them. These two anthropologies first confronted each other not in Europe but in the United States, where Franz Boas and his students challenged the theories of Lewis Henry Morgan.

It is not always appreciated how deep were the German roots of Boas's anthropology. This was partly because Boas's career was such a very long one. Some of his best-known students, including Ruth Benedict and Margaret Mead, were part of a second generation who came to him only after World War One, when he was already over sixty. By then the old battles had been won, and Boas's preoccupations had altered. I am concerned here with the earlier period and with Boas's most creative years, from the mid-1880s to the 1920s. Migration had left its mark, of course, but Boas remained still very much an ethnologist of the Berlin school.

The German tradition

Franz Boas was born in Minden, Westphalia, in 1858.[1] (Durkheim was an exact contemporary, Freud two years older.) His family was typical of the assimilated German Jewish middle-class of the time – prosperous, liberal and well-educated. Boas himself later wrote:

> The background of my early thinking was a German home in which the ideals of the revolution of 1848 were a living force. My father, liberal, but not active in public affairs; my mother, idealistic, with a lively interest in public matters, the founder about 1854 of the kindergarten of my home town, devoted to science. My parents had broken through the shackles of dogma. My father had retained an emotional affection for the ceremonial of his parental home, without allowing it to influence his intellectual freedom.[2]

After graduation and a period of military service, Boas spent the winter of 1882–1883 in Berlin. Here he came under the influence of the anatomist Rudolf Virchow, and the ethnologist Adolf Bastian, who was building up the Royal Berlin Museum of Völkskunde.[3] The two men established a new and liberal school of anthropology, which opposed the nationalist and racist ideology that was developing in Bismarck's Prussia, and Virchow himself was politically active as a liberal member of the Senate.

A leading critic of the Darwinians, Virchow rejected evolutionary determinism. He was particularly troubled by the idiosyncratic version of Darwinism promoted by his student, Ernst Haeckel, who argued that the human races had become effectively different species. Virchow countered that all races were unstable categories, with shifting boundaries. Racial mixing was widespread, if not universal. Biological traits, such as blood groups, cut across the conventional racial classifications. He was also enough of a Lamarckian to believe that the environment quickly imposed biological changes, so that local populations tended to converge. Perhaps most importantly, he insisted that cultural difference was not a sign of racial difference. Race, culture, language and nationality did not necessarily coincide. Berlin's Hugeuenot refugees 'are Germanised, just like the numerous Jews, whom we accept from Poland or Russia, and [who] have become a powerful ferment of cultural progress for us.'[4]

For his part, Bastian insisted that just as there were no pure races, so there were no pure cultures. Contacts between peoples led not only to intermarriage but to the diffusion of ideas, techniques and institutions. All cultures were historically contingent, the product of exchanges and interactions. And since cultural differences were the consequence of chance local processes – environmental pressures, migrations, trade – it followed that all history was local history. The immediate physical environment was also extremely significant for cultural development. Therefore, ethnologists should not study races or ethnic groups but 'geographical provinces'. However, the human material was the same everywhere. Every culture was inscribed upon the same foundation, the 'psychic unity of mankind'. In consequence, all cultures shared some fundamental ideas, the *Elementargedanken.*

Boas was a birthright liberal, and he naturally took the side of Virchow and Bastian on the issue of race and culture. But German universities were divided by another, philosophical, debate about the nature of science. Were the methods of the natural sciences appropriate for the study of human beings? Surely a more subjective, intuitive, approach was required to understand human motivations. As a young man, Boas was torn between his respect for the natural sciences and the appeal of a more humanistic and 'emotional' study. 'My university studies were a compromise', he wrote. 'On account of my intense emotional interest in the phenomena of the world, I studied geography; on account of my intellectual interest, I studied mathematics and physics.' But even his physics tended towards 'psychophysics'. His apprentice research involved the measurement of light intensities, which led him to consider the subjective elements in the measurement of sensations.

Broadly, the debate was between proponents of a purely physical, mechanistic form of explanation and those who argued for a historical, particularist approach, which left room for human agency. According to Lamarckian doctrine, the human body underwent alterations within a single lifetime, as a result of environmental influences. Perhaps ideas could affect the body, the mind shape the brain. Waitz had suggested that cultural variations were accidental and secondary, but he nevertheless believed that once these variations were established they could feed back and affect fundamental mental capacities and eventually precipitate changes in head shape (for head shape was, he assumed, related to mental capacities). Virchow also argued that skull proportions were plastic traits that could be modified directly by the physical environment or indirectly by mental development.

Boas was sufficiently interested in this debate to follow it up in an early piece of research. When he settled in the USA he studied the head shapes of immigrants. He apparently found that the key dimensions of the skulls of American-born individuals changed 'almost immediately after the arrival of their parents in America'. The younger the age at which a child arrived in America the narrower his face was relative to that of his parents and older siblings and the more closely it approximated to the white American mean. Boas believed that this reflected changes within that narrower immigrant skull. The child was becoming an American, inside and out.[5]

Boas switched from physics to geography, but the same issues were being urgently debated by German geographers.[6] To what extent did human beings make their own history? At one extreme, the environmental determinists argued that climate and landscape shaped not only technical adaptations and demographic trends, but even personality and ways of thinking. Other geographers placed more emphasis on human interactions, and so on history. 'The fundamental theory of world-history,' Friedrich Ratzel insisted, 'is the history of migration'.[7] Except in their most extreme forms, these positions were not necessarily mutually exclusive. Ratzel's textbook, *Völkerkunde*, published between 1885 and 1890, recognised the importance of the physical environment. Bastian himself developed the concept of the 'geographical province', a region defined both by environment and history, which, he argued, should provide the unit of study for ethnological research.

In what was to be the most intensive ethnographic fieldwork he ever attempted, Boas spent a year in Baffin Island collecting material for his doctorate on the migration routes of the Eskimo.[8] He went into the field a geographical determinist but experienced 'a thorough disillusionment'. Settlement patterns and migrations were attuned to the movements of seals and caribou, and the smoothness of the sea ice affected population densities, but geographical influences were 'so shallow that they did not throw any light on the driving forces that mold behavior.'[9] The mind was not determined by the physical environment. What was needed was a detailed history of local cultural traditions rather than a natural history of the inhabitants of a landscape.

Boas in America

Returning from Baffin Island, Boas seriously considered making New York his home. Anti-Semitism was becoming more evident in Germany, even in academic circles. However, in response to the urgings of his parents he rejoined Bastian at the ethnographic museum, where he prepared a report on his Baffin Island journey for his *habilitation* (the German university teacher's qualification). He used his thesis to criticise environmental determinism.

In 1886 he returned to North America, and spent three months on the Northwest coast of Canada, initiating his life's main work, the study of the Kwakiutl Indians and their neighbours. He decided to remain in the United States, married, and found a job as geographical editor of *Science* magazine. Now began the protracted, lonely and often painful process of establishing a position for himself in American anthropology.

In the closing years of the nineteenth century the one significant concentration of anthropologists in the USA was at the Smithsonian Institution in Washington, which housed the Bureau of American Ethnology (BAE) under the leadership of John Wesley Powell. A geologist by training, Powell was a strong advocate of Morgan's theories. Under his direction, the BAE organised the only substantial American research programme in anthropology. It was designed to extend and complete Morgan's American researches.[10] Powell's programme was, of course, unacceptable to Boas, the student of Virchow and Bastian. In 1887, the year after he had settled in the USA, he made a visit to study the Northwest Coast collection in the Smithsonian. Otis T. Mason, the first curator of ethnology at the Smithsonian museum, had arranged the exhibits to illustrate technological evolution and to bring out the underlying unity of human development. The objects from the Northwest coast were therefore distributed in a dozen different sections of the museum.

Boas complained that Mason laid out ethnographic objects as though they were specimens in a natural history collection, which could be sorted into genera and species and used to endorse a theoretical conclusion: 'like causes produce like effects. Under the same stress and resources the same inventions will arise.' Instead, Boas wanted each object to be placed together with other artefacts of a tribe or a region. A collection should be 'arranged according to tribes, in order to teach the peculiar style of each group'. 'We have to study each ethnological specimen individually in its history and in its medium, and this is the important meaning of the "geographical province" which is so frequently emphasized by A. Bastian'. In any case, 'classification is not explanation'. A rattle from Alaska might look like a rattle from British Columbia, but this did not necessarily mean that they had the same uses, or that they were the product of the same causes. Sometimes 'unlike causes produce like effects'.[11]

Powell responded that Boas's alternative was itself not viable. Tribal groups had undergone so many changes that it was impossible to classify them on ethnic grounds. He concluded that 'there is no science of ethnology, for the attempt to classify mankind in groups has failed on every hand ... The unity of mankind is the greatest induction of anthropology.'[12] As a result of this controversy, Boas found himself entrenched as a critic of the most powerful anthropological institution in the country. This did nothing to help his career prospects, since there were very few positions in anthropology outside the Smithsonian. In 1889 he was appointed to a post at the newly founded Clark University, where he stayed long enough to produce the first American PhD in anthropology, but he quarrelled with the University's founder, and by 1892 he was unemployed once more.

Yet while Boas's theoretical ideas set him against the Smithsonian people, they won him an influential sympathiser at Harvard, in F. W. Putnam.[13] A student of Agassiz, Putnam was an anti-Darwinian, inclined towards Lamarckism, and sceptical of the developmental schemes of the Smithsonian anthropologists. When he was made responsible for the anthropological section of the Chicago World Fair, Putnam made Boas his assistant. Both men expected this appointment to lead to a permanent position at the Field Museum which grew out of theWorld Fair, but the Smithsonian group secured the appointment of their protegé, Holmes.[14] However, Putnam found Boas a position as assistant curator at the American Museum of Natural History. Boas also began to teach at Columbia University. He became a full professor in 1899, and here he educated a new generation of American anthropologists.

Fieldwork

Boas's year in Baffin Island and his subsequent period in Berlin had seen him abandon environmental determinism. He had come to believe that history was of primary importance in shaping the psychology of a people – history in Ratzel's sense, essentially the history of migration and contact. As he explained in a letter to Powell in 1887, 'the phenomena such as customs, traditions and migrations are far too complex in their origin, as to enable us to study their psychological causes without a thorough knowledge of their history. I concluded it necessary to see a people, among which historical facts are of greater influence than the surroundings and selected for this purpose Northwest America'.[15]

Following his first expedition to the Northwest coast, in 1886, Boas visited the British Columbia five times between 1888 and 1894, staying for several months on each occasion, and he made further

visits after World War One. His publications on Kwakiutl ethnography eventually ran to over 5,000 printed pages.[16] Yet although
Boas did sometimes live on fairly intimate terms with the Kwakiutl,
and regularly attended ceremonies and public events, his work lacked
the directness, the personal involvement, which was later to become
a distinguishing feature of anthropological fieldwork. He was perhaps
not altogether satisfied with the nature of his own materials, and
Lowie remarked that 'he was especially appreciative of men who
had achieved what he never attempted – an intimate, yet authentic,
picture of aboriginal life. I have hardly ever heard him speak with
such veritable enthusiasm as when lauding Bogora's account of the
Chukchi, Rasmussen's of the Eskimo, Turi's of the Lapps.'[17]

Yet there were good reasons for Boas's procedures. By the end of
the nineteenth century, the Northwest coast Indians were thoroughly
enmeshed in the wide-open frontier economy and society. They were
ambivalent about their cultural heritage, and deeply suspicious of
white people. Certain ceremonies continued to be mounted, though
in a radically different setting. Others, including the *potlatch*, were
under threat from the authorities, and undertaken, if at all, in secrecy.
Boas's subject was the old way of life, and clearly this could not be
observed directly. In any case, he considered it best to let the people
speak for themselves. Together with his half-Tlingit clerk, George
Hunt, he collected vernacular texts from informants, recording
historical traditions and myths, on which, in the German tradition,
Boas laid great value, and also a magpie's collection of ethnographic
titbits, ranging from accounts of ceremonies to descriptions of
technical procedures, and including even gooseberry pie recipes.

This was how the German ethnologists proceeded. Their model
was the European tradition of Oriental studies or classical scholarship, the central aim being the compilation, annotation and translation of texts. Boas regarded interpretation as a secondary function,
which probably should not be undertaken until all the material was
published, and he issued his Kwakiutl texts with a minimum of
scholarly apparatus, or even organisation. Irving Goldman commented that 'each of the published volumes of text materials seems
to have been assembled at random. For the most part, each text
around a subject stands within the corpus of the entire work
unconnected, unannotated, and uninterpreted for the reader'.[18]
Nevertheless, the facts that they yielded could be exploited to
disprove the premature generalisations of the evolutionists. The first
targets were Morgan's dogma that all societies progressed from a

matrilineal to a patrilineal stage, and the orthodox theory of totemism.

Totems and descent

Boas initially endorsed the standard Anglo–American ideas about the evolution of marriage, descent and totemism.[19] In his first report to Tylor at the British Association, which financed his initial expedition to the Northwest coast, he dealt with the classic issues, remarking that Frazerian animal totems were to be found among the Tlingit, Tsimshian and Heiltsuk, but not among the Kwakiutl, although they were of the same linguistic stock as the Heiltsuk. However, the Kwakiutl had 'crests', and these were perhaps attenuated versions of totems. All these peoples had legends that apparently accounted for the adoption of totems by their ancestors. The totemic groups were matrilineal gentes, which were ordered into phratries (also named for animals). To the south of this cluster, however, things were very different. There 'the patriarchate prevails', clans did not associate into larger groups, or phratries, and there were no animal totems.[20]

Boas spent most of his time in the field among the Kwakiutl, who lived between the two main clusters of Northwest coast Indian tribes. He knew them best, and certainly knew them well enough to recognise that they were neither matrilineal nor patrilineal. Boas suggested that they might represent an intermediate condition between matriarchy and patriarchy. At first he thought that they had formerly been patrilineal, but by 1889 he had reversed his position. Their marriage customs 'seem to show that originally matriarchy prevailed among them'. Before his marriage a man assumed his wife's father's name and crest, 'and thus becomes a member of his wife's clan'. His children take the same name and crest, but his sons lose them on marriage. 'Thus the descent of the crest is practically in the female line, every unmarried man having his mother's crest.'[21]

These conclusions were elaborated in his 1890 report: 'the tribes speaking the Heiltsuk and Gyimano-itq dialects are in the maternal stage, and are divided into gentes having animal totems; while the southern group are in the paternal stage, and are divided into gentes which have no animal crest'. Viewed in terms of this contrast, the Kwakiutl presented a puzzle. 'The social organisation of the Kwakiutl is very difficult to understand. It appears that, in consequence of

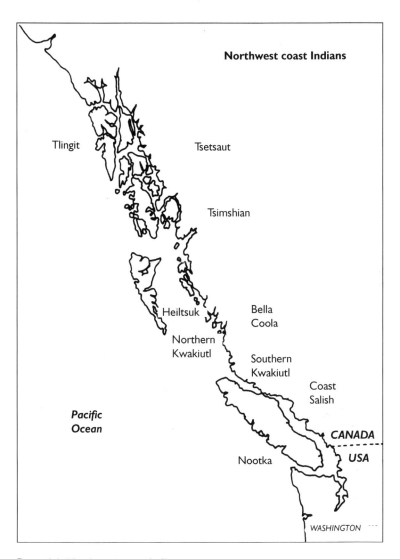

Figure 6.1 Northwest coast Indians

wars and other events, the number and arrangement of tribes and
gentes have undergone considerable changes.' The determination
of group affiliation seemed particularly complex. 'The child does
not belong by birth to the gens of his father or mother, but may be
made a member of any gens to which his father, mother, grandparents,

or great-grandparents belonged. Generally, each child is a member of another gens.'[22]

It seems obvious that these new findings weakened Boas's earlier claim that the Kwakiutl showed traces of 'matriarchy'. Were the Kwakiutl indeed really so fascinatingly transitional? In a report published in 1897, he reaffirmed the transitional status of the Kwakiutl, but reversed the direction that their historical transformation had taken. The Kwakiutl were not in the process of moving from matriarchy to patriarchy, in the orthodox Morgan fashion. Rather, as he had first suspected, they were moving in the direction of matriarchy, from an original paternal form of organisation. 'Matriarchy' was not a past but a future condition. Formerly the Kwakiutl had been organised in 'a series of village communities'. Descent had been traced in the paternal line, the members of each village being considered the descendants of a single male ancestor. Later these communities had amalgamated to form tribes and had lost their local identity. 'Maternal' clans began to consolidate. This transition from patriliny to matriliny had two basic causes: the exigencies of the new tribal organisation (but what they were Boas did not specify), and diffusion from the northern, matrilineal tribes. One mechanism was the adoption of the northern, matriarchal legends, which legitimated the transmission of rank and privileges in the female line. The Kwakiutl arrangements were so complicated because they represented 'an adaptation of maternal laws by a tribe which was on a paternal stage'.[23]

In 1890, Boas had argued that Kwakiutl legends and their system of transmitting crests showed that they had been originally (but were no longer) matriarchal and totemic. In 1897 he was drawing on much the same evidence to demonstrate that they had on the contrary been originally patriarchal, and were now in the process of becoming matriarchal. However, the traces of this transition remained somewhat exiguous, boiling down to the fact that names and crests were transmitted in the male line. Boas laid much store by the evidence of legends, but this was largely negative in character. The Kwakiutl must have been patriarchal originally, he argued, for otherwise in their legends 'the tribes would have been designated as the descendants of the ancestor's sisters, as is always the case in the legends of the northern tribes'.[24]

In a paper published in the *American Anthropologist* in 1920, Boas abandoned all talk of totems, crests, gentes or clans as misleading. Instead he offered an exegesis of the Kwakiutl concept *numaym*, a term that evidently referred to a bundle of privileges, which might include the right to a crest but was not associated with property, and had none of the classical attributes of a totem. In order to secure such privileges, a man had to have a claim through his wife or one of his parents. If a son-in-law succeeded, then the privileges were regarded as a return for the bridewealth which he had paid. There was no evidence, however, that the privileges were passed down a line of sons-in-law.[25]

This mature revision of his ethnography did not impel Boas to reconsider his theory that the Kwakiutl were making a historical transition from a paternal to something like a maternal system. On the contrary, he reaffirmed that the complex system of transmitting privileges had been superimposed upon a simpler, older, paternal, village-based social system. However, he did qualify the claim that the new system was 'maternal', or rather he conceded that his earlier formulation had been open to misinterpretation. In a 'maternal' system, rights were transmitted from a mother's brother to a sister's son. Obviously, the Kwakiutl mode of transmission, from a father-in-law to a son-in-law, was very different.

Columbia

At Columbia University, Boas introduced the German intellectual tradition into American anthropology. The students he attracted were themselves mostly of German extraction. They had come to America as children, but their homes and schools in New York city were culturally German. 'The atmosphere in which he was raised in New York was a completely German one', Paul Radin wrote of a representative member of the circle, Robert Lowie. 'All his parents' friends were Austrians, mainly Viennese, and Viennese German was the only language spoken in the home. To all intents and purposes, the United States was a foreign and somewhat shadowy land, with which one came into contact when leaving the house and with which one lost contact on reentering.' Lowie's inner life was largely 'concerned with German culture and cultural ideals'. This was manifest 'in the direction of much of his scientific work – in the influence that Haeckel, Ostwald, and Wundt once had on him, and the influence which Boas and Mach had to the end of his life.'[26]

Almost the same has been said of Kroeber. 'German was Alfred's first language', his widow wrote. 'The elder Kroebers, like their relatives and friends, wanted their children to be bilingual. They particularly wanted them to know their Goethe, Heine and Schiller and to read Shakespeare first in German translation.'[27] Other members of Boas's entourage at Columbia were from a similar cultural background, notably Goldenweiser, Sapir, and Radin himself. Most of them were Jewish, but Kroeber, who was not, remarked that the Jewish and Gentile German families alike 'took it for granted that one did not believe in religion'.[28] The Ethical Culture movement provided for the spiritual needs of many German-speaking upper-middle-class families, Gentile and Jewish, in New York. Their schools brought together Gentile and Jewish German–Americans. Kroeber was sent to Dr Sachs's Collegiate Institute, which was modelled on a European gymnasium. Four-fifths of the pupils were Jewish.[29] This was a transplanted version of the world in which Boas himself had grown up.

Boas's programme also fitted in very well with the general spirit of Columbia at the turn of the century. By 1900 the Darwinian tide had receded at Columbia, as it had somewhat earlier in the German universities. Even in England Darwinism lost ground in the last decade of the nineteenth century, where the temporary 'eclipse of Darwinism' (as Julian Huxley later called it) was accompanied by a revival of Lamarckism.[30] Lowie recalled that:

> A Columbia student who from a boy had accepted Darwinism as a dogma, who had steeped himself as an undergraduate in Herbert Spencer's *First Principles* and hailed Ernst Haeckel's *Die Welträtsel* as a definitive solution of all cosmic enigmas, was profoundly disturbed when browsing in the departmental libraries of Schermerhorn Hall or talking to age-mates who majored in zoology. Bewildering judgments turned up in the new books and journals. For William James, Herbert Spencer was a 'vague writer', and in Pearson's opinion the British philosopher cut a sorry figure when using the terms of physics. Darwin himself, esteemed for his monographs, was not always taken seriously as a theorist. In the building where our student spent most of his time Thomas Hunt Morgan, a prophet of the new dispensation, held forth on the weaknesses of the Darwinian philosophy.

But there was something bracing about this new scepticism. 'The transports of delirious rapture were succeeded by the mood of the *Katzenjammer*. What had figured as the quintessence of scientific insight suddenly shrank into a farrago of dubious hypotheses. In short, sobriety reigned once more in professional circles.'[31]

Boas's critical approach had an affinity with that of Lowie's other heroes, Mach, the empiricist philosopher, and the psychiatrist Adolf Meyer.

> They were severely scrutinizing such blanket terms as 'schizo-phrenia', 'totemism', 'matter' and trying to discover their factual basis. When later I grappled with Schurtz's notion of 'age-society' and with L. H. Morgan's of 'classificatory terms of relationship', I more or less consciously applied the principles of these scientific thinkers. We had learned to view catchwords with suspicion.[32]

If there was something very German about the intellectual style of Boas and his students, there was a definite element of ethnic confrontation in their relationship with the WASP establishment at the Smithsonian. To this was added a political strain between the liberalism of the New Yorkers and the more conservative and nationalist attitudes that dominated the nation's capital. Boas claimed that the Spanish–American war of 1898 was his 'rude awakening' to the real nature of American politics, obliging him to recognise that his adopted country was 'dominated by the same desire of aggrandise-ment that sways the narrowly confined European states'.[33] His Establishment colleagues in Washington had no such reservations.

This is not to say that a break was inevitable between the Boasians and the Smithsonian people. Relations remained correct enough for some years. In 1901 the BAE appointed Boas honorary philologist. Powell and Mason accommodated ideas taken from regional, geographical German thinking. Powell's map of American Indian language groups (which provided the centre-piece of Mason's exhibit at the Chicago World Fair) would have been perfectly acceptable to any student of Bastian.

It is difficult to avoid the conclusion that Boas deliberately set out to challenge the hegemony of the Smithsonian people. In 1904 an international conference was held at St Louis, and Boas was invited to deliver an address on the history of anthropology.[34] In his talk he represented the modern development of the discipline in terms of a struggle between two opposed positions. On the one side were the universalists, who believed that cultural traits exhibited a remarkable uniformity all over the world. Two types of explanation were advanced to account for this phenomenon, one associated with Tylor (culture evolved along the same tracks in every part of the globe), the other with Bastian (there are certain universal 'elementary ideas' which recur in every culture). The alternative view was that cultural similarities were generally the consequence of borrowing. Historical research was required to resolve the issues, and Boas instanced studies in train of European folklore.

The striking feature of the lecture is not so much what was said as what was omitted. Boas's talk was studded with examples of research and with the names of distinguished anthropologists, but he did not identify Powell and his school as the American represent-atives of the universalist tendency. As a modern commentator has remarked, Boas 'dropped a whole generation of American anthro-pologists from the historical record. There was no mention of Lewis Henry Morgan, no mention of John Wesley Powell, William Henry Holmes, Frank Hamilton Cushing, Alice G. Fletcher, and others whose work at the Bureau of American Ethnology and elsewhere was arousing the admiration of European scholars, and no mention of the man to whom Boas owed so much, F. W. Putnam.' He 'mentioned only one American anthropologist, Daniel G. Brinton, whom he called an "extremist" in his support of independent invention of myths.'[35]

The critique of evolutionism

Boas's Columbia students were presented with two tasks. One was ethnographic and documentary. There were vast gaps in the knowledge of the North American Indians, and these had to be filled. The students were expected to combine research in linguistics, folklore, material culture and social organisation. The aim was to establish the local historical relations between aboriginal cultures. Their second task was theoretical, or, rather, critical. The facts had to be allowed to speak for themselves, but they could be used to discredit evolutionist generalisations.

Lewis Henry Morgan was, in their eyes, the main source of error in American anthropology. Nevertheless, the Boasian critique of Morgan's theories was launched obliquely. The elected spokesman was one of Boas's early followers, John Reed Swanton. A rare WASP in this circle, Swanton came to work with Boas in 1900. He had studied with Putnam in Harvard, where he eventually submitted his doctoral thesis, but it was under Boas's direction that he undertook ethnographic work on the Northwest coast between 1900 and 1904.

Between 1904 and 1906, he published three major critical reviews of Morgan's theories.[36] Swanton never again published any original theoretical papers, and he later went to work – exceptionally for a Boasian – with the Smithsonian establishment. The hands were the hands of Esau, but the voice was the voice of Jacob. Swanton was a respectable American front man for Boas.

Swanton developed the line of argument that Boas had sketched in 1895. In direct contradiction to Morgan's theory, the Kwakiutl, originally patrilineal, were acculturating to the matrilineal and totemic way of life of their northern neighbours, the Tlingit, Haida and Tsimshian. Matrilineal societies in the region were if anything rather more advanced than the patrilineal societies. Nor did the patrilineal societies show traces of an early matrilineal stage. The kinship terminology did not encode the laws of some ancient and vanished marriage regulation. If two female relatives were classified together, this did not necessarily prove that once upon a time they would have been married to the same man. It might equally well signal the possibility of future marriages. For instance, a man may call his wife's sister 'wife' because she can be claimed in marriage if her sister dies. The evidence from the Northwest coast also under-mined the theory of totemism. The crests of the coastal tribes were merely personal badges, and had nothing to do with the clan structure. In any case, the clan system, totems and taboos did not form a single system. Each element could, and did, occur in isolation from the others.

These lines of attack were pursued more thoroughly by other students of Boas. Alfred Kroeber, who was Boas's first doctoral student at Columbia, began with an examination of the classificatory kinship terminology, the foundation of Morgan's edifice. He argued that Morgan's opposition between classificatory and descriptive types of kinship system was too crude. It was necessary to go beyond the individual kin terms and the relationships they designated to the 'principles or categories of relationship which underlie these'. There were eight such priniciples – *Elementargedanken* he might have said – such as generation, lineality and collaterality, age, sex and so forth. The differences between kinship terminologies arose because some peoples did not use all the eight principles, or gave them different weight. But variations in kinship terminologies had no sociological implications. 'The causes which determine the formation, choice, and similarities of terms of relationship are primarily linguistic.'[37]

Frank Speck published studies of Algonkian social organisation which showed that the basic social unit of these simple hunter-gatherers was the nuclear family. Family groups controlled specific territories.[38] This contradicted Morgan's thesis that the most primitive peoples (by definition hunters and gatherers) were organised into matrilineal hordes, without property rights and without families.

Perhaps the most powerful critique was Kroeber's monograph, *Zuni Kin and Clan*, which appeared in 1919. Frank Cushing, a close associate of Powell at the Smithsonian, had presented the Zuni as a classic matrilineal society. 'He was an extremely able man', Boas told his seminar. Then he added: 'I'm afraid his work will have to be done all over again.'[39] This task was undertaken by Kroeber, who came to the conclusion that the Zuni could not properly be described as being matrilineal at all. Their clans had ritual functions, but clan membership impinged very little on the daily affairs of any individual Zuni. Clans were 'only an ornamental excrescence upon Zuni society, whose warp is the family of actual blood relations and whose woof is the house'.[40] The clans were not localised. Indeed, the only faint sign of any matrilineal tendency was the fact that the house was transmitted from mother to daughter. The individual was attached in much the same way both to his father's and to his mother's people.

Had the Zuni perhaps once been more matrilineal? Were some of their institutions the relics of a more thoroughgoing ancient matriarchate? This sort of speculation was completely unacceptable. 'It is clear that once this method of interpretation is adopted, it can be eternally applied without let or hindrance. Every irregularity, every subsidiary feature even, can be construed as a survival, and every survival as evidence of a former different plan.'[41] The clan model simply did not apply to the Zuni. The reality had been distorted as a consequence of theoretical bias: 'it grew the fashion often to look only for clans, and to overlook actual family life, among nations whose society after all conforms in many respects to ours. I venture to believe that in many another totemic and clan-divided tribe the family of true blood-relatives is fundamental.'[42]

Morgan was not the only target. The theory of totemism was also ripe for deconstruction. In a lecture delivered at Clark University in 1909 (before an audience that included Sigmund Freud), Boas argued that totemism was 'not a single psychological problem, but embraces the most diverse psychological elements'. Moreover, 'the anthropological phenomena, which are in outward appearances alike, are, psychologically speaking, entirely distinct, and ... consequently psychological laws covering all of them cannot be deduced from them'.[43] Goldenweiser elaborated the critique and showed that totemism was not a unified institution, but a construct, whose elements might, and indeed often did, occur independently of each other.[44]

By 1920, after two decades of organised research, the critique of evolutionist anthropology had been accomplished. Lowie's books summed up the results for students and the general public.[45] New schools of anthropology were being staffed by Boasians. Kroeber and Lowie went to Berkeley, Speck to Philadelphia. The gospel spread quickly. Yet the Boasians were vulnerable to the charge that they offered nothing with which to replace the orthodoxy that they had demolished. Reviewing Lowie's *Primitive Society*, Kroeber tempered his praise. 'As long as we continue offering the world only recon-structions of specific detail, and consistently show a negativistic attitude towards broader conclusions, the world will find very little of profit in ethnology. People do want to know why'.[46] But that was the Boasian way. Empirical findings were marshalled in the first instance to attack false generalisations. As Roman Jakobson was to remark, with affectionate irony, had it fallen to Boas to announce the discovery of America he would have begun by saying that the hypothesis that there was an alternative route to India had been disproved. Then he would incidentally report what was known about the New World.[47]

Patriots and immigrants

The triumph of the Boasians was marred by a final, bitter political conflict with the Smithsonian anthropologists. During World War One, Boas and his circle were pro-German or neutral. The new director of the BAE, W. H. Holmes, led a nationalistic group of scientists in Washington who were strongly committed to the Allied cause. It turned out that one of his associates, Sylvanus G. Morley, was actually collecting information for Naval Intelligence under cover of doing archaeological work in Central America. This incident provided the occasion for the final confrontation between Boas and Holmes, whose rivalry dated back at least to the time of the Chicago Fair, when Holmes had been given the position at the Field Museum on which Boas had been counting.[48]

In 1919 Boas wrote a letter to *The Nation* denouncing men who 'have prostituted science by using it as a cover for their activities as spies'.[49] Holmes reacted vituperatively, writing to an associate about 'the traiterous article by Boas', anathematising 'Prussian control of Anthropology in this country', and demanding an end to 'the Hun regime'.[50] Boas was censured at the next meeting of the American Anthropological Association and although he had been president of the Association he narrowly escaped expulsion. Boas's students were by now established professionals, and they were able to fight his corner, but hostility towards the foreign-born and largely Jewish anthropologists continued to fester for many years. Thirty years later, it could be discerned in the polemics of Leslie White, who tried to revive Morgan's programme.[51]

Boas the theorist

My treatment of Boas and the Boasians has necessarily been shaped by the theme of this book, but while Boas's sociological contributions have been relatively neglected in most accounts of his work they constitute a significant, and integral part of his anthropology. Perhaps more contentiously, I have represented Boas as above all a theorist. Admittedly his rhetoric was fiercely empiricist. (He once told a graduate student that 'there are two kinds of people: those who have to have general conceptions into which to fit the facts; those who find the facts sufficient. I belong to the latter category'.)[52] Yet, of course, he did have a theory, if it was presented in the guise of a critique of theory, and his theory shaped his ethnographic reports even though he ostensibly gave priority to ethnographic data in the rawest form. Boas's theoretical excursions were generally illustrated by ethnographic examples, often taken from the Kwakiutl, but the empirical evidence could be made to support contradictory conclusions, as can be seen in his shifts on the question of Kwakiutl social evolution, or on the presence or absence of totems.

The best work of the Boasians combined ethnographic sensitivity and theoretical relevance, although, as Kroeber for one admitted, the final product might be unnervingly negative in tone. But, as Kroeber also remarked, people did want to know why. In the 1920s and 1930s a new generation of Boas's students turned to psychoanalysis and began to speculate about the relationships between 'culture' and 'personality'. However, a more radical critique was being prepared from outside the Boasian circle.

The neo-evolutionists

Leslie White had been trained in anthropology at Chicago by Boas's students Fay Cooper Cole and Edward Sapir, but after a visit to the Soviet Union in 1929 he was converted to Marxism, and so to the anthropology of Lewis Henry Morgan that was favoured in official circles in Russia. He now devoted himself to the revival of Morgan's reputation and to the demolition of the Boas school, against which he launched a vituperative attack.[53] Boas's critique of evolutionism and of Morgan was nothing short of obscurantism. All human societies advanced through a series of fixed stages, powered by increasing quantities of energy harnessed from the environment.

A more cautious project was developed by Julian Steward, a student of Lowie and Kroeber. He had been influenced by the geographer Carl Sauer at Berkeley, and was interested in the influence of the environment on culture, rather in the manner of the early Boas himself. Although Steward distanced himself from the unilinear evolutionism of White, the two men became leaders of a new school, which took over the Boasian stronghold at Columbia University. Two of their brilliant young followers, Elman Service and Marshall Sahlins, attempted to reconcile their conceptions of cultural evolution. All species adapted to local constraints. In the long run, however, more complex and efficient species emerged. Studies of local adaptations could be synthesised to yield larger narratives of what Marshall Sahlins termed 'general evolution'. And cultural evolution was simply an extension of biological evolution. It 'continues the evolutionary process by new means'. Finally, and as Lewis Henry Morgan would have agreed, its defining feature was 'the character of progress itself'.[54]

Detailed case studies demonstrated how local populations adapted to their environments or 'niches' with the help of technology and forms of organisation but also through rituals and taboos. Pig-killing ceremonies, human sacrifice, the Hindu taboo on the cow, all were to be explained as ways of maximising protein while safeguarding an ecological balance. Primitive societies were steady state, not interested in growth, at peace with nature. Disruptions did happen, but they were to be blamed on intrusive foreigners. Even McLennan had his day when theorists came to explain how a 'male supremacist complex' might develop as a result of population pressure, leading to war and so to female infanticide.[55]

Each evolutionary stage was correlated with a 'mode of production' such as hunting and gathering or 'swidden agriculture', with its characteristic form of social organisation. Steward and Service came up with an influential typology of the most primitive 'band societies'. These were divided into 'patrilineal bands' (as described by Radcliffe-Brown in Australia) and 'composite band societies'. The former were exogamous and patrilineal corporate units, the latter simply a collection of independent families.[56] (Steward's own experience of former hunter-gatherers was with the Shoshone, but they turned out to be an exception.) In 1962, Service set out a series of evolutionary stages in *Primitive Social Organization: An Evolutionary Approach*, which was dedicated to Steward and White. These were described more fully in a series of student textbooks, *The Hunters*, by Service, *Tribesmen*, by Sahlins, and *Peasants*, by Eric Wolf. There were also attempts to explain how primitive systems advanced. Marshall Sahlins, for instance, explained the classic shift from kin-based political systems to states, which he associated respectively with Melanesia and Polynesia, by speculating on ways in which productivity might have increased, producing a surplus which could then be extracted by a governing class.[57]

For a while, it seemed that Morgan ruled American anthropology once more.[58] The influence of the neo-evolutionist movement petered out only in the 1970s, when several of its leading members, notably Marshall Sahlins, abandoned materialism and began to treat 'culture' as a purely symbolic system, which had no obvious pay-off at all.[59] But although neo-evolutionism dropped out of fashion, the reputation of Boas and his school never recovered. However, Boas was still honoured for his contribution to one great issue. Drawing on the critique of his teacher Rudolf Virchow, Boas had crusaded against racism throughout his career in the United States. When the USA entered the war against the Axis powers, Boas took up the fight once again. In 1942, at the age of eighty-five, he was addressing a meeting at the Columbia Faculty Club on the question of racism when he had a sudden heart-attack and fell, dying, into the arms of the man sitting next to him, who was Claude Lévi-Strauss.

Chapter 7

From Rivers to Radcliffe-Brown

At the same time that Boas was building up the first doctoral programme in anthropology in the United States, at Columbia University, the first undergraduate and postgraduate courses in the discipline were being established in Britain, in the heartland of the natural sciences, at Cambridge University, by Alfred Cort Haddon, a zoologist, and a neurophysiologist, W. H. R. Rivers. The fact that Haddon and Rivers were scientists distinguished them from the lawyers and classicists who had formed the first generation of British anthropologists. Both men regarded anthropology as an undeveloped branch of the natural sciences, and one in crying need of scientific methods. Haddon would one day proudly inform the Senate of Cambridge University that 'in some respects Cambridge led the whole world in improving Anthropological methods. Certain methods introduced by Dr Rivers had revolutionised the study of Anthropology.'[1] Rivers himself told his student Layard that he hoped his tombstone would bear the inscription, 'He made ethnology a science'.[2]

Born in 1864, Rivers studied medicine at St Bartholomew's Hospital in London, graduating in 1886 and taking an MD in 1888. He began to work on problems of neurology under John Hughlings Jackson, a devoted follower of Spencer who thought of the nervous system in almost geological terms as a series of strata deposited at different periods of evolutionary history. Rivers studied experimental psychology in Jena, and then taught a course in the subject at University College London. (It was described as 'one of the earliest systematic practical courses in experimental psychology in the world, certainly the first in the this country.')[3] In 1893 he moved to Cambridge to lecture on the physiology of the sense organs, and in 1897 he was appointed to a new Lectureship in Physiological and Experimental Psychology.

A. C. Haddon claimed that he converted Rivers to anthropology by taking him on the Cambridge University Expedition to the Torres Strait in 1898. 'One of the things of which I am most proud in a somewhat long life is that I was the means of seducing Rivers from the path of virtue ... (for Psychology was then a chaste science) ... into that of Anthropology.'[4] However, it was only after retiring from his lectureship in 1907 that Rivers devoted himself entirely to ethnology, and immediately after the publication in 1914 of his *History of Melanesian Society*, which he considered to be his masterpiece, he was plucked from the field in Melanesia and recruited into the army psychiatric service. (Two of the great war poets, Siegfried Sassoon and Wilfred Owen, were his patients in a military hospital for 'shell-shocked' officers in Scotland, and among his colleagues were veterans of the Torres Strait expedition, the first British ethnological expedition, including McDougall, Myers and Seligman. Elliot Smith was another member of the team.) Rivers died suddenly in 1922. Although he was a full-time anthropologist only between the ages of 34 and 50, he was the leader of the field in Britain during the crucial years of professionalisation.

Alfred Cort Haddon,[5] nearly ten years older than Rivers, also arrived in Cambridge in 1893. He had been Professor of Zoology at the Royal College of Science in Dublin, where he had to lecture on tropical fauna and coral reefs, which he had never seen ('retailing second-hand goods over the counter', he complained).[6] T. H. Huxley encouraged him to get first-hand experience in the tropics, and in the summer of 1888 he travelled to the Torres Strait (between Australia and New Guinea). In the Pacific he collected ethnological as well as natural history specimens to sell to museums, which led him to take an interest in local crafts and traditions, and on his return he published two ethnological papers that were praised by Frazer. He now took the bold decision to concentrate in future on ethnology, even though that meant moving to an insecure position with a very small income in Cambridge. 'I admire Mrs Haddon's and your pluck immensely,' T. H. Huxley wrote, 'but after all you know there is an irreducible *minimum* of bread and butter the need of which is patent to a physiologist if not to a morphologist and I declare with sorrow that at this present writing I do not see any way by which a devotee of anthropology is to come at the bread – let alone the butter.'[7] Mrs Haddon remarked that 'You might as well starve as an anthropologist as a zoologist',[8] but in the event Haddon hung on to his post in Dublin, commuting from Cambridge. In these precarious years he used his organisational skills to mount the Cambridge Anthropological Expedition to the Torres Strait and New Guinea, which took place in 1898–1899. Shortly after his return, the university appointed him to a newly established Lectureship in Ethnology.

The Torres Strait expedition[9]

Between 1897 and 1902, Franz Boas directed the Jesup North Pacific Expedition, which recruited American and Russian ethnologists to investigate the relationship between the peoples of Asia and northwestern North America.[10] At the same time, Haddon organised the Cambridge expedition to the Torres Strait, but where Boas had a large subvention from a rich banker, Morris K. Jesup, and recruited an international team of established fieldworkers, Haddon's expedition was very much a shoestring, Cambridge affair. Aside from Haddon himself, none of its members had any experience of ethnological fieldwork. They were drawn in the first instance from among the students to whom Haddon and Rivers were lecturing in anatomy and physiology. Frazer wondered briefly whether he might not go along. Rivers hesitated until his two favourite students, C. S. Myers and William McDougall joined up. He then wrote to Haddon to say that after the recent death of his mother he felt run down and in need of a holiday. 'If you will have me, I should like to join your expedition … I have seen McDougall & Myers recently and I feel pretty sure that they would be glad if I could go with you. I think they said that they were each paying for the passage & I would do the same.'[11] Haddon was delighted, 'though I own that I felt that the psychological side was rather overweighted. I put the direction of the psychological department entirely into the hands of Rivers and for the first time psychological observations were made on a backward people in their own country by trained psychologists with adequate equipment.'[12] He recruited a linguist, S. H. Ray, who was scraping a living teaching arithmetic in a London elementary school, and two further volunteers signed up, C. G. Seligman, a pathologist and a friend of Myers, and Anthony Wilkin, a King's undergraduate, who joined as a photographer and made a speciality of material culture.

The party spent seven months in the islands of the Torres Strait between April and October, 1898, but their most detailed research was carried out in five weeks in September and October 1898 on the islands of Mer and Mabuiag. Rivers made path-breaking experiments on vision, and McDougall studied tactile sensation, but despite Haddon's initial anxiety Rivers became fascinated by what he and Haddon called 'sociological' questions.

The sociological questions that they took into the field can be reconstructed without difficulty. Rivers referred to Morgan's theory and he adopted the basic tenet of Morgan's methodology: kinship terms preserved traces of primeval social systems. Since the Torres Strait was an outpost of Australian culture, Rivers paid particular attention to what Morgan's disciple Fison had to say about Australian societies, and to Tylor's and Frazer's reflections on his work.

The *Reports of the Cambridge Anthropological Expedition to the Torres Straits* ran to six volumes. Rivers wrote up the sections on genealogies, kinship, personal names and (with Haddon) totemism. In keeping with the natural science conception of the expedition, he emphasised his methodological contribution to these fields; above all, his invention of the 'genealogical method'.[13] Genealogies or pedigrees provided a powerful tool with a variety of uses. Above all, they allowed the scientist to record the terms used for kin with a new precision. Applying this method, Rivers was able to show that kinship terms were not merely fossils, devoid of any contemporary significance. 'While going over the various names which one man would apply to others, I was occasionally told that such and such a man would stop a fight, another would bury a dead man, and so on', he noted. 'When the clues given by these occasional remarks were followed up, it was found that there were certain very definite duties and privileges attached to certain bonds of kinship.'[14] To be sure, as Morgan and Fison had argued, the system of kin terms 'has a still more important place in the community in that it is the means of regulating marriage'.[15] The terminology classified certain relatives together in a manner which 'would be a necessary result of the Australian and Fijian custom which Tylor has called "cross-cousin marriage", in which the children of brother and sister marry one another'.[16] For example, if a mother's brother is termed 'father-in-law', this is because a man has a claim to marry his mother's brother's daughter.

However, Rivers reported that the people of Mabuiag did not in fact go in for cross-cousin marriage. There were cases of sister-exchange, but he could find no traces of a system of marriage classes. 'Clans' existed, and they had totems, but the people were in a great muddle about how the totems were inherited. 'There was no doubt that there was considerable confusion in the minds of the Mabuiag people on the subject of their rules of descent, and about two years before our visit the men had a great talk about the totems and had agreed to allow some children to take the totem of the mother, but we do not know of any instance since that time in which this has taken place.'[17] The genealogies even recorded cases of marriage between persons with the same 'totem' (although Rivers decided that the persons concerned must have come from clans which had split). He concluded that the Torres Strait people no longer practised group marriage. Their marriages were 'regulated by kinship rather than by clanship'.[18] In other words, the rules of exogamy did not refer to whole clans but rather to specific categories of kin, traced genealogically. None the less, 'the system of kinship' (by which Rivers meant no more than the terminological system) 'was of fundamental importance and determined to a large extent the relations of individuals to one another'.[19] To that extent, Morgan was vindicated.

The Todas

In 1901–1902, Rivers spent some months doing field research among the Todas in South India. There were reports that the Todas had patrilineal 'clans', but the status of these groups was so uncertain that their neighbours as well as previous ethnographers had supposed them to have a 'five-clan' structure, which Rivers discovered to be a total fabrication. He concluded that neither the 'clan' nor the 'family' was a core Toda institution. The 'state of social evolution' of the Toda was 'intermediate' between a clan-based and a family-based system.[20]

Marriage was forbidden within a group termed the *puliol*. This included non-clansmen, and Rivers confessed that 'it seemed to me in several cases as if it came almost as a new idea to some of the Todas that his *puliol* included all the people of his own clan'. He concluded 'that the Todas recognise the blood-kinship as the restrictive agency rather than the bond produced by membership of the same clan'.[21] Cross-cousins were, however, frequently married (and Rivers provided statistics to prove this). 'Thus it is obviously not nearness of blood-kinship which in itself acts as a restriction on marriage, but nearness of blood-kinship of a certain kind.'[22] Marriage was regulated by individual genealogical constraints, and particular marriages were strongly influenced by material considerations relating to inheritance.

Relationship systems

Morgan promised that kinship terminologies were the golden key that would unlock ancient marriage systems. But Rivers was obliged to recognise that Morgan's theory and his methods were under siege from various directions. In 1907 he addressed some of these criticisms in a contribution to Tylor's *Festschrift*.[23] He accepted that the notion of primitive promiscuity had been effectively debunked, but he insisted that in other crucial respects Morgan's thesis was supported by the evidence. If a group of brothers did indeed collectively marry a group of sisters (which is what Rivers took 'group marriage' to mean), then father's brothers would be classed with 'father', mother's sisters with 'mother', and their children with one's own brothers and sisters. Mother's brothers, father's sisters and cross-cousins would be distinguished. Many systems of kinship terminology exhibited these features, attesting to the prior existence of systems of group marriage.

If this argument was correct, then kinship terms might signify group membership rather than positions in a genealogy. Rivers accordingly preferred to write about 'relationship systems'. In his jargon, relationship terms referred to 'status', that is, group membership, rather than to genealogically-defined 'kinship'. Admittedly he had discovered that even in the Torres Strait people used these terms to refer to genealogical position rather than to clan membership or 'status'. He thought this was probably true even in contemporary Australia. However, that was simply an index of the progress that these peoples had made from the original system of group marriage.

But Boas and his school were mounting a more systematic assault on Morgan's methods and theories. It is evident that Rivers was not aware of the whole sweep of the Boasian critique, or of its historical roots, but he was so impressed by one prong of the argument that he devoted a series of lectures at the London School of Economics in 1913 to refuting it.[24] His target was Kroeber's 1909 paper, 'Classificatory systems of relationship', in which Kroeber argued that kinship terminologies were of no sociological value but should be treated as purely linguistic or psychological material. Rivers described Kroeber's paper as 'the only explicit and clear statement of an attitude which is implicit in the work of nearly all, if not all, the opponents of Morgan since McLennan'.[25]

Precisely what either Kroeber or Rivers meant by 'psychological explanations' in this context is far from clear, but broadly this was a label for a variety of non-realist theories of semantics. Things were grouped together under one label not because they were objectively similar but because they somehow felt similar or because they were united by the internal logic of the system of classification itself. Kroeber seemed to incline to the latter option. Systems of classification of kin had an inner logic. They represented alternative combinations of universal semantic principles. However, Rivers sometimes understood Kroeber to be taking another, more obviously 'psychological', position that if relatives were grouped together into one category it was because a person felt the same emotions for them all. Either hypothesis was diametrically opposed to the basic premise of Morgan, upon which Rivers had based his own methods, and his lectures met this new challenge head on. As he said, 'the object of these lectures is to show how the various features of the classificatory system have arisen out of, and can therefore be explained historically by, social facts'. The relevant 'social facts' – or, as he also called them, 'social rights' – were obligations and claims between persons, of which the most important were claims to a wife.[26]

The best evidence for Morgan's thesis was that relationship terms and marriage rules varied together. For instance, where a man married his mother's brother's daughter he might be expected to use the same term for both his mother's brother and his wife's father. Correlations of this sort could be demonstrated in parts of the Pacific – in Fiji, for example, or the southern New Hebrides. Perhaps a man had similar feelings for his uncle and his father-in-law, Rivers observed, but that was only because he would marry his uncle's daughter, which would make his uncle his father-in-law. 'If it were not for the cross-cousin marriage, what can there be to give the mother's brother a greater psychological similarity to the father-in-law than the father's brother?'[27]

Rivers then extended the argument, borrowing heavily from Köhler's ingenious elaboration of Morgan, which had been published in German in 1897.[28] Köhler had drawn attention to two variant forms of the 'classificatory type of terminology', which he named after American Indian tribes, the Omaha and the Choctaw (nowadays the 'Crow' type). The peculiar features of these systems is that they confused generations. One cross-cousin might be termed 'father', for instance, while another cross-cousin might be termed 'son'. According to Fison and Tylor, the Australian and 'Dravidian' terminologies were consistent with a system of cross-cousin marriage or sister-exchange.

Köhler suggested that the Omaha and Choctaw systems of

classification reflected another type of group marriage. Kin of different generations were classed together because men went in for secondary marriages with women who belonged to the generation of their parents or to the generation of their children. In systems of the Omaha type 'a man also marries his wife's aunt and niece', and in the Choctaw type of system 'a woman marries both her husband's uncle and his nephew'.[29] If among the Choctaw a man calls his father's sister's son 'father' it is because his mother is actually married to his cousin. Rivers concluded that correlations of this sort demonstrated that classificatory systems of kinship terminology organised group marriage, just as Morgan had said.

Evolution and diffusion

But if Rivers remained committed to the central proposition of Morgan's method, that the terminology reflected social arrangements, particularly marriage rules, he was prepared to question features of the grand evolutionary story that Morgan derived from these data. In 1911 he took the occasion of his opening address as President of Section H of the British Association for the Advancement of Science to reveal that he was no longer wedded to evolutionary explanations in general. This lecture announced a dramatic departure from the orthodoxy of British ethnology.[30]

The shift could be defined – as Rivers in fact defined it – with reference to national traditions of anthropology. He was abandoning the traditional English assumption that everywhere in the world customs and institutions progressed through a determined series of evolutionary stages. In their place he adopted the German view that all history was local, and that cultural change was normally a consequence of the mixture of peoples.[31] A young ethnologist at the Berlin Museum, Robert Fritz Graebner, had shown that Melanesian culture was the product of migratory movements.[32] Rivers was impressed, but he objected that Graebner gave the adoption of a piece of material culture as much weight as a change in marriage rules. Material goods could be taken over quite casually, he pointed out. Even beliefs and languages could be adopted without long or profound intermixture of peoples. The only really reliable evidence of intermixture was provided by changes in what Rivers called the 'social structure', and he asserted that the social structure was very unlikely to change without 'the intimate blending of peoples'.[33] It followed that studies of social structure would provide the most reliable evidence of diffusion and migration. 'The basic idea which underlies the whole argument of this book', he wrote in his *History of Melanesian Society* 'is the deeply seated and intimate character of social structure. It seems at first sight impossible that a society can change this structure and yet continue to exist.'[34]

Graebner's essays may have precipitated Rivers's change of direction,[35] but he must have been touched by the great contemporary change in scientific thinking that Julian Huxley has called the 'eclipse of Darwinism'. It was to last for a generation, from the early twentieth century until the evolutionary synthesis of the 1930s, and it influenced biologists even in the stronghold of Cambridge. William Bateson, the man who brought Mendel to the attention of British biologists, completely rejected Darwinian theory. 'We go to Darwin for his incomparable collection of facts', he wrote in 1914. However, Darwin's 'philosophy' should be treated as a historical curiosity. 'We read his scheme of Evolution as we would those of Lucretius or of Lamarck.'[36]

Rivers nevertheless insisted that he had changed his mind as a consequence of new field discoveries. He had made a further expedition to the Pacific, where he spent about a year in 1907–1908 with G. C. Wheeler and Arthur Hocart in the Solomon Islands. Rivers and his companions did some 'intensive work' (as Rivers called it), but most of his research took the form of what he distinguished rather as 'survey-work', 'in which a number of peoples are studied sufficiently to obtain a general idea of their affinities in physique and culture',[37] and he relied largely on the help of missionaries.[38] But it was not an encounter with a particular island society or a specific ethnographic discovery to which Rivers attributed his change of mind. Rather his conversion to 'diffusionism' (as it came to be called) occurred while he struggled with the analysis of his materials – and then only at an advanced stage, for he began his book as an evolutionist account and had originally intended to entitle it *The Evolution of Melanesian Society*.[39] Even in its final form the evolutionary theme is welded rather untidily to the diffusionist story which the book tells.

The History of Melanesian Society

It is worth reviewing the argument of the *History* in some detail, not only as the culminating achievement of Rivers' ethnological career but also because the book itself – in its form as much as its content – reveals the intellectual tension between regional historical reconstructions and evolutionary theory.

It is characteristic of Rivers' intellectual culture that the issues were presented in methodological terms. 'It was only in the act of writing this book that I came gradually to realise the unsatisfactory character of current ethnological methods', he wrote in the preface to his *History*. 'From that time, method again became my chief interest, and it is primarily as a study in method that this book is put forward.' He still believed that relationship systems were 'like fossils, the hidden indications of ancient social institutions'.[40] Indeed, the main pay-off of his genealogical method was that it recorded kinship designations more accurately. What was missing in the old approach was the geographical dimension. When Rivers mapped out the spatial distribution of particular kinship classifications he was forced to recognise that regional patterns cross-cut what he had taken for evolutionary sequences. He concluded that this was because Melanesian cultures were 'complex'. They had been produced by population migrations and admixtures. Yet Rivers insisted that he was not abandoning evolutionism. 'The method of this book', he wrote, 'lies between that of the evolutionary school and that of the modern historical school of Germany. Its standpoint remains essentially evolutionary in spite of its method becoming historical, a combination forced upon me because it was with social structure that I was primarily concerned.' It was possible to combine these approaches since 'the contact of peoples and the blending of their cultures act as the chief stimuli setting in action the forces which lead to human progress'.[41]

Rivers conceived of scientific method in what was then the most up-to-date way, as a process of deduction tested by observation. The basis of his method, he wrote, was 'the formulation of a working hypothetical scheme to form a framework into which the facts are fitted, and the scheme is regarded as satisfactory only if the facts can thus be fitted so as to form a coherent whole, all parts of which are consistent with one another.'[42] His students learned this from him, and Radcliffe-Brown was later to welcome Deacon's contribution on Ambrym 'particularly by reason of the way in which it was made as the confirmation of acute reasoning that something of the sort should be there.'[43] He later described a discovery of his own in almost identical terms: 'The discovery of the Kariera system by myself in 1911 was the result of a definite search, on a surmise made before visiting Australia, but after a careful study of the Australian data in

1909, that some such system might very well exist, and that Western Australia would be a reasonable place in which to look for it.'[44] Nevertheless, Rivers insisted that deductions and inferences had to be kept distinct from 'the facts collected in the field'.[45] His *History of Melanesian Society* was accordingly divided into two volumes, the first containing summaries of observations, the second, argument.

Each of the tediously repetitive chapters of the first volume deals with a specific Melanesian society. The emphasis is on 'social organisation', by which Rivers meant the classification of kin, the moieties and clans, the rights and duties of particular relatives, and the regulation of marriage, adoption, inheritance and succession. The second volume turns to theory. It is largely devoted to the explanation of cross-cousin marriage, which was widespread in the Pacific, but Rivers also identified the problem of what he called 'anomalous' marriage forms. These were marriages between men and women who belonged to different generations. In some case there were even marriages between individuals belonging to the generations of grandparents and grandchildren. The existence of such marriages was deduced in the first place from the terminology, but stray pieces of ethnographic evidence could be cited in support. Howitt reported that among the Dieri in Australia men married the granddaughters of their brothers. There was some evidence to suggest that in Fiji and Buin a man married his father's father's wife, a custom, Rivers speculated, that had arisen in an earlier epoch, when Fiji and Buin had matrilineal moieties.

Sometimes the chain of reasoning became very long indeed. For example, Rivers claimed there were faint indications that at one time men in the Banks Islands had sexual access to their wife's sisters and brothers' wives (as would have been the case in a system of group marriage). This was no longer the case. In fact the Banks Islands terminology, which he had recorded himself, classed wife's sister and brother's wife as 'sisters'. Rivers suggested, however, 'that there is a definite association between the classing of these relatives with the sister and the cessation of such sexual relations'.[46] In other words, if the terms indicated that a particular type of marriage must have been banned, then it followed that such a marriage had once been permitted!

Having identified these 'anomalous and extraordinary' forms of intergenerational marriage, Rivers had to account for them. What might impel men to marry their great-aunts or their brothers' grandchildren? Inter-generational marriages might make sense if

primeval societies were gerontocracies, run by old men who accumu-
lated wives, marrying women of their own generation, but also
women of a younger generation. This recalls the scenarios of Atkinson
and Andrew Lang, who had picked up a hint from Darwin and
fantasised about an original condition in which a patriarch controlled
all the women of his group. But Rivers insisted that 'the monopoly
of women by the old men' did not simply result from the exercise of
force. It was governed by rules. The old men could not marry their
own daughters. They therefore resorted to the daughters of their
own daughters, or married the daughters of their brothers' daughters.
Nor were the young men left celibate. They would be supplied with
the widows and cast-offs of their elders. But a man could pass on a
wife only to a member of his own matrilineal moiety. Therefore his
wives went not to his sons or brothers' sons, but to his sons' sons
and sisters' sons.

Eventually, young men would demand the right to marry young
women. They wanted to marry their cousins, not their aunts – their
mother's brother's daughters rather than their mother's brother's
wives. This was the origin of cross-cousin marriage. Infant betrothal
was a relic of this struggle for women between men of different
generations. Ritual marriage by capture recalled actual trials of
strength between young and old men.

> The beauty of the scheme which has been advanced is that the
> explanations suggested for the four forms of marriage form a
> coherent whole. A form of marriage such as that with the wife
> of the mother's brother, which taken by itself seems anomalous
> and difficult to understand, becomes the obvious consequence
> of another form of marriage which seems still more anomalous,
> viz., marriage with the daughter's daughter; and so with the
> other marriages.[47]

Yet even if the problem was formulated in this way, an alternative
solution presented itself. These 'anomalous' marriages might be no
more than permutations of an Australian-type 'marriage class' system.
After all, Howitt had reported marriages between members of
alternate generations among the Dieri. On this line of reasoning,
Melanesia would fit into place as a natural stage in the development
of the Australian type of society. Rivers rejected this possibility on
the grounds that marriage with the mother's brother's wife was
incompatible with an Australian-type marriage class system. 'The

essence of [the Australian systems] is that members of contiguous generations belong to different classes; a man and his sister's son could never marry women of the same class, and therefore could never marry the same women.'[48]

The history of Melanesia was quite distinct from that of Australia. Melanesian society is an amalgam.[49] Peoples with a moiety system had been set on the road to social development by more advanced immigrants. Patrilineal succession, patrilineal inheritance and chieftainship were all attributable to immigrant influence. So was cross-cousin marriage, which could come into being only when paternity was recognised. So was the institution of bride-price, which arose because the immigrants were mainly men, who had to find wives from the local populations. Totemism and ancestor worship had been brought to Melanesia by the immigrant 'kava people', who believed that the dead were reincarnated in the form of animals and plants. They practised their religion in 'secret societies', but converted their wives, who taught it to their children, and so it spread. Different streams of migration accounted for differences between Melanesian and Polynesian societies.

In these ways, an appeal to diffusion allowed Rivers to account for evolution. The Melanesians went through all the conventional evolutionary stages, but as a result of contact rather than endogenous development. The argument could even be turned back to deal with the very first stages of human society. Could dual organisation itself not have been the result of the fusion of two peoples rather than being a consequence of fission, as was normally supposed? In the penultimate chapter of the second volume of his history, Rivers argued that this is precisely what had happened.

The reaction to Rivers

Rivers set the agenda for the study of primitive society in Britain, just as Boas had done in the USA, but their legacies were very different. Perhaps Columbia was more authoritarian than Cambridge. Certainly Boas was more paternalistic than Rivers. Also, Boas and his students were outsiders, while Rivers and his students were middle-class English scientists, who felt perfectly at home in the leading scientific university in the country and took for granted the ethos of élite egalitarianism that Cambridge fostered.

Nevertheless, there were limits to the radicalism of the Cambridge school. His first student, A. R. Radcliffe-Brown, turned the models of Rivers upside down, and later Cambridge students advanced alternative explanations of Melanesian marriage practices. However, they all asked the same questions as Rivers had asked, and they produced the same sort of answers. They also used the same methods. Radcliffe-Brown worked in Australia in 1910–1911 in essentially the same way as Rivers was working in Melanesia. The same could be said of his younger students, notably Layard in 1914 and Deacon in 1924. The reaction to Rivers had more to do with debates in classrooms than with new ethnographic methods or discoveries.[50]

Radcliffe-Brown and Australia

Like Haddon and Rivers, Radcliffe-Brown started off as a natural scientist, but at Cambridge he switched to moral sciences and became Rivers's first student in social anthropology.[51] His first field study took him to the Andaman Islands, and he initially analysed his Andaman data within a diffusionist framework learnt from Rivers. Around 1910 he adopted a Durkheimian approach, and in 1910–1911 he made field studies in Australia. For the next two decades, while Rivers turned his attention to Melanesia, Radcliffe-Brown was studying the Australian aborigines. He published preliminary syntheses in 1913, 1918 and 1923, and in 1930–1931 a monograph, *The Social Organization of Australian Tribes*, which was the most enduring achievement of the school of Rivers.

Since Fison, the received wisdom on Australian social structure was that marriage choices were regulated by a system of marriage 'classes'. The simplest systems had two classes, or moieties. More complex systems had four, eight, or even sixteen 'marriage classes'. In a four class system, every member of one specific group (A) had to marry into another specified group (B). Their children would belong to a third group (C), and would have to marry into a fourth group (D). The terms for kin reflected this grouping into four classes. Other social units, notably local groupings, were recent developments, foreshadowing the eclipse of the ancient system. According to Fison, these classes were the units of a system of 'group marriage', but by the turn of the century it had become widely accepted that marriage in Australia was on an individual basis (although most writers assumed that it had developed from a previous system of thoroughgoing group marriage).

An alternative line of argument could also be traced back to Fison.

He had demonstrated from first principles that if members of two moieties intermarried for more than one generation, they would be marrying 'cross-cousins'. Fison and Tylor had argued that cross-cousin marriage was a byproduct of group marriage. Rivers disagreed, on the grounds that there could not be 'cross-cousins' unless there were recognised fathers, and that this only happened at a late stage of social evolution.

Radcliffe-Brown turned all these fundamental assumptions around. The Australian systems were based on the family, marriage was between cross cousins, and the terms for kin did not determine the marriage rules but, on the contrary, reflected them. Even more radically, he denied that moieties, sections, and sub-sections were primary features of Australian society. They were not completely dropped from the model, but were displaced, becoming epiphenomena.

Radcliffe-Brown had praised Malinowski's essay on the family among the Australian aborigines,[52] and he took the central importance of the family as given. His aim was to show how the family provided the structural basis of the Australian social systems. Relationships between members of the family were extended to incorporate all the members of the tribe, kinship terms grouping more distant relatives with close kin. One treated a distant kinsman according to the norms governing relations with a close kinsman of the same category.

In all Australian communities, marriage was prescribed with a particular close relative, normally a cross-cousin. A person might marry a mother's brother's daughter, or a father's sister's daughter, or both types of cross-cousin, or a more distant cross-cousin. Each type of marriage generated an appropriate classification of relatives into two sets, roughly speaking 'in-laws' and others. From the point of view of any individual, therefore, the world of kin was divided in two; the marriageable on one side, the unmarriageable on the other. This was the true source of the 'class' system. The 'classes' did not in themselves have any effect on the system of marriage. 'The fact that a tribe has two or four named divisions tells us nothing whatever about the marriage law of the tribe, which can only be ascertained by a careful study of the system of relationship.'[53]

Australian kinship systems were divided into two types, depending on the form of cross-cousin marriage that was favoured. In Type I, marriage was with a mother's brother's daughter, and in Type II marriage was with a mother's mother's brother's daughter's daughter ('or some woman who stands to him in an equivalent relation').[54] Radcliffe-Brown's presentation of this argument was extremely formal, his papers notably brief and devoid of detail, and his two types of Australian system were presented as little more than lists of features. He identified Type I with the Kariera tribe. Either cross-cousin was marriageable, although Radcliffe-Brown analysed the Kariera system as one in which mother's brother's daughter marriage was the vital element. This marriage rule was accompanied by a division of all relatives in each generation into two categories (further divided by sex). Relatives of alternate generation were classified together (so, for example, the same term was applied to father's father, brother (and father's brother's son) and son's son). Type II, which Radcliffe-Brown identified with the Aranda, was a refinement of the Kariera system. In the Aranda system, a man married a second cousin, his mother's mother's brother's daughter's daughter. To accommodate such a marriage rule each Kariera kinship category was split in two by the Aranda, yielding four categories for each sex in each generation. Radcliffe-Brown rephrased this contrast by saying that the Kariera system required two 'descent lines' where the Aranda system required four. Each 'line' grouped together patrilineal descendants and ascendants, generating the required number of categories of kin in each generation.

The Kariera system yields four sets of kin (given the combination of alternate generations) while the Aranda with its four 'lines' yields eight classes in any two successive generations. A man could only marry a woman from one other class – that containing his mother's brother's daughter in a Kariera-type system, or a mother's mother's brother's daughter's daughter in an Aranda-type system. However, class membership was not the decisive criterion, and there were unmarriageable women in the 'marriage class' within which a man married. The classic 'marriage classes' were no more than convenient, but partial, summaries of the consequences of the system of kinship and marriage.[55]

The local groups were patrilineal 'hordes'. They were autonomous, and relationships between different hordes were maintained by intermarriage. Quite commonly a man would marry into his mother's natal horde (where his mother's brother's daughter lives), so reinforcing his links with it. In the Aranda-type system a man must try to establish links with at least four other hordes. This gives rise to a more complex form of social integration and represents a further evolutionary development. Like Fison, Radcliffe-Brown saw the local hordes as the first germ of the state. (He even drew a parallel between the constitution of an Australian tribe and that of the United States of America.)[56]

Radcliffe-Brown and Rivers

From early in 1912, when Radcliffe-Brown returned from his expedition to Australia, until early in 1914, when both he and Rivers left once more for Oceania, Rivers and Radcliffe-Brown exchanged a series of fascinating letters in which they reviewed their ideas concerning Melanesia and Australia.[57] Rivers argued that both Melanesia and Australia were 'complex' societies, the product of the mixture of different peoples, and that they could be understood only if their constituent parts were analysed out.[58] Radcliffe-Brown disagreed and he questioned the methods by which Rivers identified foreign cultural traits. Radcliffe-Brown's letters also record his first reactions to Durkheim's *Elementary Forms of the Religious Life*, which originally appeared (in French) in 1912. He thought that Durkheim was fundamentally mistaken in his Australian ethnography, but accepted the principle of his method and agreed that totemism was to be understood as a reflection of forms of social organisation. On this question again he came into conflict with Rivers. For Rivers, 'totemism' referred in the first place to a system of social organisation – essentially a system of exogamous clans. The form of religious expression was secondary. Radcliffe-Brown, however, had come to question the whole concept of exogamous clans, and he argued that totemism grew out of the 'ritual value' that was ascribed to economically important foods. As a society became increasingly differentiated, so each grouping adopted one of the valued foods as its special emblem.[59]

What Radcliffe-Brown had to say about Australia did not particularly trouble Rivers. He was concentrating upon Melanesia, and (perhaps in the light of Radcliffe-Brown's conclusions) he decided that Melanesia was not simply a more advanced form of the Australian structure. However, his later Cambridge students directly confronted his theories about Melanesia, and they produced a remarkable series of theoretically driven investigations. They would gradually reach the conclusion that the Melanesian social systems were variants of the Australian types that had been characterised by Radcliffe-Brown.

The Ambrym case

The History of Melanesian Society, published in 1914, was the central point of reference for the Cambridge-trained students who went to the Pacific after the First World War. In particular they were drawn to one problem that Rivers had constructed. The question at issue was extremely technical. Some Melanesian kinship terminologies classed together relatives who belonged to different generations. Rivers believed that these classifications signalled the existence of regular inter-generational marriages. There was, however, another possibility. The terminology might be similar to the Australian type, which grouped together grandparents and grandchildren. The significance of the question, apparently so restricted, was very great if the assumptions of the Rivers school are appreciated. If the Melanesian systems turned out to be simply variants of Australian cross-cousin marriage, then Rivers's elaborate model of gerontocracy would have to be abandoned. Indeed, his whole history of Melanesian society would lose much of its credibility.

If there was an Australian connection, it would presumably be most apparent in the earliest and purest Melanesian examples. On Rivers's reading of Melanesian social history, this meant that the crucial test would have to be made in Pentecost, or, ideally, in an even purer version of the classic Melanesian system, which Rivers thought might be found on Ambrym, since its language had what he took to be archaic features. In Ambrym, marriage with the granddaughter might exist without supposedly later complications, such as marriage with the mother's brother's wife, or with the father's father's wife, let alone cross-cousin marriage, which Rivers regarded as a very recent innovation.[60]

It was on his second visit to the New Hebrides, in 1914, that Rivers made the first systematic study of the Ambrym system. He did not actually visit Ambrym (which had been devastated by an earthquake in 1913), but he collected information from an Ambrym man, William, who was living as a teacher at a Presbyterian mission station in Tangoa. Rivers worked at first in pidgin, and later through an interpreter, a missionary, the Rev. Fred Bowie. He then sent drafts of his chapter on Ambrym to Bowie for checking. Since William was dead by this time, Bowie discussed his text with a man called Lau, who came from a village close to William's. Lau disagreed with William's account on a number of crucial points. Bowie communicated his observations to Rivers, and gave Lau's version his support.

These responses put Rivers on the spot. Quite contrary to his expectations, it appeared that the people of Ambrym were patrilineal, and lived in exogamous patrilineal villages. The other main social institution, the *vantinbul*, which regulated property relations, was also dominantly patrilineal, although sisters' sons of *vantinbul* members played some role in its affairs. Rivers discerned traces of an earlier matrilineal state in certain rituals,[61] but he had to concede that for the rest Ambrym seemed to have a lot in common with Fiji and Buin.

Rivers left the analysis of Ambrym incomplete, but to his post-war students it represented the crucial case study. There was a strong strand of opinion that the Melanesian systems would turn out to be very like the Australian. Rivers took John Layard back with him to the New Hebrides in 1914, but war broke out, and after a few weeks Rivers had to return to Britain, where he was drawn into military psychiatric work. Left behind, Layard had a severe breakdown, and was not able to write up his material until the 1940s.[62] After the war, however, a new generation of students returned to the old problems. Rivers died in 1922, and one of his former students, W. E. Armstrong, was appointed to deliver his Cambridge lectures in social anthropology.[63] Armstrong had a grounding in mathematics and he deployed abstract models in his kinship lectures to demonstrate that class systems did formerly exist in Melanesia, but that they were class systems in Radcliffe-Brown's sense. They did not regulate marriage but simply tidied up an underlying rule of cross-cousin marriage. When the post-war Cambridge anthropologists went into the field to test Rivers' theory of Melanesian culture history they were therefore primed to seek any clues that might point to the existence of a class system, though a class system which might be derived from a form of matrilateral cross-cousin marriage.

In 1922, T. T. Barnard went to the New Hebrides. Rivers had planned to accompany him, but suddenly died a few days before they set out. In the New Hebrides, Barnard met up with five Ambrym men. They could not give satisfactory answers to his questions, but the contact led Barnard to ask Professor Elliot Smith, Rivers's literary executor, whether he might examine Rivers' unpublished notes on Ambrym. Permission granted, he stumbled on the correspondence with Bowie. He devoted a chapter of his thesis to the re-analysis of this material, and concluded that the Ambrym social system was based upon six marriage classes. (These were not co-extensive with the *vantinbul* discussed by Rivers, and indeed the number of *vantinbul* in different localities was evidently quite variable.)

Members of classes A and B intermarried, classes C and D inter-married, and classes E and F intermarried. Children did not belong to the same class as their parents. The children of A men were C, of B men E and of D men F, and vice versa. Accordingly a man's son's son was a member of his own class. Since the islanders were patrilineal and patrilocal, men lived in the same local community as their sons and sons' sons. Marriageable women lived in other communities, and were classed together with their grandmothers and grand-daughters, with whom they lived.[64]

Barnard's thesis was accepted in 1924. Soon afterwards, a brilliant young Cambridge student, Bernard Deacon, went out to make a field study on Malekula in the New Hebrides, where he was to spend over a year. Deacon acknowledged the value of Armstrong's lectures, and his notes of these lectures show that Armstrong covered Radcliffe-Brown's Australian studies in some detail.[65] Nevertheless, Deacon could reasonably complain that he had not enjoyed an adequate briefing from his predecessors. He wrote to his fiancée from the field:

> Rivers of course had an elaborate theory, still the best, but his work in Ambrym later (with Layard in Malekula) seems to me to raise very great objections to its acceptance. I have never seen however, any paper of Rivers' attempting to reconcile the two, or at least stating how far he considered his Ambrym work modified his 1908 expedition work. Then in 1922 or so Barnard suggested a scheme which, so far as I understood it from hurried reading of his thesis, was almost the exact reverse of Rivers'. ...
>
> I have very little idea of what others have done here – Layard in '13, Rivers at the same time, then Barnard in 1921 or so, & Humphries ... Rivers' theory I begin to find a hindrance, I was brought up on it at Cambridge, and now it clogs me ... I am very much puzzled to know what Rivers really thought about certain things ... More particularly I want to know what Barnard thinks of Rivers' ideas. There must be more coordination of ethnological work in the field – it's useless letting people just float out & grope in the dark where they want.[66]

Deacon's own detailed fieldwork on Malekula was heartbreakingly difficult and yielded very little relevant information on social structure, but he had known all along that the crucial test of Rivers's hypothesis would have to be made on Ambrym. 'I determined, therefore, when I came out, to seek an opportunity of visiting Ambrym and going more deeply into the marriage regulations in that island.'[67]

He eventually spent six weeks on Ambrym and made what he considered a major discovery – 'something rather valuable', he wrote to his fiancée, with the proper modesty of a gentleman, 'a class system of marriage of the type of those among the Central Australian aborigines – it clarifies the whole series of problems here, besides being, I think, of considerable importance in relation to Melanesian culture in general'.[68] When he communicated his findings to Radcliffe-Brown in Sydney, Brown wrote back to say it was 'one of the most important discoveries made in Melanesia',[69] and urged Deacon to publish his report immediately. By the time the paper appeared, later in 1927, Deacon was dead. He had a sudden and fatal attack of blackwater fever, dying just short of his twenty-fourth birthday. He had been on the point of going to Sydney as a lecturer in Radcliffe-Brown's department.

Deacon's paper opened with queries about the three anomalous types of marriage that Rivers had identified in Melanesia. These were marriages between a man and his father's father's wife, or his mother's brother's widow, or his brother's daughter's daughter. If marriage with the father's father's wife occurred on a regular basis, this suggested the presence of a marriage class system on the Australian model, which in turn implied that marriage would be with a classificatory grandmother rather than with the mother of one of a man's own parents. It might have been possible to explain marriage with a classificatory granddaughter in a similar way, but Deacon questioned the very existence of 'granddaughter marriage'. Rivers had seized upon the observation of one man about an island he had not even visited, to the effect that there men married their 'granddaughters'. Deacon pointed out that in some of the terminologies in the area mother's brother's children were classified as children, and their children as grandchildren. What was at issue was really marriage with the daughter of the cross-cousin, a form of marriage that Deacon had recorded himself elsewhere in the region. This was another pointer in favour of an Australian hypothesis, since Radcliffe-Brown had recently concluded that all the Australian systems were based on matrilateral cross-cousin marriage.

The real stumbling block in the way of the Australian hypothesis was mother's brother's widow marriage, since nowhere in Australia did a man's mother's brother's widow belong to the class of marriageable women. Deacon argued that this form of marriage was an individual genealogical entitlement comparable to the levirate, and that it was part of a complex of matrilineal inheritance. These traits all indicated a fairly advanced type of social institution. If mother's brother's widow marriage was shown to be a late development (as Armstrong had also argued) then the Australian hypothesis could be salvaged. It only remained to find evidence of a Melanesian system where men could marry cross-cousins but not the mother's brother's widow. According to Deacon, Ambrym was just such an area.[70]

During his weeks in Ambrym, Deacon collected relationship systems, genealogies and statements of marriage rules, but his decisive evidence came, he wrote, 'from the remarkably lucid exposition of the class-system by the natives themselves'. This is slightly misleading, however. Judging from the indications in his paper, his informants told him that marriage involved the regular alignment of three parties in an exchange system. One informant placed three stones in a triangular pattern, and explained that 'if a woman of A married a man of C, her daughter in C would marry a man of B, her daughter's daughter in B would marry a man of A again'.[71] A second informant provided a slightly more complex version of the same model; three lines intermarried, but women were passed in either direction around the circle.

Deacon complicated the native models by introducing six 'lines' in place of three parties who engaged in exchange. This was necessary in order to discriminate all the kinship categories that were found in Ambrym. Reading his paper in the context of Armstrong's lectures and Radcliffe-Brown's Australian researches, it seems obvious that the six 'lines' derived from the lecture rooms of Cambridge rather than from the informants of Ambrym. This is probably why his model ended up looking so very much like Barnard's, despite his very different data. It was clear, in any case, that cross-cousin marriage was practised in Ambrym. However, although Deacon found traces of marriage with the mother's brother's widow in Malekula, it was unknown in Ambrym. He concluded that it had been introduced after the collapse of dual organisation and the arrival of a new immigrant culture. Properly understood, Rivers's anomalous marriages could be derived historically from a class system rather like the Australian type. The theory of Melanesian gerontocracy proposed by Rivers did not stand up.

Deacon's paper appeared in the *Journal of the Royal Anthropological Institute* accompanied by a long comment from

Radcliffe-Brown, in which he concluded that the Ambrym system was a variant of the Australian Type II system (which was based on marriage with a second cross-cousin on the mother's side, the mother's mother's brother's daughter's daughter). More broadly, it fitted into 'a single general type of kinship organization (the Dravidian–Australian type) found over a large area of South India and Ceylon … and perhaps over the whole of Australia, and in certain parts of Melanesia', a type, Radcliffe-Brown speculated, 'possibly dating back to the first peopling of Australia and Melanesia'.[72] Within five years of Rivers's death, and thirteen years after the publication of his *History of Melanesian Society*, his outstanding student had turned upside down the conjectural history of Melanesia which had been his monument.

The debate on Ambrym illustrates perfectly the procedure of Rivers and his Cambridge students. They were sceptical and daring, but within the limits of the narrow tradition of research which derived from Morgan; and they were rigorous, but without doubting the value of their basic data, the kinship terms. Boas led his students away from the traditional obsessions of Anglo–American anthropology. In Britain, only Westermarck and Malinowski escaped its domination before the 1930s, and it was largely due to Malinowski that a fresh agenda was set for the British anthropologists.

Malinowski's Melanesia

Bronislaw Malinowski 's monograph on the Australian family had been based on secondary sources. In 1914, he began to do fieldwork on his own account, first in New Guinea and then in the Trobriand Islands. In due course he delivered the most vivid firsthand ethnographic accounts of a Melanesian people that had yet been published.[73] The distance in purely descriptive terms between the Melanesia of Malinowski and the Melanesia of Rivers or Deacon was very great indeed. (Malinowski is supposed to have said that he would be the Conrad of anthropology, while Rivers was the Rider Haggard.) But he was also intent on moving anthropology beyond the theoretical agenda of Rivers and the Cambridge School.

Malinowski started from the principle that individual family relationships existed in every society. Both father and mother were always bound up with their children. Yet he accepted that there were generally also group bonds, as the whole tradition of anthropology had supposed. According to the authorities, from Maine and Morgan to Durkheim and Rivers, group bonds were primeval, individual family relationships a product of civilization. It had now been established that individual family relationships were found in even the most primitive society, and that they co-existed with group bonds. Indeed, Malinowski supposed that the clan was an outgrowth of the family, an extension of relationships with the mother or the father. But loyalties might be divided. How was a man's responsibility for his family reconciled with his duties to the clan?

Malinowski argued that men always put their own families first. Clan ties were a public, political imposition on the individual. Individual family ties were structurally in conflict with these group relationships. Private sentiments tugged against public rules. People were driven by a healthy regard for their own interests rather than by automatic submission to any authority, including the authority of tradition. But they did not generally come clean about their real interests. They paid lip service to the public morality of the clan, while doing their best to promote the private interests of their families. They said one thing and did another. This realist credo was illustrated above all by the contrast (drawn on many occasions by Malinowski) between the corporate social duty a man had to his sister's son – his heir – and the love that he felt for his own son. He passed on what he could to his son, but his estate and any office he might hold went to his sister's son. However, if he could marry his own son to the daughter of his sister, then his son's son would eventually succeed to his public position. That was why men in chiefly families were inclined to marry the daughters of their father's sisters.

Malinowski not only transformed the classic opposition between family and clan. He also milked it ingeniously for further theoretical points. For example, he argued against the Freudians that the Oedipus complex did not occur in the Trobriand Islands. A young man had no hidden resentments against his father. Instead he loathed his mother's brother because of his hold on him.[74] For the rest, however, Malinowski scorned the issues that had so pre-occupied Rivers. The old arguments were based on misleading data. Ethnographers should concern themselves with what people really did, not with vague ideological constructions. Kinship terminologies and 'kinship algebra' lost all interest once it was recognised that words were really used to change social situations, not to describe them. Marriage rules were not some lifeless obligation. If men married cross-cousins, as the Trobriand chiefs did, this was because it profited them to do so.

In 1930 Malinowski published a polemical article in *Man* in which he declared that an impasse had been reached in the study in kinship. Conjectural history and bastard algebra had debased the field, and even among experts there was confusion on fundamental issues. 'As a member of the inner ring', he wrote, 'I may say that whenever I meet Mrs Seligman or Dr Lowie or discuss matters with Radcliffe-Brown or Kroeber, I become at once aware that my partner does not understand anything in the matter, and I end usually with the feeling that this also applies to myself. This refers also to all our writings on kinship, and is fully reciprocal.' The impasse was due 'to the inheritance of false problems from anthropological tradition. We are still enmeshed in the question as to whether kinship in its origins was collective or individual, based on the family or the clan … Another false problem is that of the origins and significance of classificatory systems of nomenclature.'[75]

Malinowski was able to impose his own agenda for research after he returned to England in 1924. The London School of Economics soon displaced Cambridge as the leading department of social anthropology in Britain. It was dominated by Malinowski, a charismatic teacher whose weekly postgraduate seminars attracted and formed the young men and women who were to staff British social anthropology for the next 30 years. There was little competition. Anthropology was in the doldrums in Cambridge. Rivers had died in 1922, and when Haddon retired in 1926 he was replaced by an uninspiring ex-India Civil Service officer, T. C. Hodson. Armstrong was not given a tenured position and in the 1930s he became an economist. At Oxford, Marett was the only well-known figure, and anthropology there remained marginal, old-fashioned and uninspired. At University College London, Elliot Smith and Perry promulgated an extreme form of diffusionism (everything came from Egypt), which attracted ridicule.

For a time, Malinowski's critique of Rivers became part of the received wisdom of the discipline, alongside his new way of doing fieldwork and what he called a functionalist theory of culture. His fundamental principle was that ethnographers should study actions rather than words (unless words themselves were deeds). But at the end of the 1930s Malinowski left for the USA, and he died in New Haven in 1942. At precisely the same moment Radcliffe-Brown returned to Britain to occupy the first chair in social anthropology at Oxford. Radcliffe-Brown had been the outstanding disciple of Rivers, and then his critic, but he was still working, far more than

Malinowski, with the same view of what anthropology was about. His main lieutenants at Oxford were in reaction against Malinowski, but, imagining that they were serving Radcliffe-Brown's revolution, they revived the old anthropology in a new form.

Part IV

Descent and alliance

Primitive civilisations offer privileged cases ... because they are simple cases.

(Émile Durkheim, *The Elementary Forms of the Religious Life* (1912) 1915, p. 6)

Chapter 8

Descent theory
A phoenix from the ashes

At the worst possible time, in 1940, early in World War Two, a symposium, *African Political Systems*, announced the advent of a new model in social anthropology. Its editors, E. E. Evans-Pritchard and Meyer Fortes, were lieutenants of Radcliffe-Brown, who had been appointed to the newly established Oxford chair in social anthropology in 1937. Both Evans-Pritchard and Fortes had spent long periods in Africa in the 1930s among large, dispersed, loosely-organised populations without traditional centralised authorities. Their field experience was therefore quite different from that of the earlier generation of British ethnographers who had worked on islands in the Pacific, or among small bands of Australian Aborigines. Their initial topic was government, which had been generally ignored by the generation of Rivers and Boas and also by Radcliffe-Brown and Malinowski. After the war they published studies of kinship, heralded by another symposium, *African Systems of Kinship and Marriage*, but they paid little attention to kinship terminologies or to systems of exchange marriage, the mainstays of kinship studies from Morgan to Rivers and Radcliffe-Brown.

People began to talk about a new paradigm, 'descent theory' or 'lineage theory', but when Fortes set it out in the *American Anthropologist*, in 1953, American readers would have found some of its central features reassuringly familiar. The 'lineage' or 'descent' groups with which it was concerned were the direct descendants of Morgan's 'gentile system'. Indeed the new term, 'lineage' had been borrowed from a student of Boas, E. W. Gifford, on the advice of Radcliffe-Brown. 'I was present on this occasion', Meyer Fortes recalled. 'Evans-Pritchard was describing his Nuer observations, whereupon Radcliffe-Brown said, as he stood in front of the fireplace: "My dear Evans-Pritchard, it's perfectly simple, that's a segmentary lineage system, and you'll find a very good account of it by a man called Gifford". Thereupon Radcliffe-Brown gave us a lecture on Gifford's analysis of the Tonga system.'[1]

However, Gifford had published only a sketch of the structure and workings of Tonga 'lineages'. Evans-Pritchard and Fortes were more directly influenced by Radcliffe-Brown's Australian models, but descent theorists were particularly impressed by a paper that Radcliffe-Brown had published in 1935, entitled 'Patrilineal and matrilineal succession', in which he discussed the transmission of rights between generations. All kinship systems were based on the family, and kinship relationships were traced through both parents, but usually a person derived some elements of status from his or her father, others from his or her mother. Where rights to the most important kinds of property were transmitted through the father, the result was a patrilineal form of organisation; where they were transmitted through the mother, a matrilineal form. The differences between patrilineal and matrilineal systems (so central to the old evolutionists) were secondary. Functionally they were very similar, as Durkheim, indeed, had remarked.

African political systems

If the study of political systems had been neglected by British anthropologists in the first decades of the twentieth century, Fortes and Evans-Pritchard were reverting to some of the classic preoccupations of Victorian anthropology. Indeed, the classification of political systems that they put forward would have been familiar to the Victorians. They began with a division between states and stateless societies. 'Group A' societies had 'centralized authority, administrative machinery and judicial institutions – in short a government'. 'Group B' societies were those 'which lack centralized authority, administrative machinery, and constituted judicial institutions – in short which lack government'.[2] Like the Victorians again, they assumed that 'stateless societies' would be based on kinship. These 'stateless societies' were divided into two categories. All members of the local group are related to each other in some very small hunter-gatherer communities, and there 'political relations are coterminous with kinship relations and the political structure and kinship organization are completely fused'.[3] Larger societies of pastoralists or farmers were organised by a 'segmentary lineage system'. (The term 'segmentary' came from Durkheim. It described the structure of societies that were constituted by a series of similar and independent units and exhibited 'organic solidarity'.) However, the distinction between blood and soil was not absolute. Lineages provided the basis for settlements. 'Membership of the local community [is] … acquired as a rule through genealogical ties, real or fictional. The lineage principle takes the place of political allegiance, and the interrelations of territorial segments are directly co-ordinated with the interrelations of lineage segments.'[4]

The Nuer

The new model informed the monographs by Evans-Pritchard on the Nuer of the Southern Sudan and by Fortes on the Tallensi of northern Ghana. These provided the first plausible accounts of how quite large societies could operate in the absence of central authorities, and they quickly became accepted as paradigmatic case-studies. As Robertson Smith and Durkheim had foreseen, the secret lay in the structure of segmentary 'clans'.

Evans-Pritchard's monograph, *The Nuer* (1940), was the first of three influential volumes he was to publish on these transhumant pastoralists and agriculturalists who lived along the banks of the lower Nile. *The Nuer* itself dealt with 'social structure', a term that Evans-Pritchard used in the sense given to it by Rivers: 'By structure we mean relations between groups of persons within a system of groups'.[5] The units of this structure among the Nuer were unilineal descent groups. *Kinship and Marriage among the Nuer*, published a decade later, dealt with individual, person-to-person relationships of 'kinship'.

The largest territorial and political community among the Nuer was the tribe. This was not to be confused with an organised chieftaincy – the only office-holders were ritual 'leopard skin chiefs'. Rather, the tribe was the unit within which homicide should be compensated for by payments of blood-wealth rather than being dealt with by acts of vengeance. The tribal territory was divided into segments. At each descending level of segmentation the local groups were smaller and more cohesive. These territorial segments had no absolute political identity. They provided the context for communal action only in specific situations, and then only in opposition to like units. If a man in one village killed a man in another, all the warriors in the two villages would mobilise and confront each other, fighting until compensation was agreed. If a man in either of these villages killed a man in another district, then all the villages in the victim's district would mobilise fighters to confront men from all the villages in the district from which his assailant came. At this level the fighting would be fiercer, mediation more problematic. Evans-Pritchard identified these processes of 'fission and fusion' as the central dynamic of the segmentary political system. They were driven by the blood feud, whose 'function', he wrote, was 'to maintain the structural equilibrium between opposed tribal segments which are, nevertheless, politically fused in relation to larger units'.[6]

But it was only when viewed from the outside that Nuer politics appeared to operate in territorial terms. The secret of Nuer society lay elsewhere. The system of patrilineal descent groups provided the framework for local community organisation. The tribe, the largest territorial association, was built around a dominant clan whose members claimed to be descended in the male line from the clan founder. The clan was divided in turn into smaller descent groups, the lineages, which were formed by the patrilineal descendants of more recent ancestors. Within the clan there were several levels of 'nesting' lineage segments, which Fortes and Evans-Pritchard called maximal, major and minor lineages. These segments of the clan, the various orders of lineages, were each associated with lower levels of local organisation. They were real groups, at least potentially, since they could be called into action through the mechanism of the feud. This was a classical theme, which could be traced back to Robertson Smith, half a century earlier. In fact, Evans-Pritchard's model of the Nuer could be summarised in the very words that Robertson Smith had used of the ancient Arabs: 'The key to all divisions and aggregations of Arab groups lies in the action and reaction of two principles: that the only effective bond is a bond of blood, and that the purpose of society is to unite men for offence and defence. These two principles meet in the law of the blood-feud.'[7]

The clan and lineage groupings co-existed with territorial bonds (which Evans-Pritchard called 'community ties' or 'symbiotic ties'). Which came first – or which had priority? In *The Nuer*, Evans-Pritchard explained that blood and soil were two sides of the same coin, or as he put it, elegantly but not altogether unambiguously: 'The assimilation of community ties to lineage structure, the expression of territorial affiliation in a lineage idiom, and the expression of lineage affiliation in terms of territorial attachments, is what makes the lineage system so significant for a study of political organization.'[8]

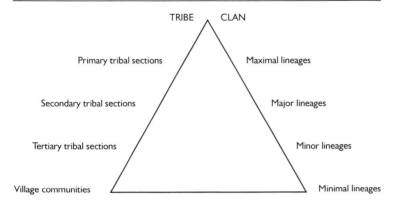

Figure 8.1   Blood and soil: Evans-Pritchard's model of Nuer social structure (from Evans-Pritchard (1940), *The Nuer*, p. 248).

Fortunately he also provided a diagram, which made the relationship between territory and descent seem much clearer (see Figure 8.1).

One of the first critics of Evans-Pritchard's monograph, a loyal pupil of Malinowski, the Africanist Audrey Richards, suggested, however, that the apparent clarity of the model had been bought at the expense of ethnographic verisimilitude. Her own field experience in Africa had taught her that:

> nothing is more remarkable than the lack of permanence of particular lineages or 'segments'; the infinite variety there is in their composition, their liability to change owing to historic factors, the strength of individual personalities and similar determinants. Such societies, in my experience, are not divided into distinct and logical systems of segments, but rather owe their being to the existence of a number of different principles of grouping.[9]

One of Evans-Pritchard's loyal young Oxford men, Max Gluckman, responded that Evans-Pritchard's detailed case materials would soon provide the empirical underpinnings for the model.[10] However, this line of defence could not be sustained for long, particularly after the publication of Evans-Pritchard's *Kinship and Marriage among the Nuer*, which appeared in 1951. That book contained detailed information on the composition of local communities which strongly suggested that the relationship between the Nuer ethnography and the Nuer model, or between territory and descent, was less clear-cut than Evans-Pritchard had suggested in *The Nuer*.

In essays on the Nuer that Evans-Pritchard published in *Sudan Notes and Records* in the 1930s, he had in fact remarked that the system of territorial political groups did not mesh neatly with the system of clans and lineages. Far from brushing off this lack of fit, he had specifically drawn attention to it. It showed, so he suggested, that the Nuer were in a state of transition from a pure lineage system to a territorially-based polity. Generations of war and expansion 'broke up clans and lineages to an extent which must have greatly impaired the unifying influence of kinship'. The larger descent groups split into 'small lineages' which were 'in frequent feud with their relatives and neighbours. This means that community of living tended to supplant community of blood as the essential principle of social cohesion though in a society based upon ties of kinship change took place by assimilating symbiotic [i.e. territorial] ties to kinship ties.'[11] Of course, that was precisely what an adherent of the classical model (Maine, say, or Morgan) would have expected. Originally the Nuer had been organised into clans. Now they were making progress, developing a political system based upon territorial groups. This seems to have been Evans-Pritchard's own view, since he suggested that the remnants of the clan system now constituted 'the main obstacle to political development'.[12]

However, five years on, *The Nuer* made no mention of a possible movement from a clan system to a territorial system. In this book Evans-Pritchard adopted a functionalist model: the two modes of organisation were treated as contemporary. Just as family and clan co-existed in Malinowski's ethnography, so here clan and territory, blood and soil, operated in tandem. Why then did the lineage segments not in fact match up neatly with the territorial segments? Evans-Pritchard did not attempt to argue along the lines proposed by Gluckman, that the model captured the empirical form of actual groups out there, camped across the flood-plains of the White Nile. However, the empirical discrepancies could no longer be attributed to the inevitably untidy processes of historical transition. Evans-Pritchard's solution was to argue that the lineage system existed on a different level of reality from the territorial system. The lineage system was an ideological construct, a way of thinking and talking about the actual camps and villages and their relationships with each other. It was 'a system of values linking tribal segments and providing the idiom in which their relations can be expressed and directed'.[13]

The idiom was of decisive importance since values were primary; but the ideology did not determine what people did in practice.

Given this new formulation, the contrasts between the model and what Evans-Pritchard and Fortes sometimes termed 'the actualities' were no longer a source of embarrassment. Evans-Pritchard, indeed, came to glory in the lack of fit between the rules and values (which constituted the reality for Radcliffe-Brown), and the practice (on which Malinowski insisted). 'The underlying agnatic [or patrilineal] principle is … in glaring contrast to social actualities. But the actualities are always changing and passing while the principle endures'.[14] He even seemed to suggest that the more the Nuer practice diverged from the model, the more fundamental must be the values that the model encapsulated.

> I suggest that it is the clear, consistent, and deeply rooted lineage structure of the Nuer which permits persons and families to move about and attach themselves so freely, for shorter or longer periods, to whatever community they choose by whatever cognatic or affinal tie they find it convenient to emphasize; and that it is on account of the firm values of the structure that this flux does not cause confusion or bring about social disintegration. It would seem it may be partly because the agnatic principle is unchallenged in Nuer society that the tracing of descent through women is so prominent and matrilocality so prevalent. However much the actual configurations of kinship clusters may vary and change, the lineage structure is invariable and stable.[15]

As one commentator pointed out, the implication was that 'if the principles were challenged, descent through women would be less prominent and matrilocality less prevalent'.[16] That seems unlikely, yet Evans-Pritchard suggested, in a similar vein, that although Nuer marriage prohibitions covered a number of relatives on the mother's side of the family, this just went to show how powerful their patrilineal bias must be. 'Nuer make any kind of cognatic relationship to several degrees a bar to marriage, and, at least so it seems to me, it is a bar to marriage because of the fundamental agnatic principle running through Nuer society.'[17] In short, if the values were sufficiently powerful then they would permit great divergences of practice, and even allow contradictions in the rules. The appeal was to faith, not to acts.

Some critics, however, pointed out that the model does not capture basic Nuer values. Indeed, certain Nuer values appear to contradict it. This is a vital issue in the assessment of the model, and once again it is instructive to reconsider Evans-Pritchard's early essays in *Sudan Notes and Records*. Here he described the difficult fieldwork conditions he faced, and remarked on the rapid changes that had overtaken the Nuer. In consequence, he confessed:

> I was more successful, for these reasons, in grasping their kinship system and the daily contacts of cattle camp life than the organization of the less tangible clan and tribal groups ... in the case of the second I had to rely largely upon what little information could be dragged out of the occasional informants by question and answer methods of enquiry. I am therefore compelled to generalise upon what may sometimes be insufficient data and to regard some of my conclusions as working hypotheses though I feel that I have drawn the outlines correctly.[18]

Whatever the reasons, Evans-Pritchard's difficulties with the 'less tangible clan and tribal groups' were apparently shared by the Nuer themselves. 'What exactly is meant by lineage and clan?' he asked rhetorically. 'One thing is fairly certain, namely, that the Nuer do not think in group abstractions called clans. In fact, as far as I am aware, he has no word meaning clan and you cannot ask a man an equivalent of "What is your clan?"'[19]

These scrupulously-recorded uncertainties suggest that the Nuer would have had difficulty in constructing a way of life that was based upon the values of clan and lineage. But some years later, in *The Nuer*, although no further fieldwork had supervened, Evans-Pritchard gave a very different impression, writing that:

> it is only when one already knows the clans and their lineages and their various ritual symbols, as the Nuer does, that one can easily place a man's clan through his lineage or by his spear-name and honorific salutation, for Nuer speak fluently in terms of lineage. A lineage is *thok mac*, the hearth, or *thok dwiel*, the entrance to the hut, or one may talk of *kar*, a branch.[20]

Apparently the Nuer had achieved a fresh precision by abandoning a 'clan' model for a 'lineage' model, just as Radcliffe-Brown, or perhaps Gifford, had advocated. But what was their idea of 'lineages' of which they 'speak fluently'?

A Nuer rarely talks about his lineage as distinct from his community, and in contrast to other lineages which form part of it, outside a ceremonial context. I have watched a Nuer who knew precisely what I wanted, trying on my behalf to discover from a stranger the name of his lineage. He often found great initial difficulty in making the man understand the information required of him, for Nuer think generally in terms of local divisions and of the relationships between them, and an attempt to discover lineage affiliations apart from their community relations, and outside a ceremonial context, generally led to misunderstanding in the opening stages of an inquiry.[21]

When Evans-Pritchard elicited a Nuer diagram of 'clan' or 'lineage' relations, it was not at all like the tree-and-branch imagery that he favoured. Instead, his informant drew a focus, with lines radiating out from it. As Lladislaw Holy pointed out, this was a map of a particular set of territorial relations.[22] Evans Pritchard in fact conceded that this particular man visualised the social system 'primarily as actual relations between groups of kinsmen within local communities rather than as a tree of descent'.[23]

Apparently the Nuer lacked even the basic vocabulary for a folk model that might correspond, however loosely, with Evans-Pritchard's model of the segmentary lineage system. In any case, it is hardly credible that their commitment to agnatic values *explains* how it is that all sorts of relatives, tracing ties through fathers or mothers or wives, could become members of a local community. Evidently the Nuer model provided a reliable guide neither to Nuer behaviour nor to Nuer values. The model must rather be read as an attempt to translate the classic evolutionist stages of political development into aspects of a single structure. In Evans-Pritchard's account, blood and soil become two dimensions of a single system. Time (and so descent) and space (and so residence) are the points of reference of alternative idioms in which actors can talk about their political relationships. But even the Nuer are not like *The Nuer.*

The Tallensi

Meyer Fortes's analysis of the segmentary structure of Tallensi society provides an instructive counterpoint to Evans-Pritchard's Nuer model. Less elegant, less hermetic, Fortes's account is even more revealing of the problems that arose when descent theory was applied to order ethnographic observations. Fortes shared

Evans-Pritchard's view that the social structure depended on a system of values: 'the centre of gravity of the equilibrium characteristic of a stable and homogeneous primitive society lies in its scheme of cultural values'.[24] But Fortes was not prepared to retreat entirely to a world of values. Rather than indulging in the Father Brown paradoxes which so delighted Evans-Pritchard, he tried to stretch the model, to make it more accommodating. As Audrey Richards had suggested, the price was a sacrifice of analytic precision and, at worst, fuzziness.

The Tallensi, a scattered population of farmers in northern Ghana, were like the Nuer to the extent that they lacked kings and chiefs. (Actually there were chiefs of a sort, but Fortes paid little attention to their role.) As among the Nuer, family relationships were very important, and patrilineal ties ordered political affiliations. Following Evans-Pritchard, Fortes treated unilineal descent groups separately from the network of individual kinship relations. Like Evans-Pritchard again, he devoted a separate monograph to each type of organisation.[25]

The Tallensi population was divided between the autochthonous Talis and the immigrant Namoos, who assumed a position of political superiority. The most detailed account of a clan structure that Fortes provided actually dealt with the dominant section of the Namoos. However, he argued that the Namoo–Tali stratification was secondary. Tallensi society was an egalitarian and uncentralised congeries of local communities. These local communities were organised on the basis of unilineal descent groups, and were linked to other unilineal descent groups in 'fields of clanship'.

The associations of lineages did not have a coherent structure like the Nuer pattern of 'nesting' segments. Nor were they mechanically ordered by genealogical connection, however fictitious. Clan ties were constituted in all sorts of ways. They might be based upon spatial proximity with no genealogical framework. Indeed, it was often difficult to distinguish clan ties from neighbourhood relationships. Some clans had a rule of exogamy, others were endogamous. Fortes also recorded that 'lineages belonging to the same clan, or to a series of linked clans ... do not have completely congruent fields of clanship'. 'Clanship ties cut across clans ... a clan is the region where the fields of clanship of two or more lineages have the maximum overlap'.[26] Some clans, however, were ordered upon principles so uncertain that Fortes was obliged to distinguish a further category of 'extra-clan ties of clanship'.

The lineages within (or overlapping) the clan were elaborately distinguished into levels. 'We thus have a hierarchy of lineage segments: the effective minimal lineage or segment, the nuclear lineage or segment, the inner lineage or segment, the medial lineage or segment, the section or major segment, the maximal lineage'.[27] However, it was not easy to distinguish these segments in operation. 'As usual in Tali social organization no rigorous criterion can be found.'[28] Having reached this point, Fortes must have been tempted to follow Evans-Pritchard and beat a retreat to the level of values. But he conceded that the Tallensi did not articulate these supposedly fundamental principles. 'These distinctions are not made by the natives ... it should be noted that the Tallensi have no term for the lineage.'[29]

Fortes paid particular attention to the function of interpersonal relationships of kinship. Like the Nuer the Tallensi were supposedly strongly patrilineal, yet in both cases ties traced through the mother were very significant. For Evans-Pritchard they were simply an area of play that could be exploited with safety precisely because the central patrilineal structure was so secure. Fortes argued, like Malinowski, that domestic relations of kinship served very specific functions; they were a special sphere of moral sentiments and emotional attachments. Malinowski had described how the father among the matrilineal Trobriander Islanders provided sympathy and support, while the public political relationships of the matrilineage were typically full of tension. Among the patrilineal Tallensi, relationships on the mother's side of the family had a similar supportive function, giving each man a personal set of allies that differentiated him from other members of his lineage. Fortes called these ties through the mother in a patrilineal system, or through the father in a matrilineal system, relationships of 'complementary filiation'. Personal relationships of kinship also stretched beyond the clan. Networks of cross-cutting ties linked individuals across political boundaries and so helped to sustain the political structure itself.

The most subtle presentation of Fortes's thesis is to be found in an essay on another West African society, the Ashanti. The Ashanti were in many respects a 'matrilineal society', but R. S. Rattray, the early ethnographer (a correspondent of Frazer), had reported that they were moving towards a patrilineal condition, and that they had both matrilineages and patrilineages. Moreover, the family group was emerging in Ashanti, signalling the passage to a more advanced condition. Fortes applied the Malinowskian principle that 'clan' and 'family' co-existed, but operated in tension with each other, and he suggested that this tension worked itself out in different ways during the life cycle. When a young couple first married, they were still attached to their respective matrilineages. As their children began to grow up, so the ties of the children to the father became more significant, and the individual family tended to form a single residential unit. Then the adolescent children left home to live with their mother's brother, and the mother followed them to her brother's home. The family had its own specific functions, but these were particularly important only while the children were growing up.[30] Fortes generalised the argument in his essay 'The structure of unilineal descent groups'.

> It appears that there is a tendency for interests, rights and loyalties to be divided on broadly complementary lines, into those that have the sanction of law or other public institutions for the enforcement of good conduct, and those that rely on religion, morality, conscience and sentiment for due observance. Where corporate descent groups exist the former seem to be generally tied to the descent groups, the latter to the complementary line of filiation.[31]

Elaboration and reaction

In the 1950s British social anthropology entered a period of rapid institutional growth, and, from the outside, it appeared to be a coherent school. Every recruit had to do a spell of fieldwork on the Malinowskian model (and for a while it seemed that this fieldwork had to be in Africa); and the observations they brought home had to be fitted into the mould of the new descent theory. Segmentary lineage systems now turned up virtually everywhere. A new symposium, *Tribes Without Rulers*, brought together the work of a coming generation of 'lineage theorists', all working in Africa, most of them trained by Evans-Pritchard and Fortes at Oxford.[32] The systems that they described seemed astonishingly uniform; indeed, virtually indistinguishable from each other. Further, it now appeared that these lineage structures explained all sorts of apparently unrelated phenomena. Max Gluckman appealed to the lineage structure to account for differential divorce rates.[33] Max Marwick used it to explain the incidence of witchcraft accusations.[34] Ancestor worship, burial rituals, the position of women, all came down to the structure of unilineal descent groups. There were some intermediary cases, not true states yet not unambiguously 'stateless', and Aidan Southall, working in East Africa, invented a new type of political system, the 'segmentary state', to bridge the gap between lineage-based societies and the state.[35]

But by the 1960s loyal followers of Malinowski were beginning to formulate a coherent critique of lineage theory. They had a nagging feeling, which Audrey Richards had expressed immediately on reading *The Nuer*, that the descent models were too neat, too abstract, to capture the nitty-gritty of social life. Anthropologists should not ignore the 'actualities'. The most comprehensive attack on descent theory along these lines was formulated by Edmund Leach, a former student of Malinowski and a close associate of Raymond Firth. In a monograph on a Sri Lankan village, *Pul Eliya*, published in 1961, he virtually accused the descent theorists of writing science fiction.

> In Evans-Pritchard's studies of the Nuer and also in Fortes's studies of the Tallensi unilineal descent turns out to be largely an ideal concept to which the empirical facts are only adapted by means of fictions. Both societies are treated as extreme examples of patrilineal organization. The evident importance attached to matrilateral and affinal kinship connections is not so much explained as explained away.[36]

Not only did the descent theorists ignore inconvenient facts. They looked for explanations in quite the wrong places. People's behaviour was not governed by principles of kinship and descent. Their strategies could not be captured by the rigid models of descent theory. Social systems had to allow room for manoeuvre and manipulation.[37] Communities were not elaborate ideological constructions. They were loose and quarrelsome associations of competitive individuals who were making a living as best they could in a particular landscape. A Sri Lankan village was 'simply a collection of individuals who derive their livelihood from a piece of territory laid out in a particular way'.[38]

The classic anthropological opposition was between the principles of blood and of soil. Lineage theory assumed that blood ties were decisive in 'stateless societies'. On Leach's argument, everything in Pul Eliya was rooted in the soil. 'Pul Eliya is a society in which locality and not descent forms the basis of corporate grouping; it is a very simple and perhaps almost obvious finding, yet it seems to me to have very important implications for anthropological theory and method'.[39] Admittedly, the villagers did talk a lot about kinship, but kinship was just an idiom, a way of talking about property relationships. If genealogical relationships did not conform with the real dispositions of property and power, they were massaged into appropriate patterns.

The impact of Leach's critique was weakened because he manifestly underplayed the independent significance of at least certain kinship relationships in Pul Eliya. There was another obvious difficulty. His case-study dealt with a village in Sri Lanka. Who would have expected these Asian peasants to operate African-style segmentary lineages? Indeed, in making Pul Eliya a test of descent theory, Leach was paying a massive tribute to its influence. By the same token, however, the critique stung, since the pretensions of lineage theory had become very great indeed. And in essence Leach's critique was independent of the case-study. His claim was that descent theorists paid too much attention to ideological constructs and not enough to what was really going on. And were these the constructs of the actors – or of the anthropologists? 'It might even be the case that "the structure of unilineal descent groups" is a *total* fiction; illuminating no doubt, like other theological ideas, but still a fiction.'[40]

Raymond Firth suggested that descent groups did not have to be either matrilineal or patrilineal. In Oceania, apparently, descent groups could be set up in a perfectly satisfactory way on the basis of 'cognatic descent'.[41] That was a quibble, however. A more persuasive critique of descent theory was developed by anthropologists studying societies in Highland New Guinea that were, on the face of it, perfect candidates for the orthodox treatment. There were no powerful central authorities in the Highlands. Patrilineal descent was emphasised. And indeed one of the first and most influential monographs, by Mervyn Meggitt, applied the Africanist model with little modification to a Highland tribe, the Mae-Enga.[42] Yet although Meggitt's study was at least as sophisticated as the best of the Africanist descent studies, it provoked an immediate reaction among other fieldworkers.

The reaction was anticipated by a British Africanist descent theorist, John Barnes, who had recently been appointed to a chair at the Australian National University, which was the centre of the new wave of New Guinea studies. On board ship, travelling out to

Australia, without the resources – and distractions – of a library, he reflected on the contrasts between Africa and New Guinea and wrote a brief but extremely influential paper.

> The people of the New Guinea Highlands first became accessible for study at a time when anthropological discussion was dominated by the analyses of political and kinship systems that had recently been made in Africa. Ethnographers working in New Guinea were able to present interim accounts of the poly-segmentary stateless systems of the Highlands with less effort and greater speed by making use of the advances in under-standing already achieved by their colleagues who had studied similar social systems in Africa. Yet it has become clear that Highland societies fit awkwardly into African moulds.[43]

To begin with, local groups often included large numbers of people related to the core members by kinship ties traced through women, or by marriage bonds. Some of these might be men of influence, since status distinctions within the local community did not depend on descent. Barnes contrasted the variety of affiliations found in a typical Highland New Guinea village with the apparently solidary group structures of the Tallensi, and concluded that there was no 'predictability or regularity in the segmentary pattern' of Highland societies.[44]

His colleague, Paula Brown, complained that:

> we may be hard put to decide, for example, whether descent groups are mainly agnatic with numerous accretions, or cognatic with a patrilineal basis. We find that people are more mobile than any rules of descent and residence should warrant, that genealogies are too short to be helpful, that we don't know what 'corporate' means when applied to some groups, that local and descent groups are fragmented and change their alignments.[45]

Other commentators suggested that the problem was one of levels of abstraction. As Laura Langness put it, 'the comparisons made are often between jural rules (ideologies) of the lineal-segmentary societies of Africa, and presumed (but not actual) statistical norms of New Guinea'.[46] This suggested that the New Guinea studies might be comparable to the African, if all concerned restricted themselves to the level of values. But Highland values seemed to be very different from the values that had been described by Evans-Pritchard and Fortes and their students in Africa. Locality was greatly emphasised. There was even a widespread belief that living in the same place and eating the same food created kinship. These difficulties drove some anthropologists to deny that there was any necessary connection between ideology and practice in descent systems. 'In major territorial descent groups, there is no particular relation between the descent ideology and group composition', Marshall Sahlins argued. 'A descent doctrine does not express group composition but imposes itself upon the composition.'[47]

In any case, far from seeking safety in the world of values, the Australian-based ethnographers of New Guinea were inclined to concentrate upon actions. And if one looked at the situation on the ground, then perhaps New Guinea was not so peculiar after all. Even the Tallensi and the Nuer did not rigidly follow the precepts of the descent model when it came to the organization of local groups. Phyllis Kaberry pointed out that 'an analysis of some Nuer communities reveals that they have a number of the characteristics attributed by Barnes to many Highland societies'.[48]

Damaged by these criticisms, descent theory was confronted in the 1960s with an alternative and even more ambitious model. This was the 'alliance theory' of Claude Lévi-Strauss, which put marriage exchange systems and kinship terminologies on the agenda once again. Edmund Leach became an exponent of alliance theory, and in a widely-read polemical exchange in *Man* he claimed that Fortes, 'while recognizing that ties of affinity have comparable importance to ties of descent, disguises the former under his expression "complementary filiation"'.[49]

By the 1970s descent theory was in retreat. It had failed to establish significant bases outside the British school, and even within Britain it was beset by opponents, old and new: the diehard Malinowskians; the ethnographers of Pacific societies; and the new 'alliance theorists', who followed Lévi-Strauss. There was a moment when it seemed that a revival was on the cards. In Paris, a new wave of neo-Marxist theorists tried to resuscitate the ideas of Engels with the help of the British models. The segmentary lineage system was transformed into the 'lineage mode of production', in which old men exploited young men and women.[50] This translation of Fortes and Evans-Pritchard's model into the language of class analysis did not catch on, but it did briefly create a market for reprints of Morgan.

Chapter 9

Towards the intellect
Alliance theory and totemism

It is a nice irony that the structuralism of Claude Lévi-Strauss, the most avant-garde theoretical fashion of the 1960s, should have taken for its subject matter Victorian speculations about primitive society.

Born in 1908, Lévi-Strauss graduated in philosophy from the Sorbonne in 1931, and he went out to Brazil in 1935 intending to put philosophy to an empirical test.[1] ('I had gone to the ends of the earth to look for what Rousseau calls "the almost imperceptible stages of man's beginnings"', he wrote in *Tristes Tropiques*.)[2] Two issues engaged him in particular. The first was the intuition of Rousseau, his favourite philosopher, that the principles of social justice go back to the very origins of society. Among the Nambikwara Indians of the Mato Grosso, Lévi-Strauss identified the political principles idealised by Rousseau: equality, and leadership by assent. One Nambikwara chief with whom he became friendly told him that he had accepted his election only with the utmost reluctance, and Lévi-Strauss recalled with 'astonishment and admiration' that this was precisely what a Brazilian Indian had told Montaigne four centuries earlier.[3] The Nambikwara assumption of equality was rooted in the practice of reciprocity, and people imagined that they stood in a similarly egalitarian and reciprocal relationship with the natural world, and with the dead.

Exchange and reciprocity were, of course, famous themes in French sociology. A generation earlier, Durkheim's nephew Marcel Mauss had identified exchange as the fundamental mechanism of the social life of 'archaic societies'.[4] Lévi-Strauss argued that this was not true just of 'archaic societies' (a category which, in any case, he rejected). Reciprocity was the foundation of all social relationships. It could be seen spontaneously at work even in Paris, or at least in the south of France, where people would exchange identical glasses of wine with strangers who wandered into their cafés. In 1949 he published a long and formidably technical book, *The Elementary Structures of Kinship*, in which he argued that kinship systems had evolved as a mechanism for the exchange of women in marriage. The incest taboo, the first rule, obliged people to enter into this most fundamental of exchanges, and so to establish societies.

The second philosophical question that Lévi-Strauss took into the field in Brazil had been raised by Immanuel Kant. If people have an intuitive knowledge of categories of time and space, as Kant believed, then these must be universal. But are our categories shared by the Nambikwara? It was not even agreed that they were rational beings. Brazilian Indians believed that shamans could transform themselves into jaguars, and speak to animals. Yet beneath the irrational surface a sort of reason might be discerned. In Lévi-Strauss's early essays, the rationality of the Nambikwara was demonstrated in a way that had become conventional in anthropology. He reported that his informants were sceptical, sensible, down-to-earth, and competent practical biologists. They accepted magical ideas only when there seemed to be evidence for them, or if no obvious alternative explanation was available. It was later, during his wartime exile, that he discovered a deeper source of human reason.

Lévi-Strauss escaped from occupied France at the end of 1940 and he lived in New York between 1941 and 1945. Here he met a fellow exile, the Russian linguist Roman Jakobson, who had also come to the city as a refugee in 1941. Lévi-Strauss remarked approvingly that Jakobson was a polymath and 'interested in everything – painting, avant-garde poetry, anthropology, computers, biology ...'[5] (The first number of the journal founded by Lévi-Strauss, *L'Homme*, would carry a structuralist analysis of Baudelaire's *Les Chats* by Lévi-Strauss and Jakobson.) Jakobson was also a leading figure in theoretical linguistics. His special subject was phonology, the most technical and sophisticated branch of linguistics at the time. And his claim was that he had split the atom of linguistics, the phoneme. The phoneme had been viewed as the smallest significant component of language, but according to Jakobson it was itself a bundle of what he called distinctive features. These were made up in turn of pairs of contrasting elements (voiced vs. voiceless consonants, for example). These binary oppositions were universally available, although in any particular language only some were put to use. This tendency to form binary oppositions reflected a fundamental disposition of the brain.

Lévi-Strauss concluded that linguistics had achieved the stature of a true science, universal and objective, penetrating beneath the surface of appearances to the hidden inner mechanics of nature. Anthropology should follow its lead. The sorts of things that anthropologists studied – systems of classification, myths, kinship systems and rules of marriage – were collective, symbolic productions very much like languages. His ambition was to show that they are governed by a deep structure of contrasting features, although this structure remained unconscious, like the phonological rules of language that govern speech. Ultimately, these structures were determined by features of the human brain itself. It is there that Kant's mental universals are to be found, not in the mind of God.

While in New York, Lévi-Strauss also made contact with Franz Boas and his circle, Robert Lowie in particular, and he devoted himself to ethnological research, spending many hours in the famous New York Public Library. ('Every morning I went to the New York Public Library. What I know of anthropology I learned during those years.')[6] He wrote a brief monograph on the Nambikwara in 1941, over which the spirit of Rousseau hovers, and he began work on a hugely ambitious comparative project, on systems of marriage.

Lévi-Strauss recalled that his interest in kinship began when he read Marcel Granet's monograph on Chinese kinship, published in 1939, shortly before his departure from France,[7] but it would be interesting to discover what he read as he pursued his researches in the Public Library, and to know to what extent his reading was guided by others. The Boasians certainly influenced him, and Lowie read the manuscript of his *Elementary Structures*, returning it with the ambiguous observation that it was 'in the grand style',[8] but Lévi-Strauss was very impressed by Lewis Henry Morgan, which suggests that he was by no means an orthodox Boasian even at this point. My guess is that he read a great deal, stimulated by long talks on great themes with Roman Jakobson, but idiosyncratically, and with very little outside advice, and that his starting-point, or at least his main point of reference, was Volume 2 of Frazer's *Folklore in the Old Testament*, a book (first published in 1918) which is discussed again and again in the pages of the *Elementary Structures of Kinship*.

Frazer's theory of cross-cousin marriage

Chapter 4 in Volume 2 of Frazer's *Folklore in the Old Testament* is entitled 'Jacob's Marriage'. In characteristic Frazerian style, a classical episode is described – here Jacob's marriages to his cousins, the two daughters of his mother's brother, Laban – and the question is posed whether Jacob was following established customs, and whether these were current beyond Ancient Israel, perhaps even typical of primitive societies.

> The customs in question may conveniently be distinguished as three in number, namely; first, marriage with a cousin, and in particular the marriage of a man with his mother's brother's daughter, or, to put it conversely, the marriage of a woman with her father's sister's son; second, the marriage of a man with two sisters in their lifetime, the elder sister being married before the younger; and third, the practice of a son-in-law serving his father-in-law for a wife.[9]

Frazer dealt mainly with cross-cousin marriage and he treated the other customs more cursorily. He followed his usual method, which was to pile up parallel instances from 'primitive societies', and then to identify a common function that might motivate them all. The pursuit was characteristically leisurely and meandering, and the final product, the chapter on Jacob's marriage, would make a substantial modern book: it runs to almost 300 printed pages.

In his reflections on Australian marriage classes, Fison had demonstrated that the relatives whom Tylor termed 'cross-cousins', the children of a man's father's sister and of his mother's brother, were never members of his own moiety. This was the case whether the moieties were matrilineal or patrilineal, or if a system of patrilineal moieties was superimposed upon a system of matrilineal moieties. Because they were not members of the moiety, cross-cousins were marriageable. In consequence, the terminology distinguished cross-cousins from siblings and from the children of two brothers or two sisters, who *were* members of one and the same moiety and who therefore could not be married. The moiety system fostered marriage between cross-cousins, but Tylor believed that the practice of marrying cross-cousins persisted after the moiety framework itself had been abandoned.

In his usual fashion, Frazer began by trying to define the 'custom' involved. In many societies there was a curious opposition between 'cross-cousins' and the children of two brothers or of two sisters, whom he proposed to call 'ortho-cousins'. Commonly, cross-cousins were marriageable, ortho-cousins were not. In some societies, however, one but not the other type of cross-cousin was marriageable; usually, where such a distinction was made, a man could marry a mother's brother's daughter but not a father's sister's daughter. Preferential marriage with the mother's brother's daughter was widely distributed. It had been well documented in south India, and elsewhere in Asia it was found among the Chin and Kachin of Burma and among the Gilyaks of Siberia. The custom could also be found in the Americas, Africa, Indonesia, New Guinea and Australia.

The next question was, 'Why is the marriage of cross-cousins favoured?'[10] Frazer naturally looked for an answer first of all in Australia. Here he discovered an economic rationale for the exchange of women in marriage. In Australia a man acquired a wife in exchange for a sister or a daughter, for he had nothing else to offer. The exchange of sisters or daughters was therefore a form of barter in a society 'where women had a high economic value as labourers, but where private property was as yet at so rudimentary a stage that a man had practically no equivalent to give for a wife except another woman'.[11] These exchange partnerships tended to stabilise. If two men were satisfied with the exchange of their sisters, then their sons might exchange sisters in turn. 'The same economic motive might lead the offspring of such unions, who would be cross-cousins, to marry each other, and thus in the easiest and most natural manner the custom of cross-cousin marriage would arise and be perpetuated'.[12] The men in the second generation would be marrying wives who were double cross-cousins – mother's brother's daughters who were at the same time father's sister's daughters.

Although the economic motive for cross-cousin marriage could only be demonstrated in a few specific cases, Frazer argued that it must explain the custom of cross-cousin marriage wherever it was to be found, 'for under the surface alike of savagery and of civilization the economic forces are as constant and uniform in their operation as the forces of nature, of which, indeed, they are merely a peculiarly complex manifestation'.[13] However, an alternative economic explanation of some forms of cross-cousin marriage had been proposed by F. E. Richards, an ethnographer working in India, who speculated that cross-cousin marriage was a way of evading inconvenient rules of inheritance.[14] For example, a man who lived in one of India's matrilineal societies had to accept that his possessions would pass to a nephew. On the other hand, he would know very well that Hindu law insisted on the division of an estate between all a man's children. He might therefore marry his daughter to a sister's son in order to

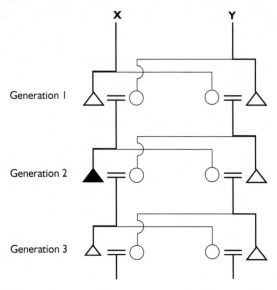

Figure 9.1 Sister exchange over two generations leads to marriage with a double cross-cousin. A man marries a woman who is at once his mother's brother's daughter and his father's sister's daughter. (Diagram by Alan Barnard.)

allow her to share in his estate after his death. Frazer admitted this explanation as a special case, and remarked that it could be seen as 'a sort of compromise between matrilineal succession and Brahmanic law'.[15] Malinowski seems to have borrowed from this argument when he explained aristocratic marriages with the father's sister's daughter in the Trobriand Islands as a tactic for evading the rule of matrilineal succession.

Yet even if Frazer was on the right track, he had to recognise that his economic hypothesis resolved only one part of the puzzle. Economic motives might explain a preference for cross-cousin marriage, but it could not explain why marriage was so widely forbidden between the children of two brothers, or the children of two sisters. Like Tylor before him, Frazer argued that where marriage was prohibited with these ortho-cousins, this was a relic of a former moiety system. Moieties had been introduced to stop men marrying their sisters. A by-product of the incest taboo was that a man could not marry an ortho-cousin, since they were members of his own moiety. When moieties died away, the prohibition on marriage with ortho-cousins survived.

The ban on marriages between ortho-cousins might go back to the moiety structure, but Frazer was reluctant to adopt Tylor's deduction that cross-cousin marriage was also a relic of a vanished structure of dual organisation. If this were the case, then his economic explanation for the custom was redundant. However, Frazer thought that sister-exchange must have been introduced even before moieties were invented. Cross-cousin marriage derived directly from sister-exchange. Therefore, 'it is possible and indeed probable that the practice of cousin marriage and the preference for it long preceded the two-class system of exogamy'.[16]

In practice, Frazer was not entirely consistent. He conceded that both the preference for cross-cousin marriage and the ban on ortho-cousin marriage might be traced back to an original moiety structure. 'Hence wherever the dual organization exists or has formerly existed, we may expect to find the preference for the marriage of cross-cousins and the prohibition of the marriage of ortho-cousins.'[17] If there were any traces of a former state of dual organisation – totemic exogamy, for example, or a classificatory kinship terminology – then Frazer expected to find a system of cross-cousin marriage. And he was able to show that cross-cousin marriage was common in the areas for which dual organisation had been reported.

But if the rule of exogamy was the baseline of all these practices, how had exogamy arisen? Tylor believed that exogamy had beneficial social consequences since it generated alliances. For Frazer the ban on marriage with kin followed from a general improvement in moral character, but the sources of this refinement remained obscure. 'The general cause which I have assumed for the successive changes in marriage customs which we have now passed under review is a growing aversion to the marriage of persons nearly related to each other by blood. Into the origin of that aversion I shall not here inquire; the problem is one of the darkest and most difficult in the whole history of society.'[18]

Elaborating the thesis

Frazer's accumulation of ethnographic instances was perhaps more immediately stimulating than his arguments, and in any case alternative theories were abundantly available. Rivers, for one, had proposed a very different theory of the origin of cross-cousin marriage. According to Rivers, cross-cousin marriage in Melanesia derived from a previous rule that allowed a man to marry the wife of his mother's brother. Frazer objected that marriage with the mother's brother's wife 'appears to have been rare and exceptional in other parts of the world.'[19] Moreover, if Rivers was correct, then cross-cousin marriage must have been a late development in the evolution of kinship systems, following even the recognition of paternity. Tylor and Frazer believed that on the contrary it was very primitive, the consequence of sister exchange, or of an original structure of dual organisation.

In any case, the theory of Rivers was discredited by his own students. Fison's abstract model proved to be more suggestive, and it inspired other transformations. T. C. Hodson pointed to an association between cross-cousin marriage and the existence of more than two intermarrying groups.[20] Reo Fortune showed that each regime of cousin marriage produced a characteristic long-term pattern of exchange relationships.[21] The French scholar, Marcel Granet, who so influenced Lévi-Strauss, tried to show that the Chinese had followed the same evolutionary route as the Australians. Beginning with a four-section system rather like that of the Kariera, but based upon matrilocal marriage, they had later developed an eight-class patrilineal system in which marriage was preferred with the mother's brother's daughter.[22]

Finally, Durkheim's theory had its adherents. Leiden University in the Netherlands was a centre of research on Indonesia, which was then a Dutch colony, and J. P. B. de Josselin de Jong and his students began to publish analyses of cousin marriage practices that on some points anticipated the ideas of Lévi-Strauss.[23] In 1935 one of de Josselin de Jong's associates, F. A. E. van Wouden, published a thesis on Indonesian marriage systems, for which he borrowed Tylor's term 'connubium'.[23] Indonesia had many systems of cross-cousin marriage, and van Wouden made the classical assumption that cross-cousin marriage was rooted in a system of dual descent. He also drew on Durkheim and Mauss's essay, *Primitive Classification*, which argued that a society with dual organisation, that is, with moieties, would develop a matching dual classification of the universe.[24]

Other Leiden anthropologists were inspired to seek systematic series of dual oppositions in the structure of various Indonesian artefacts and ideologies. De Josselin de Jong defined an Indonesian culture area that was characterised by double descent, cross-cousin marriage and oppositional classificatory forms.[25] The theory was Durkheim's, but the methodological approach was inspired by

Radcliffe-Brown's treatment of the Australian systems as local variations on a common regional theme.[26]

Lévi-Strauss's theory of marriage exchange

Lévi-Strauss was the first to offer a full-blown alternative to Frazer, albeit an alternative that was essentially a transformation. He granted Frazer the 'credit for being the first to call attention to the structural similarity between marriage by exchange [of sisters] and cross-cousin marriage, and for establishing the real connection between the two.'[27] However, he pointed out that Frazer had failed to establish a necessary connection between the practice of cross-cousin marriage and the prohibition on marriage with the children of two brothers or of two sisters, which he had termed 'ortho-cousins'. He attributed Frazer's failure to his mistaken notion of what exchange is about. Frazer's savage had 'the mentality of *Homo Oeconomicus* as conceived of by nineteenth-century philosophers'.[28] But economic calculation and barter are not primitive social practices. One must grasp exchange 'as a mere aspect of a total structure of reciprocity which … was immediately and intuitively apprehended by social man'.[29] This gnomic observation can only be understood by referring it back to its inspiration in the work of Marcel Mauss.

In 1924, Mauss had published a brief essay on 'the gift' (*le don*), which was subtitled 'The form and cause (*raison*) of exchange in archaic societies'. The theme of the essay is that exchange in primitive societies is not directly comparable to 'economic' transactions in contemporary societies. Primitive peoples have an ethic of reciprocity. This has been destroyed in capitalist systems and must be recovered if a socialist society is to be possible. The ancient exchange systems were characterised by the fact that exchanges took place between groups – tribes, clans or families – rather than between individuals. These exchanges were not voluntary. There was a compulsion to give, to receive, and to make an appropriate return. Finally, people did not exchange only what we would consider to be economic goods. They exchanged courtesies, rituals and entertainments, dances and feast, and assistance at times of war. Most remarkably, they exchanged women and children in the same way.

Lévi-Strauss took the argument even further. The principles of exchange and reciprocity are burned into the human unconscious. They are 'fundamental structures of the human mind'.[30] According to Lévi-Strauss, they could be observed even in the thinking of Western children. Mauss's principle of reciprocity becomes an unconscious but universal rule, like a rule underlying a grammatical structure or defining a phoneme; in short like the principles which were described in Jakobson's linguistics. It was very different from Frazer's straightforward notion of economic rationality that might lead, for example, to the barter of women. Beginning with this imperative to exchange, Lévi-Strauss proposed a single explanation not only for cross-cousin marriage but also for sister-exchange, dual organisation and rules of exogamy (including the prohibition on marriage with ortho-cousins). All these kinship institutions were mechanisms for ensuring the exchange of women in marriage.

The starting point was the prohibition of incest. This rule, the first law of society, was the necessary precondition for systems of exchange. Once incest had been banned, a man could no longer marry his sister. Instead, she became his ticket of entry into social life. Marrying her to another man, he entered into relations of reciprocity. 'As soon as I am forbidden a woman, she thereby becomes available to another man, and somewhere else a man renounces a woman who thereby becomes available to me,' Lévi-Strauss explained. The rule of exogamy 'is instituted only in order to guarantee and establish, directly or, immediately or mediately, an exchange.'[31]

Like Durkheim and Mauss, Lévi-Strauss assumed that 'primitive' peoples operate in groups, and that marriage exchanges would therefore take place between descent groups operating as units. In its simplest form, the exchange of women follows one of two modes. Women may be exchanged directly between two groups. This direct give-and-take Lévi-Strauss calls restricted exchange. It may be a straightforward deal, in which two men exchange their sisters in marriage, but it may be an institutionalised relationship between two groups, the men in the one group always marrying women in the other. This is a moiety system. Alternatively, women may be exchanged indirectly between three or more groups. This leads to what Lévi-Strauss calls generalised exchange. 'Generalized exchange establishes a system of operations conducted "on credit". A surrenders a daughter or a sister to B, who surrenders one to C, who, in turn, will surrender one to A. This is its simplest formula.'[32] In either sister-exchange or dual organisation, both kinds of cross-cousin are marriageable. In generalised exchange, only the mother's brother's daughter may be married. The father's sister's daughter cannot be

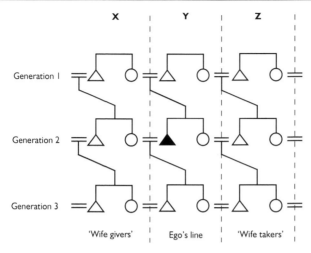

Figure 9.2 Generalised exchange: marriage with the mother's brother's daughter. (Diagram by Alan Barnard.)

taken as a wife. (If a systematic series of mother's brother's daughter marriages are drawn in a model, it will be seen that women are circulating in one direction between fixed lines of men. See Figure 9.2.)

Lévi-Strauss remarked that generalised exchange can join an unlimited series of groups in a single exchange cycle, while dual organisation only integrates two primary social units. It is therefore a more effective means of generating social solidarity. (Radcliffe-Brown had made a similar argument. The Aranda system allowed people to make alliances with more local groups than was the case in the simpler Kariera system.)

Lévi-Strauss believed that dual organisation was most common in Australia, while the most important concentration of systems of generalised exchange was in Asia. Following Frazer, he identified the Burmese tribes and the Gilyak of Siberia as the most thorough-going contemporary exponents of this form of marriage exchange, and he suggested that they represented the remnants of a widespread system which once spanned the whole of China, as Granet had, apparently, demonstrated. Generalised exchange (or at least system-atic marriages with the mother's brother's daughter) was also common in South India, as Frazer had noted. However, Lévi-Strauss argued that there was so much political instability in this region that people would have been reluctant to engage in long speculative cycles of exchange. Anxious marriage partners would demand a more

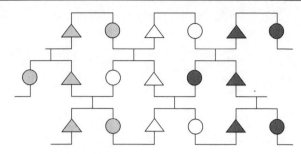

Figure 9.3   Delayed direct exchange: marriage with the father's sister's daughter. (Diagram by Alan Barnard.)

immediate return. The temptation would then be to revert to the simplest form of direct exchange, the exchange of sisters (as had happened in Melanesia, according to Rivers), but Lévi-Strauss suggested that in South India people opted for a slightly more sophisticated mechanism, a deferred but direct return – I give you my sister, and you give your daughter to my son. The effect was to resurrect the hidden possibility of marriage with the father's sister's daughter.

In terms that Frazer might well have used, Lévi-Strauss argued that 'marriage with the father's sister's daughter contrasts with other forms of cross-cousin marriage as an economy based on exchange for cash contrasts with economies permitting operations on deferred terms.'[33] This was the poor man's version of marriage exchange. It offered some security in conditions of political uncertainty, when people are reluctant to gamble on the long term. But it did not establish ties between an extended series of local groups.

Lévi-Strauss's book was dedicated to Lewis Henry Morgan, and he accepted Morgan's principle that the kinship terminology provides definitive evidence of the system of marriage. Any system of dual organisation or cross-cousin marriage is based upon a dichoto- misation of the world of kin. On the one hand there are affines, the wife-givers and wife-takers; on the other hand, there are unmarriage- able relatives. This opposition between kin and affines persists from generation to generation. In a system of generalised exchange, the kinship terminology will characteristically oppose cross-cousins on the mother's side with other cousins and with siblings. It is also likely to identify the parents of these cross-cousins with affines. The term for mother's brother, for example, will often be the same as the term for wife's father.

By the time that Lévi-Strauss was writing, the leading anthropologists in Britain and America – Malinowski, Radcliffe-Brown,
Lowie and Kroeber – had come to the conclusion that the nuclear
family was universal. Moreover, it was the main generating force
behind all kinship systems and kinship terminologies. Lévi-Strauss
rejected this orthodox view, but he did not revert to the classic
evolutionist model, according to which the family appeared only at
a late stage of human development. Instead, arguing from the primacy
of exchange, he insisted that the basic unit of any kinship system
was made up of a nuclear family *plus a wife-giver*. It included not
only a man, his wife and their child, but also his wife's brother, his
affine. Built into this 'atom of kinship' were the two opposed and
fundamental principles of consanguinity and affinity.[34]

By substituting a mental structure of 'reciprocity' for Frazer's
more earthy notion of barter, Lévi-Strauss was able to offer a deductive, unitary theory that accounted at one stroke for exogamy, dual
organisation and cross-cousin marriage. In the central chapters of
his book he also developed a model to show how systematic matrilateral cross-cousin marriage could order social groups in a whole
society. Moreover, he used this model to reanalyse a number of
ethnographic cases. All this was certainly most impressive, and yet
there was an obvious danger that Lévi-Strauss's theory was actually
too powerful. If the generative principles of reciprocity and exchange
were universal, burned into the human mind, why were all kinship
systems not based upon cross-cousin marriage or dual organisation?
Yet many, including our own, were not. Did we lack the primitive
drive towards reciprocity (as Mauss, indeed, had hinted)? On the
other hand, if Lévi-Strauss's theory applied only to a small group of
primitive societies, then how could cross-cousin marriage and dual
organisation express universal principles of human mentality?

Lévi-Strauss recognised that he had dealt with only one category
of human marriage systems. He termed these 'elementary structures'
or 'closed systems' and opposed them to 'complex structures' or
'open systems', in which the choice of a wife was governed by
principles that did not derive from the kinship system at all, but had
to do with such considerations as the wealth or power of her relatives,
or simply with personal chemistry. These systems were still governed
by the negative rule of exogamy, and so in some sense reciprocity
and exchange might be at work, although it was not easy to specify
quite how they operated. But Lévi-Strauss's dialectical cast of mind
suggested that the binary oppositions might be mediated. The systems

that American anthropologists called 'Crow–Omaha' were an intermediate type, without a positive marriage rule but with extremely wide-ranging prohibitions. Typically a man could not marry into the clans of any of his four grandparents. Moreover, these rules operated in rather small societies, with few clans, so that there were not many women whom a man could marry. In these circumstances the negative rules might produce a statistical pattern of marriages that linked local groups in an enduring structure.[35]

Leach and the Kachin

Lévi-Strauss's remarkable solution to Frazer's puzzle immediately stimulated a series of commentaries. The first major critical reaction was an essay by Edmund Leach, published in 1951, and entitled 'The structural implications of matrilateral cross-cousin marriage'.

Leach was a student of Malinowski. He was therefore conditioned to expect that rules were there to be broken, and that all individuals actively pursue their own interests. Moreover, he had actually spent the best part of the previous decade with the Kachin, first as an ethnographer and then, during the Japanese occupation of Burma, as a guerrilla. The Kachin had provided Lévi-Strauss with one of his main case-studies of a system of cross-cousin marriage, but Leach was immediately aware that he had got the Kachin material wrong on several crucial points, sometimes even mixing up reports on the Kachin with data on neighbouring groups. Even where Lévi-Strauss had got it right, he was dealing only with Kachin ideology. But Leach admitted that Lévi-Strauss had obliged him to see the Kachin data in a new way, and his point of departure was Lévi-Strauss's model of a society based on systematic marriage with the mother's brother's daughter.

Yet Leach's goal was very different. He was not concerned with mental universals and unconscious principles of reciprocity but rather with a concrete, historical society and with the way in which real individuals within it conducted their affairs, promoted their own interests, and thought about their world. The Kachin ideology depicted a system of groups that married in a circle. In practice, however, the system was radically unbalanced. There was a built-in status difference between wife-givers, who were equals or superiors, and wife-takers, who were equals or inferiors. The system was therefore not driven by Mauss's principle of reciprocity. The flow of wives was just one aspect of a series of unequal exchanges. In order to get a wife, a man was obliged to pay a brideprice, and he often had to accept what was virtually the position of a feudal inferior. The marriage system was therefore to be understood as one facet of a broader structure of political and economic transactions between people of different status. As Leach summarised the situation:

1   From a *political* aspect, chief is to headman as feudal Lord of the Manor is to customary freeholder.
2   From a *kinship* aspect, chief is to headman as *mayu* to *dama*, that is as father-in-law to son-in-law.
3   From a *territorial* aspect, the kinship status of the headman's lineage in respect to that of the chief is held to validate the tenure of land.
4   From an *economic* aspect the effect of matrilateral cross-cousin marriage is that, on balance, the headman's lineage constantly pays wealth to the chief's lineage in the form of bridewealth.[36]

In 1954 Leach published an ambitious monograph on the Kachin, *Political Systems of Highland Burma*, in which he played a dialectical game with Fortes and Evans-Pritchard's famous Types A and B societies, states and segmentary lineage system. According to Leach, some Kachin communities were very like African segmentary lineage systems (although with systematic cross-cousin marriage). Others were hierarchical states. He argued that in fact they lurched from feudal hierarchy to radical republicanism because they were constructed upon a fundamental contradiction between a lineage system, in which all lineages must be equal, and a system of unilateral transmission of wives, which implied hierarchy.

This was an impressive synthesis of descent and alliance models. However, there was a fundamental ambiguity about Leach's real objective. Earlier he had criticised Lévi-Strauss for neglecting the tactics, the political realities, which explained the marriage choices that people were making. In *Political Systems* he flirted with an idealist vision of the anthropologist's task. Was his book about what Kachin politicians really did, or about the way in which the Kachin thought that an ideal world should work? Increasingly he took a very un-Malinowskian point of view on this question, and he admitted in his preface to the 1964 reprint of *Political Systems of Highland Burma* that 'my own attempt to find systemic ordering in historical events depends upon the changing evaluation of verbal categories and is, in the final analysis, illusory'. It may be that even a sceptical adoption of Lévi-Strauss's approach imposed a certain idealism; certainly the other main transformation of Lévi-Strauss's theory was to take a radically idealist path.

Leiden, Needham and Dumont

The Durkheimians of the Leiden school were impressed to discover that Lévi-Strauss was working along the same lines as themselves. Their anthropology seminar worked its way through Lévi-Strauss's massive book in the course of the academic year 1950–1951, and in 1952 de Josselin de Jong published the first extended appreciation of *The Elementary Structures of Kinship*. (Since his essay was published in English, it served for nearly 20 years as the main primer on Lévi-Strauss's theory for anthropologists unable to read French).[37]

Rodney Needham, a young British social anthropologist specialising in Indonesia, was a member of this de Josselin de Jong seminar. On his return to Britain he became one of the leading promoters of Lévi-Strauss's monograph, which he described in the most effusive terms as 'a masterpiece, a sociological classic of the first rank'.[38] True, like de Josselin de Jong himself, he was not a blind advocate. 'I do not by any means think it is perfect', Needham wrote, and he specified some of the many things that the master had wrong. However, it was not his particular criticisms that were to get him into hot water; it was rather his innocent attempt to make the argument clearer.

Unlike Leach, Needham was a formalist. The Malinowskian concern with practice was foreign to him. He believed that people would be obliged to follow the rules in prescriptive systems. That was why, after all, the rules were called prescriptions. In societies that prescribed, for example, marriage with a mother's brother's daughter, men would have to marry either a daughter of their actual mother's brother, or a woman who was classified as a relative of the same type in the kinship terminology. To be sure, there were societies, in the Trobriand Islands, for instance, where it might suit some men to marry a cousin for political reasons, but choices of this sort should be treated as 'preferences'. They were not required, not 'prescriptive'. What Lévi-Strauss had done was to identify a specific type of primitive society, in which marriage was prescribed within a particular marriage class. He had also demonstrated that societies of this type had characteristic forms of classifying relatives (basically, into two sets, marriageable and unmarriageable). But Lévi-Strauss had nothing to say about societies in which people might say that it was best, if at all possible, to marry (for example) a mother's brother's daughter, as among the Tswana common people, or a father's brother's daughter, as among Tswana aristocrats.[39] These were preferences, not prescriptions, which were a different matter entirely.

Needham fostered Lévi-Strauss's reputation, translated one of his key essays,[40] and supervised the English translation of his masterpiece on kinship and marriage. At the last moment, Lévi-Strauss contributed a new preface for this translation. With an insouciance that would have been admired by de Gaulle himself, he devoted it largely to the repudiation of Needham's interpretation of his thesis.

> Following Needham, several writers today assert that my book is only concerned with prescriptive systems, or, to be more exact (since one need only glance through it to be assured of the contrary), that such had been my intention had I not confused the two forms. But if the champions of this distinction had been correct in believing that prescriptive systems are few and far between, a most curious consequence would have resulted: I would have written a very fat book which since 1952 [the year in which J. P. B. de Josselin de Jong published his commentary] has aroused all sorts of commentaries and discussions despite its being concerned with such rare facts and so limited a field that it is difficult to understand of what interest it could be with regard to a general theory of kinship.

Prescriptions described the rules of the game, preferences referred to statistical outcomes: 'a preferential system is prescriptive when envisaged at the model level; a prescriptive system must be preferential when envisaged on the level of reality.'[41] From now on there was no more implacable critic of Lévi-Strauss's thesis than Rodney Needham. He even tried to revive the reputation of Rivers's friend Hocart, because he had followed McLennan and cast doubt upon the sociological significance of kinship terms.

Another significant reinterpretation of Lévi-Strauss's theory was developed by a French scholar, Louis Dumont. In 1953, Dumont had published an essay on Dravidian kinship terminology, arguing that it divided the universe of kin into consanguineal relatives on the one hand and permanent affines on the other.[42] In 1957 he developed his ideas in a long essay, *Hierarchy and Marriage Alliance in South Indian Kinship*, which he dedicated to Lévi-Strauss. Although

he insisted that his analysis was 'quite in accordance with Professor
Lévi-Strauss's broad view of South Indian kinship',[43] its effect was
to give priority to the system of categories generated by the terminology. The key proposition was that 'the terminology provides a
common, regional conceptual framework, making affinity the equal
of consanguinity'.[44] The expression of this terminology in actual
marriages with cross-cousins was evidently only a potentiality, of
subsidiary importance to the semantic structure. Dumont later
collected these essays in a volume whose title, *Affinity as Value*,
captured perfectly his distinctly idealist view of marriage relationships.

Needham took up Dumont's argument and pressed it further. He
had persuaded himself that alliance theory applied only where a
man was obliged to marry a woman who belonged to a particular
category of relatives. The category was designated by the relationship
terminology. Needham now argued that it was here, at the level of
words for kin, that alliance systems had their true being. Whether
or not the classifications were translated into marriage rules was a
secondary issue, and it did not matter at all whether people actually
married in accordance with any such rules. Alliance was just a
conceptual possibility; prescriptive alliance no more than a form of
classification. 'This type of organization is defined by the terminology', Needham proclaimed, 'and the terminology is constituted
by the regularity of a constant relation that articulates lines and
categories'.[45]

African lineages again

Lévi-Strauss himself did care about marriage choices, and in fact he
had suggested that if the actual marriage choices in complex societies
were analysed, it would be apparent that even here there is a pattern,
although not one encoded in positive marriage rules. In the Crow–
Omaha systems, in which marriage was forbidden with anyone from
the same clan as any grandparent, the incest rules were so expansive
that they would act in effect very like positive marriage rules, to
direct marriages within a specific target group.

This thesis was put to the test by Françoise Héritier, in a study
of a community in Burkina Faso, the Samo. The Samo have all
the conventional attributes of an 'Omaha' system, and yet despite
the elaborate armoury of prohibitions they apparently do have a
pattern of marriage alliances with (distant) relatives, as Lévi-Strauss

predicted. Despite elaborate computer manipulation of the data, Héritier could not say whether the Samo actively prefer to marry kin, or whether (given a small population and many prohibitions) they simply have no alternative, or whether, indeed, they were rather practising a form of neighbourhood endogamy, since some 70 per cent of the marriages in her sample were between residents of three closely allied villages. Any of these possibilities might be reconciled with Lévi-Strauss's expectations. But what was the significance of this statistical pattern, of which the actors were unaware? Lévi-Strauss had suggested that the statistical tendency would be 'sufficient to place the society in question in the same group as a theoretical society in which everyone would marry according to the rule, and of which the former can best be understood as an approximation.'[46] It was not easy to work out the implications of this principle.

It was also not clear what the Samo marriage prohibitions actually amounted to. They were first presented in conventional terms as prohibitions on marriage with women from particular lineages, but once again doubts cropped up about the true nature of African lineages. Héritier herself demonstrated a sophisticated uncertainty about the significance or even the reality of these lineages. 'From the point of view of their function with respect to marriage,' she wrote, 'the principle of unilineality, so apparent in the semi-complex systems of the Crow–Omaha type, is not really fundamental; it is above all a principle of order and simplification.'[47] 'Lineages' were therefore just ways of tidying up or summarising the incest regulations, conveniently though inexactly (for some non-lineal kin were also unmarriageable). The lineages become epiphenomena, like Australian classes in Radcliffe-Brown's theory, where they were similarly presented as rough and ready summaries of the kinship terminology, which really determined marriage choices. Apparently, Samo 'lineages' are not exogamous groups, any more than Australian marriage classes regulate marriage. Yet if 'alliance' is not a system of exchange between groups, it is difficult to see what Lévi-Strauss's theory explains. On the other hand, if an alliance structure is simply a classificatory scheme that divides relatives into two classes, as Dumont and Needham supposed, then what is its effect on social life?

To put it another way, was the alliance system a statistical pattern of real marriage choices, a plan of action, or a way of thinking? Or, as Lévi-Strauss originally suggested, is it all three at once? In his 'Overture' to *The Raw and the Cooked*, the first volume of his series of studies of American mythology, Lévi-Strauss signalled a retreat from the field of sociology and a return to the project of Jakobson's structuralism, which studied social productions (language the great example) in order to find evidence of something deeper and more fundamental; ultimately, to find pointers to the structure of the human mind itself. Marriage systems were perhaps the wrong place to start looking for these deep mental structures, Lévi-Strauss now suggested, since they were inevitably contaminated by real-life constraints and tactics. He therefore turned his attention instead to the other great subject of Victorian anthropology, totemism, which Frazer had also subjected to one of his encyclopaedic reviews.

Totemism again

In 1962, Lévi-Strauss published a brief essay, *Totemism* (or *Totemism Today*, in the French), and then a follow-up, a monograph entitled *La Pensée Sauvage*. He began by comparing the totemism of Victorian anthropology with the early psychiatric notion of hysteria. Hysteria had been invented in order to distinguish a class of others, the mad. Totemism set up another class of people in opposition to ourselves, people who were ignorant of logic and who confused the basic categories of Nature and Culture. Freud, however, had demonstrated that many of the processes identified with hysteria were commonplace in everyday psychology, and Lévi-Strauss set out to show that our own mental processes were shot through with traces of savage thought.

Boas and his followers had made totemism one of the targets of their critique of evolutionism, and demonstrated that the various features classically associated with totemism did not necessarily occur together. 'When we speak of totemism we actually confuse two problems', Lévi-Strauss explained.

> The first problem is that posed by the frequent identification of human beings with plants or animals, and which has to do with very general views of the relations between man and nature, relations which concern art and magic as much as society and religion. The second problem is that of the designation of groups based on kinship, which may be done with the aid of animal or vegetable terms but also in many other ways. The term 'totemism' covers only cases in which there is a coincidence of the two orders.[48]

But why should social groups so often be named for animals and plants? And why were totems sacred? Durkheim had argued that any emblem of a social group was made the object of ritual and so became sacred. Radcliffe-Brown reversed the argument. Animals and plants that were particularly important for subsistence were assigned a ritual value, and they were therefore chosen to serve as the symbols of a social group. Lévi-Strauss disagreed with both, and in his support he invoked Rousseau. Rousseau had imagined that in the passage from nature to culture the intellect would have become more crucial than instinct and emotion. And one of the first intellectual acts would have been to impose a classification upon the natural world. At first human beings would have felt that they were identical to other people and also to animals. As they began to distinguish themselves from animals and from each other, so they distinguished animals into different species. 'It is because man originally felt himself identical to all those like him (among which, as Rousseau explicitly says, we must include animals) that he came to acquire the capacity to distinguish *himself* as he distinguishes *them*, i.e., to use the diversity of species as conceptual support for social differentiation.'[49]

Totemism is precisely such a system of classification. Durkheim and Mauss had supposed that the social system was the fundamental reality. The classification of the natural environment followed the model of the social structure. It was a projection of society into nature.[50] Lévi-Strauss argued that *la pensée sauvage* classifies social groups and natural species at the same time, and in relation to one another. It establishes a system of homologies between Nature and Culture, without privileging the social world. The relationship between the social series and the natural series of categories is a metaphorical one. Species x stands to species y as social group A stands to social group B. The attention paid to natural species had nothing to do with what people liked to eat. They were so important because they are easy to classify. People can latch on to any one of a number of possible superficial resemblances and differences and distinguish pairs of species as flying things vs. creatures that crawl, meat-eaters vs. vegetarians, etc. The conclusion is 'that natural species are chosen not because they are "good to eat" but because they are "good to think"'.[51]

Lévi-Strauss insists that the tropes of *la pensée sauvage* are ethically superior to the utilitarian ends–means mode of thought of modern rationalism. It is a way of thinking that treats our relationships with nature on the analogy of social relationships, and takes it for granted that both should be governed by the principle of reciprocity. In *Tristes Tropiques*, he had lamented the disruption of the Neolithic world, with its respect for Nature. 'What did I propose?', he ruminated, many years later, in answer to a question from an interviewer. 'To found the rights of man not, as we have done since the American and French Revolutions, on the unique and privileged character of one living species, but instead to see it as a special case of the rights of all species.' Moving in that direction, we will 'find ourselves on an equal footing with the practical attitude that "primitive" peoples, the ones studied by anthropologists, have regarding nature.'[52]

> Although situated in history, these societies seem to have developed or retained a particular wisdom which impels them to resist desperately any modification in their structure that would enable history to burst into their midst. Those which, recently still, best protected their distinctive character appear to be societies inspired by the dominant concern to persevere in their existence. The way in which they exploit the environment guarantees both a modest standard of living and the conservation of natural resources. In spite of the diversity of their marriage rules, a demographer can recognize in them the common characteristic of rigorously limiting the birth-rate and keeping it constant. Finally, a political life, based on consensus and allowing no other decisions than those taken unanimously, seems conceived to exclude that driving force of collective life which makes use of the contrasts between power and opposition, majority and minority, exploiters and exploited.[53]

Lévi-Strauss is deeply pessimistic about the future of primitive societies, but his writings helped to prepare the ground for a revival of the theory of primitive society in a new form, as a political programme. Civilisation is a destroyer. The only way to reinvigorate cultural diversity, and to restore a sustainable relationship between Nature and Culture, is to bring back primitive society.

Part V

Back to the beginning

The primitives create little in the way of order in their culture. Nowadays we call them underdeveloped peoples. But they generate very little entropy in their society. In general, these societies are egalitarian, mechanically so, regulated by the rule of unanimity ... The civilised, on the contrary, create a great deal of order in culture, as can be seen in the technology and the great works of civilisation, but they also generate much entropy in their society: social conflicts, political battles, all things against which, as we have seen, the primitives secure themselves, in a manner perhaps more conscious and systematic than we may have supposed.

(Lévi-Strauss in G. Charbonnier, *Entretiens avec Claude Lévi-Strauss* (1961), p. 47)

Chapter 10

The return of the native

On Human Rights Day 1992, the United Nations proclaimed an International Year of the World's Indigenous People. In 1995, a Decade for Indigenous Peoples was launched and a Forum of Indigenous Peoples established. Unfortunately, the inaugural meeting of the Working Group was disrupted by gatecrashers. A self-styled delegation of South African Boers turned up and demanded to be allowed to participate on the grounds that they too were indigenous people, whose traditional culture, moreover, was under threat from the new African National Congress government. They were unceremoniously ejected, and no doubt their motives were far from pure, but the drama might usefully have drawn attention to the difficulty of defining and identifying Indigenous People.

The loaded terms *native* and *indigenous* are the subject of much debate in activist circles.[1] *Native* still has a colonial ring in many parts of the world, although it has become an acceptable label in North America, where it is generally capitalised (Native), perhaps in order to suggest that it refers to a nation of some sort. Indeed, the term *First Nations* is often used as an alternative designation in Canada and the USA. In international discourse, however, the term *indigenous* is usually preferred. This sounds somewhat foreign to English ears, but perhaps it comes across as more scientific.

At the same time, the names used for particular indigenous peoples have undergone changes, Saami, for example, being preferred to Lapp, Inuit to Eskimo, and San to Bushman. As is so often the way with this sort of relabelling, 'San' turns out to be a pejorative Hottentot – or Khoekhoe – term for Bushmen, connoting vagabonds and bandits.[2] But the principle is defensible. It is a good idea to call people by names they recognise and find acceptable.

Nevertheless, discredited old arguments may lurk behind new

words. Culture has become a common euphemism for race. Similarly, in the rhetoric of the indigenous peoples movement 'native' or 'indigenous' are often euphemisms for what used to be termed primitive.[3] Indeed, one of the major NGOs in this field, Survival International, began life as the Primitive Peoples' Fund. It has since changed its name, but clinging to the same anachronistic anthropology it now promotes itself as a movement 'for tribal peoples'. Once this equivalence between 'indigenous' and 'primitive', 'tribal', 'hunting' or 'nomadic' peoples is grasped, it is easier to understand why the Secretary General of the United Nations should have glossed 'indigenous peoples' as 'nomads or hunting people'.[4] The Indigenous Peoples Forum was dominated by delegations speaking for Inuit, San, Australian Aborigines, Amazonian peoples, etc. These are precisely the quintessential 'primitive societies' of classical anthropological discourse.

Not only has the ghostly category of 'primitive peoples' been restored to life under a new label. The UN Secretary General of the day, Dr Boutros Boutros-Ghali, identified common problems that these peoples suffered in the modern world. They had been 'relegated to reserved territories or confined to inaccessible or inhospitable regions' and in many cases 'seemed doomed to extinction'. Governments treated them as 'subversive' because they 'did not share the sedentary lifestyle or the culture of the majority. Nations of farmers tended to view nomads or hunting peoples with fear or contempt.' However, the Secretary General noted that 'a welcome change is taking place on national and international levels'. The unique way of life of indigenous peoples had at last come to be appreciated at its true value. Organisations of indigenous people had been formed. Collective rights in historical homelands were being recognised, and land claims pressed with some success.[5]

The Secretary General was certainly right to identify new international thinking on these issues. The *ILO Convention no. 169 (1989) Concerning Indigenous and Tribal Peoples in Independent Countries* laid down that national governments should allow indigenous peoples to participate in making decisions that affect them, that they should set their own development priorities, and that they should be given back lands that they traditionally occupied. This convention has been ratified by Denmark and Norway among European states, and by Bolivia, Costa Rica, Guatemala, Honduras, Mexico, Paraguay and Peru in Latin America. However, no African or Asian state has adopted it. More recently a United Nations Draft

Declaration on the Rights of Indigenous Peoples has been negotiated, but because of persistent opposition from a number of African states it has not yet been put before the General Assembly.[6]

Towards a critique

The rhetoric of the indigenous peoples movement rests on widely accepted premises that are nevertheless open to serious challenge, not least from anthropologists. The initial assumption is that descendants of the original inhabitants of a country should have privileged rights, perhaps even exclusive rights, to its resources. Conversely, immigrants are simply guests, and should behave accordingly. These propositions are popular with extreme right-wing parties in Europe, although the argument is seldom pushed to its logical conclusion since it is well-known that the history of all European countries is a history of successive migrations. Even in the most extreme nationalist circles it is not generally argued that, for instance, descendants of the Celts should be given special privileges throughout Britain, which should be denied to descendants of Saxons, Romans, Vikings, Normans, and, of course, all later immigrants. But where hunters and nomadic herders are concerned, the principle is sometimes taken even further. It is then argued that they represent not merely the first inhabitants of a country but the original human populations of the world. In a certain sense primitive, aboriginal, humankind's first-comers, theirs is also the natural state of humanity. If that is so, then perhaps it follows that their rights must take precedence over those of farmers and, of course, city dwellers.

Yet the distinction between hunters and farmers is not always self-evident. In Africa, the Kalahari Bushmen and the Congo Pygmies interacted with farming neighbours for centuries, probably for at least a millennium, before the colonial period. Exchanges with farmers and traders are crucial for their economy, and their foraging activities are geared to this broader economic context. Moreover, the divide between a foraging and a farming or herding way of life is not necessarily hard and fast. People may forage for some seasons, even some years, but fall back on other activities when times are tough. Conversely, farmers collect firewood and certain foods, and may be driven back on foraging as a result of war or natural disasters, and Saami herders, for example, both hunt and herd reindeer.[7]

Nor does hunting mean the same thing everywhere. Inuit commercial hunters flourished for centuries in Canada's far north, in time embracing the new technologies of hunting rifles, motorised sleighs and radio communications, but this trade has been in decline for decades, and the consumer boycott of furs has made further inroads in the rump of the industry. From the 1950s the Canadian government implemented a policy of sedenterisation. Today there are still a few part-time commercial hunters, and some men still hunt for recreation, as elsewhere in North America, but hunting is a marginal activity. Louis-Jacques Dorais concludes bluntly that 'Inuit society, in many respects, is as modern as its Euro–American counterpart'.[8] Ethnographers have emphasised the continuing importance of what one author describes as 'the imagery rather than the subsistence aspects of hunting',[9] but much the same could be said of the place of hunting in the imagery of North American male suburbanites.

Several generations – in some cases many centuries – of European settlement have also greatly complicated the picture. For example, in parts of what is now Quebec native hunters began to trade with French fur buyers in the late fifteenth century. France staked a claim to sovereignty in 1534, and in the next century many local people converted to Christianity and adopted the French language. Some native leaders were given land grants and trading monopolies, and substantial numbers fought with the French against the English. The British acquired Quebec in 1763, introducing new political and economic structures. A century later Quebec became part of Canada and underwent further political and economic changes. Colonialism was a protean beast, and the course of local history was in many ways very different even in neighbouring Newfoundland and Labrador, which only became part of Canada in 1949. World-wide, the only constant is that local ways of life and group identities of all colonised peoples have been subjected to a variety of pressures, and they have seldom, if ever, remained stable over the long term.

Obviously the way of life of modern hunters or herders is only remotely related to that of hunters and herders who lived thousands of years ago. It is nevertheless often assumed that each descendant of former hunters is the carrier of an ancient culture. In familiar, romantic fashion, this culture is associated with spiritual rather than with material values. It is unique, and expresses the genius of a native people. To be sure, it is conceded (even angrily insisted) that the authentic culture may survive only in rural enclaves, since (again in good romantic style) native cultures are represented as being everywhere under threat from an intrusive material civilisation associated with cities, with stock markets, and with foreigners. However, it is argued that the essence survives, and can be nursed back to health if the resources are provided. The alternative is represented in the bleakest terms. The loss of culture is sometimes spoken of as a form of genocide. Even in less apocalyptic discourses it is taken for granted that a people which loses its culture has been robbed of its identity, and that the diminution of cultural variation represents a significant loss for all humanity.

Dr Boutros-Ghali accordingly insisted that the indigenous peoples movement is not only about land, or hunting rights. It is, even more fundamentally, concerned with culture and identity. Indeed, beyond the conventional list of individual human rights something new was at issue. 'Henceforth we realize that human rights cover not only individual rights', Boutros-Ghali claimed, 'but also collective rights, historical rights. We are discovering the "new human rights," which include, first and foremost, cultural rights ... We might even say that there can be no human rights unless cultural authenticity is preserved.'[10] He did not consider the obvious difficulty that 'collective rights' might come into conflict with 'individual rights', nor did he enquire why cultural rights should suddenly have become so prominent in international discourse.[11]

Finally, there is a strong ecological thread in the indigenous peoples rhetoric. According to the dogma, and despite the reservations expressed by some anthropologists,[12] hunters are supposed to be in tune with nature in a way that the exploitative and greedy farmers are not. Boutros-Ghali summed up the doctrine in appropriately clichéd language – 'It is now clearly understood that many indigenous people live in greater harmony with the natural environment than do the inhabitants of industrialised consumer societies.'[13]

Some activists wish that the modern heirs of ancient hunter-gatherer populations would take up hunting again, and restore the age-old environmental balance. Such hopes are not justified by experience. In Greenland, the Inuit-led Home Rule government regards hunting as anachronistic and objectionable, and favours the exploitation of non-renewable resources.[14] The Inupiat of Alaska's North Slope have supported oil drilling on the coastal plain of the Arctic National Wildlife Refuge (although they are opposed by the Gwich'in Indians). The Alaska Native Claims Settlement Act (1971) created 12 Native-controlled profit-making corporations, which now export resources to Japan and Korea. Kirk Dombrowski has described the interplay between US government agencies, agro-businesses and native leaders in the development of the Alaska Native Timber policies. Industrial timber and pulp producers in Southeast Alaska recognised Native claims for tactical reasons, since this allowed them to evade environmental laws that were intended to curb production. Dombrowski also reports that 'two classes of Natives' have emerged. One is made up of people who became shareholders in terms of the Alaska Native Claims Settlement Act of 1971. The other, born afterwards, and known as 'New Natives', are not shareholders, and they do not participate in the profits of the native corporations. For these reasons, locally-led evangelical Christian churches oppose the indigenist movement.[15]

Land rights

Leaving aside the question of how the land might be used, land claims on behalf of former 'nomads' typically raise very tricky issues.[16] Courts have found that it is difficult to establish the boundaries of lands hunted by former generations, or to grasp how ancestral populations understood rights to resources and rights in land. They must also consider whether rights exercised by hunters are in some way equivalent to rights that arise from clearing virgin lands for agriculture, or to other common law entitlements. Finally, they must decide whether native chiefs legally entered into treaties that alienated some or all of their lands.

Some activists argue that too much emphasis is placed on treaties which may have been poorly understood by the natives, and they argue that courts should recognise that there are different cultural modes of encoding historical settlements. Hugh Brody, who has become a leading theorist of the Canadian First Nations movement, favours recourse to unwritten historical resources, and in line with other Canadian activists he suggests that if there are no appropriate oral traditions the court should take evidence from shamans, who are able to see in dreams the arrangements that their ancestors made with the first European settlers.[17]

Brody concedes that questions may be asked about the factual status of oral traditions, let alone the dreams of shamans, but he insists that there is a reliable test of the historical value of these accounts. It all depends on who tells them. 'For the peoples of the Northwest Coast,' he writes, 'as to any hunter-gatherer society or, indeed, any oral culture, words spoken by chiefs are a natural and inevitable basis for truth.'[18] Now the word of a chief may carry weight, where chiefs exist, but it will not necessarily be accepted as 'a natural and inevitable basis for truth' by anyone other than, perhaps, the most loyal and trusting subjects of that chief. It is surely regrettable if advocates of native rights grant powers to chiefs that they would be reluctant to allow to mere kings or emperors, or even to elected presidents. Anyway, while some of the native peoples of Canada did have hereditary chiefs, in other cases, and particularly in the case of hunter-gatherers, it is far from certain that chiefs were recognised before the office was established by colonial authorities. There are also frequent disputes about who should be chief, and land claims regularly pit native against native, chief against chief (and anthropologist against anthropologist). Precisely because myths function as charters, there are inevitably competing stories, and disputes often rage over who owns a particular story and who has the right to use it to back up claims to resources.

Other problems arise when myths are compared with historical or archaeological evidence. As a consultant to Canada's Royal Commission on Aboriginal Peoples in the 1990s, Hugh Brody organised an historical workshop. Archaeologists explained that the Arctic was colonised across the Bering Straits, by way of a land bridge that connected Siberia and Alaska.

> One of the workshop participants was a woman from a Cree community who was enrolled in a PhD programme at a prestigious American university [Brody reports]. She was not happy about the Bering Strait theory. She pointed out that her people, and most 'Indian' people, do not believe that archaeologists know anything about the origins of human life in the Americas. The idea that people first came as immigrants from Asia was, she said, absurd. It went against all that her people knew … There had been no immigration, but an emergence … She would have nothing to do with so-called scholarship that discredited these central tenets of aboriginal oral culture.[19]

This objection broke up the workshop. Brody recalls feeling confused. Could something be true at the University of Toronto but false in Kispiox?

Yet the Cree student had good reason to be troubled. If their ancestors were themselves immigrants, then perhaps the Cree may not after all be so very different from the Pilgrim Fathers who crossed on the Mayflower, or even from the huddled masses who streamed across the Atlantic in the 1890s. To be sure, the great population movements from Siberia across the Bering Straits began a very long time ago, but it was still relatively late in the history of the colonisation of the world by fully modern humans. According to a recent authoritative review, 'nothing found thus far challenges the view that significant human population movements through the area occurred only after the peak of the last glaciation, 16,000 years BC'[20] These migrations then continued for many millennia. The first wave passed quickly to the south, and the Arctic and sub-Arctic were settled at a later stage. The ancestral Aleut–Inuit may have begun to colonise the far north only in the past 4,000 years. The ancestors of the Cree are dated from 3,000 years ago,[21] while the proto-Athapascans are dated from 2,000 years ago.[22]

Precisely whose ancestors came, and when, may also be problematic, and, of course, over the centuries communities migrated, merged, died out, or changed their languages and altered their allegiances. 'Archaeologically well-known populations that predate the last 4,000 years may never be assigned clear linguistic identities', a modern authority concludes.[23] It is therefore difficult to sort out the various strains that intermingled to produce the native populations with whom the first Europeans made contact in Alaska and in the far north of Canada. However, it cannot be doubted that some of the First Nations were not merely immigrants but actually colonisers. Innu, for instance, entered the Quebec–Labrador peninsula only 1,800 years ago, displacing and assimilating earlier populations.[24]

Ever-changing colonial and national contexts have added layers of complexity to the histories of populations that derived from the precolonial communities, and with the best will in the world it may not be possible to return to a pre-Columbian state of nature. In Labrador (to continue with a Canadian example), an organisation called the Innu Nation demands the restoration of ancestral lands.[25] One difficulty they face is that the northern portion of their claim overlaps land claimed by another ethnic movement, the Labrador Inuit Association. A further complication is that this area is also home to another category of people, originally of European stock, known locally as the Settlers. Their presence raises a problem of a different order, one of principle. There have been several generations of intermarriage between Settlers and Inuit; both Inuit and Settlers are often bilingual; and their way of life is similar.[26] If the phrase has any meaning, one might surely say that they share a common culture, although apparently not a common identity. Settlers are accepted under certain conditions as members by the Labrador Inuit Association, but the Innu Nation regard them as their main adversaries, and the government excludes Settlers from collective land claims and treats them as squatters because they cannot prove aboriginal bloodlines. On the other hand, a person who has lived his or her whole life in, say, St John's in Newfoundland, and does not speak a word of a native language, may be granted aboriginal status in Labrador if he or she can claim a sufficient proportion of aboriginal ancestry.

In practice, the Canadian government accepts that native claims to land are based not only on descent, but on a calibrated measure of descent. You have rights only if you have a certain number of appropriate grandparents (although in Canada the law excludes 'aboriginal' women who had married men not recognised as Indians). This might fairly be called the Nuremberg principle. A drift to racism may be inevitable where so-called cultural identity becomes the basis for rights, since any cultural test (knowledge of a language, for example) will exclude some who might lay claim to an identity on grounds of descent. In the indigenous peoples movement, descent is tacitly assumed to represent the bedrock of collective identity.

The Canadian situation is not unique. Courts in Australia, New Zealand and the USA have also been persuaded to grant land rights to indigenous peoples. In many Latin American countries there have been mass movements of 'indigenous peoples' that purport to speak for a majority of the population, a form of ethnic nationalism with which I am not concerned here. But there are also movements of small minorities of 'hunting peoples' who demand the return of ancestral homelands, and their claims have been sympathetically considered by some Latin American governments. In most Asian and African countries, however, government policy has been firmly (not to say oppressively) assimilationist with respect to minorities of formerly foraging peoples and nomads. Occasionally, as in the case of the Bushmen of Botswana and Namibia, they have been treated as victims of poverty, who require economic aid.

Bushmen (or San) in Botswana and South Africa

The case of Botswana is instructive. On 19 April 2002, a Botswana court refused to order the government to continue to provide services to people living in the Central Kalahari Game Reserve. The claim of Bushmen or San living in the Reserve had been supported by a number of NGOs, notably Survival International, which organised vigils outside Botswana embassies, and the judgement was given prominent coverage in the world press. *The Times* of London, for example under the headline 'Last Bushmen Lose Fight For Right to be Nomads' reported that 'sub-Saharan Africa's last nomadic people have lost a legal battle against being evicted from their ancient homeland, ending 40,000 years of a hunter-gatherer lifestyle.'[27]

Even when Botswana was still a British colony (the Bechuanaland Protectorate), Bushman policy had attracted international attention from time to time. In 1958 the colonial government appointed a Bushman Survey Officer, George Silberbauer, a district commissioner who had been trained in anthropology, and was engaged in post-graduate research on the G/wi speakers west of Ghanzi. He was commissioned to review the situation of the Bushmen and to come up with a fresh policy. In his report, Silberbauer estimated the country's Bushman population at around 25,000, but he noted that only some 6,000 lived by hunting and gathering and so should be classified as what he called 'wild' Bushmen, which he glossed as Bushmen who made their living by hunting and gathering, and who were permanently settled in remote areas of the Kalahari.[28]

Silberbauer's main proposal was that the government should establish a game reserve in the G/wi area, in which only 'wild' G/wi and, in the east of the reserve, some G//ana, would be allowed to hunt. The Government accepted this recommendation and the Central Kalahari Game Reserve was established in 1961 with a territory of 130,000 square kilometres, and an estimated Bushman population of some 3,000, although some hundreds of Kgalagari cattle-farmers also found themselves within its borders. The second largest game reserve in Africa, the Central Kalahari Game Reserve is about the same size as Bangladesh or Nepal, and larger than South Korea or Portugal.

The original policy was radically incoherent. Was this supposed to be a reserve for wild animals or for 'wild Bushmen'? And who could live there, and what rights would they enjoy? A few non-G/wi Bushmen migrated into the reserve, but they were not entirely welcome. What about the Kgalagari pastoralists who had herded their cattle there before the proclamation of the reserve? And what about the majority of Bushmen in the country, who had no claims there at all? When the Bechuanaland Protectorate became an independent state under the name of Botswana in 1966, its new political class was generally unsympathetic to the policy behind the Reserve, and tended to remark that there was a clear parallel with the Bantustan policy of the apartheid regime in South Africa. The Botswana government – like its colonial predecessor – was nevertheless prepared at first to make allowances in order to allay international concerns.

The situation in the Central Kalahari Game Reserve had, however, been changing.[29] Silberbauer himself had taken the radical step of sinking a borehole at his main camp at Xade in 1961. He was reluctant to let the Bushmen use it, but Xade, with its permanent water supply, became the centre of a new settlement after his own departure. The Botswana government built a school and clinic, and the residents of Xade began to farm and keep livestock. However, during the drought years of the late 1970s and early 1980s many people left the reserve, although perhaps intending to return. (/Gwi had long been accustomed to labour migration to the nearby Ghanzi farms when times were tough.) The population of the Reserve dropped from around 3,000 in the early 1960s to 1,300 in the mid 1980s, most of whom were settled in Xade. There were also significant numbers of Bantu-speaking Kgalagari people herding livestock within its borders.

In due course, the government developed a new policy. Two settlements were established outside the Reserve and provided with schools and clinics, and the Bushmen were encouraged to congregate there, with some success. There were two main reasons for the change in official thinking. First, environmentalists complained that residents were keeping donkeys and goats which interfered with the game, and that they were engaged in poaching. This was to turn the conventional appeal to environmental values against the Bushmen. Second, officials were committed to a national policy of bringing aid and development to what were called Remote Area Dwellers, a term coined precisely to avoid ethnic discrimination. Officials regarded the special provisions made for people in the Reserve as an expensive anomaly. 'We as Government simply believe that it is totally unfair to leave a portion of our citizens undeveloped under the pretext that we are allowing them to practise their culture',[30] a Minister of Local Government told the Botswana Centre for Human Rights in January 2002. Yet while senior members of government rejected the argument from culture, there was a feeling that the Bushmen were simply backward, and had to be civilised. The Permanent Secretary in the Ministry of Local Government was reported in the press as remarking, in terms which would have been familiar to his colonial predecessors, that 'Botswana owns the Basarwa and it will own Basarwa until it ceases to be a country; and they will never be allowed to walk around in skins again'.[31] President Mogwe himself commented that the San were 'stone age creatures' who might 'perish' like the dodo if they did not move with the times.[32]

In May and June 1997, over 1,100 people were moved in trucks to the new settlements outside the reserve, where the usual depressing concomitants of forced resettlement soon manifested themselves in the form of alcoholism, domestic violence, and the spread of petty crime. In November 2001 the government announced that it would no longer provide public services or welfare payments to anyone remaining in the Game Reserve. At this point five to six hundred people remained within its borders, a number that had been swelled by the return of disgruntled families who did not appreciate life in the new villages set up by the government. It was an appeal on their behalf for services to be restored that the court rejected in April 2002. These actions were taken in the face of international protests. Indeed, there was something of a backlash in government circles against the activities of NGOs, notably Survival International.[33] The Botswana government has concluded that some international agencies are proposing what amounts to a form of apartheid, and are sabotaging a rational policy of development.

On the face of it, the situation in the new South Africa is very different to that in Botswana. Bushmen, or San, within South Africa were generally believed to have died out or to have been assimilated by the late nineteenth century. Most of the Hottentots, or Khoi, had been acculturated to the so-called Coloured group, although there are some bilingual Afrikaans–Nama speakers in the northern Cape. Moreover, at the time of the political transition the ANC was unsympathetic to any movement of ethnic assertion within the country. In 1996, when he was Deputy President, Thabo Mbeki celebrated the Khoi and San as South Africa's first freedom fighters, but in the conviction that they had since passed from the scene.[34] The government was evidently caught by surprise when the indigenous peoples movement was taken up by UN agencies, and NGOs in South Africa began to champion the cause of the country's own indigenous peoples.

The first to achieve prominence was the Griqua movement, or rather movements, since there were competing organisations that claimed to speak for the Griqua people. The Griqua emerged on the frontier of the Cape colony in the late eighteenth century. At first they called themselves *Basters*, but the missionaries persuaded them to adopt a less shocking name. They were largely Khoi, or Hottentot, by ancestry, but they were Christians and spoke Dutch. Equipped with horses and guns, they operated as cattle ranchers and free-booters. In 1804 they settled under the auspices of the London Missionary Society at Klaarwater, later called Griquatown. In the course of the next generation the community split, there were various migrations, and treaties were made and abrogated with the Boer republics. Later in the nineteenth century, descendants of the original community, by now largely landless, were divided between three widely separated settlements, and increasingly assimilated into the broader Cape Coloured society.[35] Under apartheid, many Griquas were initially classified with the Bantu speakers, but they managed to get themselves reclassified as Coloureds, which was a more privileged situation. In the 1990s, however, some Griqua politicians declared that they were Khoi and San, and, therefore, indigenous people. They demanded restitution of ancestral lands and represen-tation in the House of Traditional Leaders. Support was forthcoming from the United Nations Indigenous Peoples' Forum.

The government was ready to treat with them, but became frustrated when the various Griqua spokesmen refused to agree on a single representative body for purposes of negotiation. To sort out the claims to leadership, officials consulted government anthro-pologists. Ironically, this was a return to the practices of the apartheid regime. These self-same government anthropologists had been accustomed to similar duties when they were employed by the Department of Bantu Affairs. Now, redeployed to the Department of Constitutional Development, they found themselves faced with the familiar task of identifying the traditional leader, although as it happens they were unsuccessful on this occasion. The rival claimants to the Griqua leadership only came together for brief official visits from Nelson Mandela or the American ambassador. Today the various Griqua settlements seem to have opted rather more enthusiastically for participation in evangelical Christian movements.[36]

On another front, however, the South African government did make a grand gesture. A ‡Khomani San Association was set up to make claims to rights in the Kalahari Gemsbok Park, another enormous game reserve, which had been proclaimed in 1931. There were only about a dozen people in South Africa who could still speak the ‡Khomani language, but the movement was strongly supported by an NGO based in Cape Town. Rather vaguely specified rights of 'ownership' in the park were symbolically handed over to the '‡Khomani people'. People classified as ‡Khomani were also allowed to graze stock in certain areas. This more specific and practical right was crucial. As Steven Robins has pointed out, while 'San livestock farmers are often perceived to be less authentically San by donors, for many Kalahari San, goats and sheep have been, and continue to be, their main strategy for survival.'[37] Unfortunately, these privileges have created tensions between those now classified as ‡Khomani and other local residents, who had been classified as 'Coloured' under apartheid. And just as under apartheid, people have been obliged to reformulate their ethnic identities in order to get access to resources. Another ethnographer reported that one informant 'says he is not a San, but he is part of them by virtue of his grandmother having been a "pure San", she had according to him the correct phenotypic features.'[38]

The change of ANC policy is at least in part a response to agitation by NGOs, with their international connections.[39] The government could not ignore these pressures while it harboured ambitions to be recognised as Africa's leading actor in the field of human rights. Moreover, ANC leaders were committed to gestures of restitution for the injustices of apartheid. Symbolic acts of solidarity with San are now popular, and on the occasion of South Africa's Sixth Freedom Day, on 27 April 2000, President Mbeki unveiled the new national coat of arms, which displayed at its centre two figures from a Bushman rock painting. Below is a text from an extinct Cape Bushman language, *!ke e: /xarra //ke*, which has been translated as 'Unity in Diversity', the motto of the New South Africa, although the precise meaning of this passage in an obscure, dead language is a matter of some scholarly controversy.[40] (The motto of the old Union of South Africa was Unity is Strength.) The advantages of this official gesture are nevertheless apparent enough. None of South Africa's eleven official languages is being privileged. The only ethnic group that is given special status has long vanished from the scene. And the new symbol may boost South Africa's reputation in the field of human rights, since in some circles today the litmus test is a government's policy on indigenous peoples.

Survival strategies

The indigenous peoples movement has been fostered by the UN and the World Bank, by international development agencies and NGOs. Despite the fact that the ideas behind the movement are very dubious, the motivation is surely generous. Whatever the reasons behind it, a grant of land to poor people may be a good thing, even if very large tracts of land are sometimes being handed over to extremely small communities – or rather, to small categories of people defined in terms of descent. But I am doubtful about the justice or good sense of most of these initiatives. Policies based on false analysis distract attention from real local issues. They are unlikely to promote the common good. And they will certainly create new problems. Wherever special land and hunting rights have been extended to so-called indigenous peoples, local ethnic frictions are exacerbated. These grants also foster appeals to uncomfortably racist criteria for favouring, or excluding, individuals or communities. New identities are fabricated, and spokespeople identified who are bound to be unrepresentative, and who might be effectively the creation of political parties and NGOs. These spokespeople demand recognition for alternative ways of understanding the world, but ironically enough they do so in the idiom of Western culture theory. Since the representations of identity are so far from the realities on the ground, and since the relative wealth of the NGOs and the locals is so disparate, these movements are unlikely to be democratic.

Some anthropologists have argued that although the rhetoric of indigenous peoples activists may come across as essentialist and romantic, it is effective, perhaps the only effective way of advancing the interests of these peoples. The arguments should be assessed in strategic terms, rather than treated as serious scholarly theses. Moreover, they are flexible, adapting to circumstance. Beth Conklin reports, for example, that the environmental arguments in favour of land grants to indigenous peoples have been discredited in Brazil. Indigenous leaders have been implicated in too many well-publicised instances of ecological vandalism. Some activists therefore prefer to emphasise the ancient folk wisdom of 'shamans'. Conklin explains that this allows them 'to construct new discourses about indigenous peoples' identities' by appealing to fashionable ideas about 'indigenous knowledge'. There are further advantages. Brazilian nationalists were reluctant to alienate vast swathes of forest to particular ethnic minorities, but they are happy to agree that native experts have some sort of collective copyright in ancient medical lore. Awkward questions about political representation can also be avoided. 'Whereas the figure of the "chief" can raise the empirically testable question of whether a certain individual has or deserves his people's support,' Conklin suggests, 'the figure of the shaman circumvents such questions'.[41] In other words, spiritual leaders are not required to be democrats.

The strategic argument is, however, unpersuasive, even in its own terms. As James Suzman remarks:

> The precarious status of San peoples in southern Africa, for example, shows first that it is not always possible to identify who is indigenous and who is not, secondly that those peoples best placed to claim the privileges due to indigenes are not necessarily those most in need of assistance, and thirdly that a focus on indigenousness may well reinforce the very structures of discrimination that disadvantage these peoples in the first place.[42]

In any case, anthropologists should surely not wish to pretend that they believe in ideas which they know very well are intellectually indefensible. Are they supposed to criticise Victorian evolutionism when it is invoked to justify discrimination against a minority group, but endorse it, or keep silent, when the same logic is used to support land claims on behalf of the same minority?

Why have these discredited ways of thinking become so influential once again? As always, our conceptions of the primitive are best understood as counters in our own current ideological debates. The image of the primitive is often constructed today to suit the Greens and the anti-globalisation movement. Authentic natives represent a world that is the opposite to our own (imagined here as rapaciously materialist). It is a world to which we should, apparently, wish to be returned, a world in which culture does not challenge nature. At the same time, the movement exploits the very general European belief that authentic citizenship must be based on ties of blood to ancestral soil. In Europe today, this principle is used to justify anti-immigrant policies. The obverse of this, however, is the painless concession that faraway natives should be allowed to hunt in their own Bantustans. And so the indigenous peoples movement garners support across the political spectrum for a variety of different, even contradictory reasons. (The founder of Survival International, Robin Hanbury-Tennison, recently achieved new prominence as chief executive of the Countrywide Alliance, a movement formed to oppose the banning of fox hunting in Britain.) But whatever the political inspiration, the conventional lines of argument currently used to justify 'indigenous' land claims rely on obsolete anthropological notions and on a romantic and false ethnographic vision. Fostering essentialist ideologies of culture and identity, they may have dangerous political consequences.

Chapter 11

Conclusion

The idea of primitive social structure that crystallised in the late nineteenth century was remarkably simple. Primitive society was originally an organic whole. It then split into two or more identical blocks, made up of exogamous, corporate descent groups. There were no families. Women and goods were held in common by the men of each group. Marriage took the form of regular exchanges between them.

Anthropologists worked on this conception for more than a century. The prototype of primitive society became an ideal type, which directed and ordered empirical studies. Finally it evolved into a model that lent itself to formal manipulation, particularly in the field of kinship studies. Kinship itself became the technical core of social anthropology. At least until the 1970s, it was the insiders' special field, the least accessible, the most jargon-ridden, the most apt to use abstract models. It was perhaps an even more surprising construct than primitive society. An accidental by-product of Morgan's philology, it depended on the unlikely premises that all kinship terminologies were readily classified in a few broad types, and that they reflected long-dead practices, in particular, marriage forms. However, kinship models lent themselves to the most dazzling play of variations and so helped to sustain scientific interest in the structure of primitive society.

It went without saying that primitive society had an appropriate religion, and it was widely agreed that this was totemism or fetishism, a form of nature worship, or the worship of animals or plants as ancestors. Fustel thought that religion was the source of all social forms. Durkheim protested that it reflected social institutions. Boas tried to show that the clans, exogamy and totems were quite distinct, and might have nothing to do with each other. Finally, after almost exactly a century of speculation and debate, Lévi-Strauss recast totemism as a universal way of thinking about Nature and Society, draining it of any specifically religious character. But if totemism has lost its old status, animism lives on in the census reports of many Third World countries. (So many Christians, so many Muslims, so many 'animists'.) However, today it is 'shamanism' which is widely thought of as the original and natural religion. A New Age cult for the Old World, it promises personal communion with the other world, and it is studied more enthusiastically as a source of spiritual rather than sociological insights.

Theories of the origin of private property and the state have changed less radically. Maine, Morgan, Engels and many twentieth-century archaeologists shared the same basic assumptions. The original primitive societies were anarchic, or perhaps democratic, or maybe they were patriarchal dictatorships. Certainly they practised communism. However, as agriculture developed, kin-based commun-ities gave way to territorially-based associations, which gradually grew into states, or which were conquered and subjugated by more advanced neighbours. Nevertheless, there were endless debates about what, precisely, constituted a state, a primitive state, or an 'early state'.[1]

The only part of the original vision to survive virtually unques-tioned was the thesis that primitive societies lived in a self-regulating symbiotic relationship with nature. In the 1960s, a whole school of American anthropologists tried to show that social arrangements, rituals, beliefs and economic practices formed a perpetual motion machine that miraculously maintained a perfect balance between human beings and the natural environment. Shamans knew all about it. Any untoward developments were written off as the fault of outsiders, although the grim story of the self-immolation of the isolated society of Easter Island might serve as a counter example, should one be needed.[2] In any case, this is the image of primitive society that is most potent today, in an age of great anxiety about the environment.

Out of the box

To be sure, there were debates, some quite ferocious, challenges to the orthodoxy, at times radical, but the prototype proved to be remarkably resilient. Even when it was set against ethnographic descriptions, reality did sometimes seem to match up (most famously in Evans-Pritchard's account of the Nuer). Where there were obvious discrepancies, a particular society could be presented as a local variant or a transitional form. In the USA, however, Franz Boas and his students produced a barrage of ethnographic counter examples that were specifically designed to blow away the props that underpinned Morgan's model (which had become almost an official doctrine, institutionalised in the Bureau of American Ethnology at the Smithsonian Institution in Washington DC). Lowie's textbooks, published in the 1920s, summed up a generation of anti-evolutionist criticism from the Boas school: the family was universal; territorial bonds were always significant; matrilineal societies were not necessarily less developed than patrilineal societies; totemism was a fantasy.[3] A cautious man, Lowie hung on to some of the older ideas (notably the reflectionist theory of kin terms), but he wrote as a successful revolutionary, or so he believed.

At the London School of Economics, Westermarck presented a different critique of Victorian theories of the family. Unlike Boas, Westermarck wrote as a Darwinian. He criticised Morgan and McLennan not as evolutionists but as false evolutionists. In the 1920s, his young colleague Bronislaw Malinowski introduced a more realistic, individualist sociology as an alternative to the accepted notion that primitive peoples operated only in groups. To understand what was going on it was vital to understand individual motives and tactics, and to appreciate that actions were liable to diverge from stated ideals. Even among the matrilineal Trobrianders, relationships between fathers and children counted in practice for a great deal, despite the fact that the people evidently denied the father's role in procreation. Nor did the natives bother much with theological speculations. What mattered was practical magic, which alleviated anxieties. Social practices were ways of getting things done.

Terms of reference

By the early 1920s, the Victorian theory of primitive society was in a poor state of repair. When it was taught in the more advanced university departments of anthropology, it was presented only to be demolished. Grounded in ethnographic studies, the critique seemed to carry all before it. And yet while the old orthodoxy was down, it was not out. One problem with the criticisms of the Boasians and of Malinowski was that however cogent their objections to orthodox propositions, they did not seem to offer any coherent alternative.

Boas was criticised for always fussing about details and never thinking about the big picture, Malinowski for not providing a systematic model of kinship.[4] It is true that while Boas stuck with the old issues, Malinowski did sometimes argue that the questions themselves were wholly misleading, but his students could not escape the demand for systematic accounts of primitive types of social system. Malinowski himself was always ready to make large comparisons between savages and civilised people, or at least with businessmen in Vienna or London, even if his intention was to suggest that they had a great deal in common.

In the end, the critiques of Boas and Malinowski were not decisive because they could not displace the terms of reference that had been established within the anthropological tradition. There was also the accident that both Boas and Malinowski died during World War Two. In Britain, Radcliffe-Brown, Fortes and Evans-Pritchard resuscitated the ideas of Maine and Durkheim, and even of Fustel and Robertson Smith, although they purged their theories of evolutionist residues. Lévi-Strauss reanimated some features of Morgan's kinship theory. In the USA, Leslie White, Julian Steward and G. P. Murdock revived other aspects of his programme, and they found support in the coming generation. There was a 'band' type of society, a 'peasant' type, and so on, in each of which a particular kind of technology generated appropriate forms of social and political relationship. The features that the new generation of American evolutionists emphasised were again rather traditional; kin-groups were contrasted with territorial groups, the mode of descent was regarded as crucial, and (in the more Marxist examples) special attention was paid to the emergence of social stratification. Murdock, no Marxist, revived Tylor's methods and Morgan's preoccupations. These American scholars effectively continued the old tradition of American anthropology, blocking out the Boasian intervention. In effect, they all retained the prototype of primitive society, but used it as a model with which to analyse particular ethnographic cases.

Three factors explain why the classic idea of primitive society was so 'good to think'. The theory generated a specialised tradition of puzzle-solving; it yielded a succession of transformations that could accommodate any special interests; and it referred to ultimate social concerns – the state, citizenship, the family and so on. It did not, however, impose particular political conclusions. The idea of primitive society served imperialists and nationalists, anarchists and

Marxists, and now it is proving helpful to the Green movement. Any ideological current could use primitive society as a foil because primitive society is the mirror image of modern society or, rather, primitive society inverts some strategically significant features that are attributed to modern society. Both terms of the opposition are equally imaginary, but they sustain each other. It turns out that the idea of primitive society is perhaps even more potent when projected against an image of the future, a future in which, so we are told, we will all inhabit a global village, set in a wasteland.

Whatever the reasons for its persistence, the theory was hard to shake. Ethnographic counter-instances could be dismissed as interesting exceptions. New theoretical propositions were introduced, but they yielded reformulations of old ideas. The primitive himself was rebranded, as labels like barbarian, savage, primitive, or even 'stone age' came to seem insulting. For a time 'preliterate' was a favourite euphemism, which must have pleased the shade of Thomas Aquinas. Today a politically correct alternative is available in the term 'indigenous people'. But the barbarian is still the same person, the eternal Mr Hyde to our Dr Jekyll. Love him or loathe him.

Research on hunter-gatherers – or former hunter-gatherers – and pastoral nomads is still infused by the classic conceptions, and as Evie Plaice remarks, anthropology may be in some danger of becoming 'the academic wing of the indigenous rights movement, whose role is to advocate the rights of vulnerable cultural minorities'.[5] The old ideas are also staples of popular culture. TV programmes regularly pretend to document the final hopeless resistance of 'vanishing peoples', the last survivors of the stone age.

However, this branch of anthropology seems to have parted company from the mainstream. Anthropology can no longer be defined as the study of primitive societies. This is not necessarily because primitive society is universally recognised to be a fiction. Rather, anthropologists have changed the subject. Cultural and social anthropology today has very largely abandoned the study of social institutions. American anthropologists typically define their discipline as the study of culture, by which they mean systems of values and symbolic representations,[6] and they struggle, probably unavailingly, to assert a proprietary interest in this glamorous if slippery property. However, since they preach that every culture has equal value, they are inclined to regard any attempt to distinguish 'primitive culture' from 'civilisation' as not only mistaken but oppressive. Meanwhile, on the margins, there is a third tradition of anthropology, which pays special attention to biological processes and claims to be the true heir to the programme of Darwin. It too has imperial designs, and it is colonising some of the deserted strongholds of the theory of primitive society.

My own hope is that although certain things have been done badly in the past, we may still aspire to do them better in the future. There is room enough for more sociologically sophisticated accounts of societies very different from those that we imagine we know in the modern, industrial, west. Families, patterns of intermarriage, kinship networks, settlement patterns, political processes, religious practices, ecological relations, all require accurate description and analysis. The best contemporary ethnographies situate the small-scale communities or networks that they study in their relationships with neighbours and with the state, and they take into account regional and international migrations and economic processes. Social anthropology can still aspire to extend the range of the social sciences by testing their propositions in other conditions. Ethnographers should engage ethnocentric social scientists in discussions about the less familiar social processes and views of the world that they have studied. Perhaps as we come to know others better, as people with similar capacities, forming societies of a comparable sort, faced with common dilemmas, we may also understand more about ourselves.

However, this book is intended as a historical critique rather than a programme for future research. 'One practises science – and above all sociology – against the grain of one's education as much as with it', Pierre Bourdieu wrote. 'And only history can free us from history.'[7] My aim has been to loosen the bonds of our history by making explicit one particular theoretical tradition, and by demonstrating the way in which it has held us in its grip.

Notes

Preface

1 This is based on a paper I published in *Current Anthropology* in 2003, but draws also on the debates that followed.
2 Adam Kuper, *The Chosen Primate*, 1994.

I The myth of primitive society

1 E. B. Tylor, 1865, *Researches into the Early History of Mankind*, p. 277.
2 See J. W. Burrow, 1981, *A Liberal Descent: Victorian Historians and the English Past*.
3 Richard Klein, 1989, *The Human Career*.
4 Lewis Binford, 1989, 'Isolating the transition to cultural adaptations' in E. Trinkhaus (ed.) *The Emergence of Modern Humans*, pp. 35–6.
5 Richard Lee and Irven DeVore (eds) 1968, *Man the Hunter*, p. ix.
6 R. B. Lee, 1979, *The !Kung San: Men, Women and Work in a Foraging Society*.
7 Marshall Sahlins, 1972, 'The original affluent society' in Sahlins *Stone Age Economics*, Chapter 1.
8 These theories were launched in Lee and DeVore, *Man the Hunter*.
9 Edwin N. Wilmsen, 1989, *Land Filled With Flies: A Political Economy of the Kalahari*.
10 See Alan Barnard, 1992, *Hunters and Herders of Southern Africa*.
11 George W. Stocking, Jr, 1987, *Victorian Anthropology*, Chapter 7.
12 Claude Lévi-Strauss, 1981, *The Naked Man*, p. 675.
13 Claude Lévi-Strauss, 1963, *Structural Anthropology*, p. 230.
14 Henry Maine, 1883, *Dissertations on Early Law and Custom*, pp. 218–19.
15 Howard E. Gruber, 1974, *Darwin on Man*, p. 281.
16 Adrian Desmond and James Moore, 1991, *Darwin*, p. 250.
17 Charles Darwin, 1871, *The Descent of Man, and Selection in Relation to Sex*, p. 81.
18 Darwin, *Descent of Man*, p. 906.
19 Darwin, *Descent of Man*, p. 196.
20 Darwin, *Descent of Man*, p. 199.
21 Darwin, *Descent of Man*, p. 220.
22 Darwin, *Descent of Man*, p. 200.

23 Darwin, *Descent of Man*, p. 203.
24 Darwin, *Descent of Man*, pp. 195–6.
25 J. W. Burrow, 1966, *Evolution and Society*, p. 114.
26 Janet Browne, 2002, *Charles Darwin: The Power of Place*, p. 94.
27 For a full account of the famous Oxford meeting see Janet Browne, *Charles Darwin: The Power of Place*, pp. 118–25.
28 Burrow, *Evolution and Society*, p. 115.
29 R. R. Marett, 1936, *Tylor*, p. 19.
30 The index to the authoritative biography, Robert Ackerman's (1987) *J. G. Frazer*, has only three glancing references to Darwin.
31 R. R. Marett, 1911, *Anthropology*, pp. 8–9.
32 See Peter J. Bowler, 1983, *The Eclipse of Darwinism*.
33 Quoted in L. J. Jordanova, 1984, *Lamarck*, p. 106.
34 George W. Stocking, 1987, *Victorian Anthropology*, Chapter 5.
35 Darwin, *Descent of Man*, p. 224.

2 Barbarian, savage, primitive

1 Thucydides, 431 BCE, *History of the Peloponnesian War*, Book 1, Chapter 1. (Trans. Richard Crawley.) Simon Hornblower, however, points out that 'barbarian-speaking Karians' are mentioned in the Iliad (ii. 867). See Hornblower, 1991, *A Commentary on Thucydides*, Vol. 1, p. 17.
2 Edith Hall, 1989, *Inventing the Barbarian: Greek Self-definition through Tragedy*, p. 1.
3 See Simon Hornblower, 2004, 'Herodotus' in Adam and Jessica Kuper (eds) *The Social Science Encyclopedia*, 3rd edition.
4 François Hartog, 1988, *The Mirror of Herodotus: The Representation of the Other in the Writing of History*.
5 Herodotus, *History*, 2.35.
6 Hartog, *The Mirror of Herodotus*, p. 324.
7 Aristotle, 350 BCE, *Politics. Book 1 Part l, and Book Three Part XIV*. Translated by Benjamin Jowett.
8 Edith Hall 1996 (commentary), *Aeschylus Persians*.
9 Edith Hall, *The Invention of the Barbarian*, pp. 211–23.
10 Aristotle, *Politics*, II.
11 Michel de Montaigne, 1578, 'Of cannibals', *The Complete Works of Montaigne*, translated by Donald M. Frame, 1948, p. 152.
12 Montaigne, 'Of cannibals', p. 153.
13 Montaigne, 'Of cannibals', p. 156.
14 Michael Wintroub, 1998, 'Civilizing the savage and making a king: the royal entry festival of Henri II'.
15 Montaigne, 'Of cannibals', p. 159.
16 Montaigne, 'Of cannibals', p. 150.
17 Edward Gibbon (1741 edition), *The History of the Decline and Fall of the Roman Empire*, Chapter 51, p. 464, footnote to the discussion of the Berbers.
18 Aristotle, *Politics*, Book 1, Part l.
19 A. O. Lovejoy and G. Boas, 1935, *Primitivism and Related Ideas in Antiquity*.
20 Cited by W. R. Jones, 1971, *The Image of the Barbarian in Medieval Europe*, p. 382.

21 See Anthony Pagden, 1982, *The Fall of Natural Man: The American Indian and the Origins of Comparative Ethnology*, especially Chapters 6 and 7.
22 See Pagden, *The Fall of Natural Man*, and Margaret T. Hodgen, 1964, *Early Anthropology in the Sixteenth and Seventeenth Centuries*.
23 Thomas Hobbes, 1660, *Leviathan*, III, 114.
24 Hobbes, *Leviathan*, Part 1, Chapter XIII, II.
25 John Locke, 1690, *The Second Treatise of Civil Government*, Chapter 5, paragraph 49.
26 Denis Diderot, 1773, *Supplément au Voyage de Bougainville*.
27 See Jean Starobinski, 1993, 'The word *civilization*' in *Blessings in Disguise*.
28 Montesquieu [1748] 1914, *Spirit of the Laws*, Book XVIII, II.
29 Auguste Comte [1839] 1983, *Auguste Comte and Positivism: The Essential Writings*, p. 71.
30 Cited by Ronald L. Meek, 1976, *Social Science and the Ignoble Savage*, which discusses the development of the four-stage theory.
31 William Robertson, 1777, *The History of the Discovery and Settlement of America*.
32 Adam Ferguson, 1767, *An Essay on the History of Civil Society*, Part 2, Section 1.
33 For a full account of the encounter between Darwin and the Fuegians, see Nick Hazelwood, 2000, *Savage: The Life and Times of Jemmy Button*.
34 Robert Fitzroy (ed.) 1839, *Narrative of the Surveying Voyages of H.M.S. Adventure and Beagle Between the Years 1826 and 1836*, pp. 120–2.
35 Charles Darwin, 1974, *The Descent of Man*, 2nd edition, pp. 919–20.
36 Nick Hazelwood, 2000, *Savage: The Life and Times of Jeremy Button*, citation p. 67.
37 F. Burckhardt and S. Smith (eds), 1984, *The Correspondence of Charles Darwin*, Vol. 1 (1821–1836), p. 434.
38 R. D. Keynes (ed.) 1979, *The Beagle Record*, pp. 222–3.
39 Charles Darwin, 1839, *Journal of Researches into the Geology and Natural History of the Various Countries visited by H.M.S. 'Beagle'*, Chapter X.
40 R. D. Keynes (ed.), 1988, *Charles Darwin's Beagle Diary*, p. 223.
41 Keynes, *Beagle Record*, pp. 222–4.
42 Keynes, *Beagle Record*, pp. 141–2.
43 Keynes, *Beagle Record*, p. 221.
44 FitzRoy, *Narrative*, pp. 323–7.
45 Keynes, *Beagle Record*, p. 221.
46 Darwin, *Journal of Researches*, Chapter X.
47 Keynes (ed.), *Diary*, p. 384.
48 Frederick Burkhardt *et al.* (eds), 1997, *The Correspondence of Charles Darwin*, Vol. 10, p. 71.
49 Janet Browne, 1995, *Charles Darwin: Voyaging*, p. 382.
50 Darwin, *Descent of Man*, p. 276.

3 Henry Maine's patriarchal theory

1 Maine's early life is poorly documented. Lady Maine destroyed her husband's papers and threw away his letters from famous writers after cutting off their signatures for sale. There was no typical Victorian 'Life and Letters'. The *Life*

and Speeches of Sir Henry Maine by W. Stokes contains only a brief memoir as preface to long extracts from his speeches. However, an excellent modern biography was published in 1969 by George Feaver, *From Status to Contract: A Biography of Sir Henry Maine, 1822–1888*. His contribution to legal scholarship is described by R. C. J. Cocks in *Sir Henry Maine: A Study in Victorian Jurisprudence* (1988). A conference was held to mark Maine's centenary, in 1988, which resulted in a book edited by Alan Diamond and published under the title *The Victorian Achievement of Sir Henry Maine* (1991). It presents appraisals of various aspects of his career.

2 J. W. Burrow, 1974, 'The village community and the uses of history in late 19th century England', in Neil McKendrick (ed.) *Historical Perspectives: Studies in English Thought and Society*, p. 255.

3 I have drawn heavily on E. Stokes (1959), *The English Utilitarians and India*. See also Gordon Johnson, 'India and Henry Maine', and C. A. Bayly, 'Maine and change in nineteenth century India', both in Alan Diamond (ed.), 1991, *The Victorian Achievement of Sir Henry Maine*.

4 Stokes took this striking remark as the motto for his *English Utilitarians and India*.

5 James Mill, 1817, *The History of British India*, Vol. 2, p. 167.

6 Cited by Stokes, *English Utilitarians and India*, p. 219.

7 Cited by Feaver, *From Status to Contract*, pp. 102–3.

8 Maine's debt to these writers is discussed in Vinogradoff, 1904, *The Teaching of Sir Henry Maine*, Cocks, 1988, *Sir Henry Maine: A Study in Victorian Jurisprudence*, and Peter Stein, 1980, *Legal Evolution: The Story of an Idea*. For a lucid account of Savigny's career and ideas see Kantorowicz, 1937, 'Savigny and the historical school of law', and also M. Smith, 1895, 'Four German jurists', which discusses Jhering. See P. Atiyah, 1979, *The Rise and Fall of Freedom of Contract*, for an assessment of the central arguments.

9 See J. W. Burrow, 1981, *A Liberal Descent: Victorian Historians and the English Past*.

10 In his essay on the 'German school of history', published in 1886, Lord Acton identified Maine, with Savigny, Grimm, Humboldt and Ritter, as a leading figure of this 'school'. 'They trifled for a time with fancy, but they doubled the horizons of Europe. They admitted India to an equality with Greece, mediaeval Rome with classical.' Reprinted in Acton, 1907, *Historical Essays and Studies*, p. 346.

11 Henry Maine, 1861, *Ancient Law*, p. 76.

12 *Ancient Law*, p. 85.

13 *Ancient Law*, p. 88.

14 *Ancient Law*, p. 116.

15 *Ancient Law*, p. 118.

16 Loc. cit.

17 James Mill, 1817, *History of British India*, Vol. 1, p. 146.

18 John Kemble, 1849, *The Saxons in England*, pp. 56–7.

19 *Ancient Law*, p. 141.

20 *Ancient Law*, p. 143.

21 *Ancient Law*, p. 145.

22 *Ancient Law*, p. 124.

23 *Ancient Law*, p. 125.

24 *Ancient Law*, pp. 127–8.

25 *Ancient Law*, p. 163.

26 *Ancient Law*, p. 165.
27 *Ancient Law*, pp. 7–8.
28 L. Fuller, 1967, *Legal Fictions*, gives an account of Bentham's and Maine's theories. The citations from Bentham are taken from Fuller.
29 See Fuller, *Legal Fictions*, pp. 59–63.
30 *Ancient Law*, p. 25.
31 *Ancient Law*, p. 252.
32 Clive Dewey, 1991, 'The influence of Sir Henry Maine on agrarian policy in India', in Alan Diamond (ed.) *The Victorian Achievement of Sir Henry Maine*.
33 Quoted in Feaver, *From Status to Contract*, p. 25.
34 *Ancient Law*, p. 252.
35 G. Campbell, 1852, *Modern India: A Sketch of the System of Civil Government*, p. 86.
36 Feaver, *From Status to Contract*, p. 179.
37 Feaver, *From Status to Contract*, p. 73.
38 Feaver, *From Status to Contract*, pp. 87–8.
39 Feaver, *From Status to Contract*, p. 90.
40 Louis Dumont, 1966, 'The "village community" from Munro to Maine' p. 85. Cf. Dewey, 1972, 'Images of the village community' and Srinivas, 1975, 'The Indian village: myth and reality'.
41 Dewey, 'The influence of Maine on agrarian policy in India', p. 359.
42 See Vinogradoff, 1892, *Villainage in England*. Cf. Meinhard, 1975, 'The matrilineal principle in early Teutonic kinship'.
43 Fustel de Coulanges, *La Cité Antique*, p. 3.
44 Fustel de Coulanges, *La Cité Antique*, p. 41.
45 Fustel de Coulanges, *La Cité Antique*, p. 60.
46 Fustel de Coulanges, *La Cité Antique*, p. 58.
47 Fustel de Coulanges, *La Cité Antique*, p. 96.
48 Fustel de Coulanges, *La Cité Antique*, p. 135.
49 Fustel de Coulanges, *La Cité Antique*, p. 149.
50 Fustel de Coulanges, *La Cité Antique*, p. 265.
51 Fustel de Coulanges, *La Cité Antique*, p. 464.
52 A. D. Momigliano, [1970] 1994, 'The ancient city of Fustel de Coulanges', Sally Humphreys, 1983, *Family, Women and Death: Comparative Studies*.
53 E. Durkheim [1893] 1915, *The Division of Labour in Society*, p. 154.
54 R. A. Jones, 1993, 'Durkheim and La Cité antique: an essay on the origins of Durkheim's sociology of religion'.
55 Tylor's obituary appeared in *The Academy* in 1881. *Primitive Marriage* was reprinted together with other essays under the title *Studies in Ancient History* in 1876. (That is the edition used here.) In 1885, McLennan's brother edited and completed further writings and published them under the title *Patriarchal Theory*.
56 In a chapter dealing with Bachofen in his *Studies in Ancient History* (1876), McLennan charged that Bachofen was 'mystic' and unreadable, and counselled readers to consult Giraud-Teulon's French summary of Bachofen's argument (*La mère chez certains people de l'antiquité*, 1867). Giraud-Teulon for his part cited Baron Eckstein as a predecessor of Bachofen. Ferdinand Eckstein (1790–1861) studied philology and Sanskrit in Germany early in the nineteenth century and wrote books about German and Indian history.
57 J. F. McLennan, 1876, *Studies in Ancient History*, p. 132.

58 McLennan, *Primitive Marriage*, p. 196.
59 McLennan, *Primitive Marriage*, p. 333.
60 Peter Rivière, 1970, 'Introduction' to McLennan's *Primitive Marriage*, pp. xxxiii and xxxv.
61 McLennan, *Studies in Ancient History*, pp. xiv–xv.
62 McLennan, *Studies in Ancient History*, p.7.
63 Maine, 1883, *Dissertations on Early Law and Custom*, pp. 199–200.
64 Maine, 1875, *Lectures on the Early History of Institutions*, p. 67.
65 Maine, *Dissertations on Early Law and Custom*, pp. 199–200.
66 Maine, *Dissertations on Early Law and Custom*, p. 209.

4 Lewis Henry Morgan and *Ancient Society*

1 See Blake McKelvey, 1946, 'When science was on trial in Rochester: 1850–1890'.
2 J. S.McIlvaine, 1923, 'The life and works of Lewis H. Morgan, LL.D.: an address at his funeral', p. 57.
3 See Winthorp Hudson, 1965, *Religion in America*; James Moore, 1979, *The Post-Darwinian Controversies*, and R. Wilson, 1967, *Darwin and the American Intellectuals*.
4 Quoted in Hudson, *Religion in America*, p. 267.
5 McIlvaine, 'The life and works of Lewis H. Morgan', p. 56.
6 See William Stanton, 1960, *The Leopard's Spots: Scientific Attitudes toward Race in America 1815–1859*.
7 See Ernst Mayr, 1959, 'Agassiz, Darwin and evolution'. The citation from Agassiz occurs on p. 171.
8 Lewis Henry Morgan, 1868, *The American Beaver and His Works*.
9 See Peter Bowler, 1975, 'The changing meaning of "evolution"'.
10 Charles Darwin, 1859, *The Origin of Species*, p. 314.
11 J. S. McIlvaine, 1867, 'Malthusianism'.
12 McIlvaine, 'The life and works of Lewis H. Morgan'.
13 See C. Resek, 1960, *Lewis Henry Morgan*, p. 9.
14 See R. Bieder, 1980, 'The Grand Order of the Iroquois: influences on Lewis Henry Morgan's ethnology', and Thomas R. Trautmann, 1987, *Lewis Henry Morgan and the Invention of Kinship*, Chapter 3.
15 George Grote, 1851 (3rd edition), *History of Greece*.
16 Lewis Henry Morgan, 1851, *League of the Ho-de-no-sau-nee, or Iroquois*, pp. 56–7.
17 Morgan, *The League of the Iroquois*, p. 81.
18 L. White, 1957, 'How Morgan came to write *Systems of Consanguinity and Affinity*', p. 257.
19 Op. cit., p. 262.
20 See Blake McKelvey, 1946, 'When science was on trial in Rochester: 1850–1890'.
21 Lewis Henry Morgan, 1871, *Systems of Consanguinity and Affinity of the Human Family*, p. 3.
22 Cited in Bernard J. Stern, 1931, *Lewis Henry Morgan*, p. 73.

23 Samuel Haven, 1856, 'Archaeology of the United States', *Smithsonian Contributions to Knowledge*, VIII, pp. 1–168.
24 Haven, 'Archaeology of the United States', p. 65.
25 Haven, 'Archaeology of the United States', p. 67. This was a simplification. For a sophisticated contemporary discussion of agglutination, see Max Müller, 1861, *Lectures on the Science of Language*, especially Chapter 8.
26 Haven, 'Archaeology of the United States', pp. 158–9.
27 Müller in Bunsen, 1854, *Outlines of the Philosophy of Universal History, Applied to Language and Religion*, Vol. 1, p. 478.
28 McIlvaine, 'The life and works of Lewis H. Morgan', pp. 50–1.
29 Stern, *Lewis Henry Morgan*, p. 27.
30 Morgan, *Systems of Consanguinity and Affinity of the Human Family*, p. 508.
31 Morgan, *Systems of Consanguinity and Affinity of the Human Family*, p. 12.
32 Morgan, *Systems of Consanguinity and Affinity of the Human Family*, p. 472.
33 Quoted by Resek, *Lewis Henry Morgan*, pp. 96–7.
34 McIlvaine, 'The life and works of Lewis H. Morgan', pp. 51–2.
35 Quoted in Resek, *Lewis Henry Morgan*, p. 94.
36 Resek, *Lewis Henry Morgan*, p. 92.
37 Thomas R. Trautmann, 1987, *Lewis Henry Morgan and the Invention of Kinship*, pp. 158–68.
38 Quoted in Resek, *Lewis Henry Morgan*, p. 98.
39 Morgan, 1868, 'A conjectural solution of the origin of the classificatory system of relationship', p. 465.
40 Morgan, *Systems of Consanguinity and Affinity*, p. 481.
41 Morgan, *Systems of Consanguinity and Affinity*, p. 492.
42 Morgan, 'A conjectural solution of the origin of the classificatory system of relationship', pp. 463–4.
43 McKelvey, 'When science was on trial in Rochester', pp. 11–12.
44 Lewis Henry Morgan, 1877, *Ancient Society*, p. 6.
45 Morgan, *Ancient Society*, p. 12.
46 *Ancient Society*, p. 533.
47 Stern, *Lewis Henry Morgan*, p. 141.
48 Morgan, *Ancient Society*, p. 186.
49 Morgan, *Ancient Society*, pp. 186–7, footnote.
50 Morgan, *Ancient Society*, p. 222.
51 Morgan, *Ancient Society*, p. 247.
52 Morgan, *Ancient Society*, p. 340.
53 Morgan, *Ancient Society*, p. 341.
54 Morgan, *Ancient Society*, p. 554.
55 See A. Bailey and J. Llobera, 1981, *The Asiatic Mode of Production*.
56 See L. Krader, 1974, *The Ethnological Notebooks of Karl Marx*.
57 Preface to *The Origin of the Family, Private Property and the State*, originally published in German in 1884.
58 Engels, *The Origin of the Family, Private Property and the State*, 1972 English edition, p. 128.
59 Engels, *The Origin of the Family, Private Property and the State*, pp. 145–6.
60 McLennan, 1876, *Studies in Ancient History*, p. 366.

5 The question of totemism

1 K. Theodore Hoppen, 1998, *The Mid-Victorian Generation: 1846–1886*, p. 427.
2 O. Chadwick, 1970, *The Victorian Church*, Vol. 2, p. 35.
3 See George W. Stocking, Jr, 1987, *Victorian Anthropology*, pp. 150–6.
4 Quoted by Burrow, 1966, *Evolution and Society*, pp. 228–9.
5 Stocking, *Victorian Anthropology*, pp. 157–8.
6 Tylor, *Primitive Culture*, Vol. 2, p. 12.
7 Tylor, *Primitive Culture*, p. 84.
8 E. B. Tylor, 1866, 'The religion of savages', p. 77.
9 This famous definition is given in the opening sentence of Tylor's *Primitive Culture*.
10 See Adam Kuper, 1999, *Culture: The Anthropologists' Account*, Chapter 1.
11 Andrew Lang in H. Balfour *et al.*, 1907, *Anthropological Essays Presented to E. B. Tylor*.
12 R. A. Downie, *Frazer and the Golden Bough*, p. 76.
13 J. F. McLennan, 1869, 'The worship of animals and plants, Part 1, p. 422.
14 Grey's remarkably concise description specified: '1st. That children of either sex, always take the family name of their mother. 2nd. That a man cannot marry a woman of his own family name.' He also remarked that each 'family' had an animal or vegetable crest, a *kobong*, and commented: 'A certain mysterious connection exists between a family and its *kobong*, so that a member of the family will never kill an animal of the species to which the *kobong* belongs.' George Grey, 1841, *Journals of Two Expeditions of Discovery in North-Western Australia*, Vol. 2, pp. 226–8.
15 See John Black and George Chrystal, 1912, *The Life of William Robertson Smith*.
16 Julius Wellhausen [1883] 1885, *Prolegomena to the History of Israel*.
17 Robertson Smith, 1889, *Religion of the Semites*, p. 86.
18 Robertson Smith, *Religion of the Semites*, p. 88.
19 Robertson Smith, *Religion of the Semites*, p. 84.
20 Cited in T. Beidelman, 1974, *W. Robertson Smith*, p. 21.
21 Robertson Smith, 1885, *Kinship and Marriage in Early Arabia*, pp. 187–8.
22 Robertson Smith, *Religion of the Semites*, p. 214.
23 Robertson Smith, *Religion of the Semites*, p. 18.
24 Robertson Smith, *Religion of the Semites*, p. 85.
25 Robertson Smith, *Religion of the Semites*, p. 53.
26 Robertson Smith, *Religion of the Semites*, p. 243 and p. 271.
27 Robertson Smith, *Religion of the Semites*, p. 294.
28 Roberston Smith, *Religion of the Semites*, p. 345.
29 Robertson Smith, *Religion of the Semites* (1st edition) p. 393.
30 J. G. Frazer, 1894, 'William Robertson Smith', pp. 800–7.
31 Robert Ackerman, 1987, *J. G. Frazer: His Life and Work*, p. 60.
32 T. O. Beidelman, *W. Robertson Smith*, p. 24.
33 Baldwin Spencer, 1928, *Wanderings in Wild Australia*, Vol. 1, p. 184.
34 J. G. Frazer, 1887, *Totemism*, p. 3.
35 Frazer, *Totemism*, p. 95.
36 Wilhelm Mannhardt, 1875, *Der Baumkultus der Germanen und ihrer Nachbarstämme*.
37 Frazer, *The Golden Bough*, Vol. 2, p. 363.

38 Frazer, 1900, 2nd edition of *The Golden Bough*, Vol. 1, p. 3. Cf. R. Ackermann, 1975, 'Frazer on myth and ritual'.

39 Bernard J. Stern, 1930, 'Selections from the letters of Lorimer Fison and A. W. Hotitt to Lewis Henry Morgan', p. 271.

40 R. R. Marett and T. K. Penniman (eds) 1932, *Spencer's Scientific Correspondence with Sir J. G. Frazer*, p. 22.

41 For a good account of Fison's research in Australia see L. R. Hiatt, 1996, *Arguments about Aborigines*, pp. 41–6.

42 See B. Stern, 1930, 'Selections from the letters of Lorimer Fison and A. W. Howitt to Lewis Henry Morgan'.

43 Lorimer Fison and A. W. Howitt, 1880, *Kamilaroi and Kurnai*, p. 23.

44 Fison and Howitt, *Kamilaroi and Kurnai*, p. 32.

45 Fison and Howitt, *Kamilaroi and Kurnai*, p. 40.

46 L. R. Hiatt argues, however, 'that *de facto* group marriage occurred on a small scale among the Aborigines, never as a total system of the kind postulated by Fison and Howitt but as an option, usually informal but sometimes formal, within regimes favouring polygyny. Undoubtedly kin classification of the Australian type was compatible with it, and might even be said to have been conducive to it.' L. R. Hiatt, 1996, *Arguments about Aborigines*, p. 55.

47 Fison and Howitt, *Kamilaroi and Kurnai*, p. 29.

48 Stern, 'Selections from the letters of Lorimer Fison and A. W. Howitt to Lewis Henry Morgan', p. 268.

49 Fison and Howitt, *Kamilaroi and Kurnai*, pp. 95–6.

50 Fison and Howitt, 1885, 'On the deme and the horde'.

51 Fison and Howitt, *Kamilaroi and Kurnai*, pp. 67–8.

52 Fison and Howitt, *Kamilaroi and Kurnai*, pp. 58 and 60.

53 Fison and Howitt, *Kamilaroi and Kurnai*, p. 297.

54 E. B. Tylor, 1889, 'On a method of investigating the development of institutions; applied to laws of marriage and descent', p. 256.

55 Tylor, 'On a method of investigating the development of institutions; applied to laws of marriage and descent', p. 262.

56 Tylor, 'On a method of investigating the development of institutions; applied to laws of marriage and descent', p. 263.

57 Tylor, 'On a method of investigating the development of institutions; applied to laws of marriage and descent', pp. 267–8.

58 Spencer, *Wanderings in Wild Australia*, Vol. 1, p. 185.

59 Spencer, *Wanderings in Wild Australia*, Vol. 1, p. 185.

60 Mulvaney and Calaby, 1984, *So Much That is New*, p. 174.

61 Mulvaney and Calaby, *So Much That is New*, p. 169.

62 Mulvaney and Calaby, *So Much That is New*, p. 172.

63 Marett and Penniman, *Spencer's Scientific Correspondence*, p. 79. In fact Fison did follow up questions raised by McLennan's theory of totemism. See *Kamilaroi and Kurnai* pp. 165–71.

64 Marett and Penniman, *Spencer's Scientific Correspondence*, p. 58.

65 Marett and Penniman, *Spencer's Scientific Correspondence*, pp. 22 and 23.

66 Frazer, 1909, 'Howitt and Fison', p. 171.

67 Frazer, 1900, 'Preface' to the second edition of *The Golden Bough*, p. xix.

68 Marett and Penniman, *Spencer's Scientific Correspondence*, pp. 45–54.

69 E. B. Tylor, 'Remarks on totemism', pp. 144 and 148.

70 Frazer, *Totemism and Exogamy*, Vol. 4, p. 14.

71 Frazer, *Totemism and Exogamy*, Vol. 4, p. 10.
72 Frazer, *Totemism and Exogamy*, Vol. 4, p. 124.
73 A. Goldenweiser, 1910, 'Totemism, an analytical study'.
74 E. Westermarck, 1927, *Memories of My Life*.
75 K. Wikman, 1940, 'Letters from Edward B. Tylor and Alfred Russel Wallace to Edward Westermarck'.
76 E. Westermarck, 1891, *History of Human Marriage*, pp. 14 and 15.
77 See his letters in Wikman, 'Letters from Edward B. Tylor ... to Edward Westermarck'.
78 See Michael W. Young, 2004, *Malinowski: Odyssey of an Anthropologist*, pp. 172–84.
79 Darwin, 1874 (2nd edition) *The Descent of Man*, p. 901.
80 Still the best general account of Durkheim is Stephen Lukes, 1973, *Emile Durkheim: His Life and Work*.
81 V. Karady, 1969 (ed.) *Marcel Mauss, Oeuvres*, Vol. 3, p. 475.
82 Karady, *Marcel Mauss, Oeuvres*, Vol. 3, pp. 480–1.
83 Frédéric Le Play, 1884, *L'Organisation de la famille, selon le vrai modèle signalé par l'histoire de toutes les races et de tous les temps*.
84 Charles Letrourneau, 1888, *L'évolution du mariage et de la famille*.
85 See P. A. Corning, 1982, 'Durkheim and Spencer'.
86 See V. Karady, 1981, 'French ethnology and the Durkheimian breakthrough'.
87 E. Durkheim, 1893, *De la division du travail social: étude sur l'organistion des sociétés supérieures*.
88 V. Karady (ed.), 1975, *Emile Durkheim, Textes*, Vol. 3, p. 73.
89 Karady, *Emile Durkheim, Textes*, Vol. 3, p. 25.
90 E. Durkheim, 1898, 'La prohibition de l'inceste', p. 39.
91 See Lukes, *Durkheim*, and the essays by R. A. Jones on Durkheim's theory of religion – 1977, 'On understanding a sociological classic'; 1981, 'Robertson Smith, Durkheim, and sacrifice'; 1985, 'Durkheim, totemism and the Intichiuma'; and 1986, 'Durkheim, Frazer and Smith'.
92 E. Durkheim, [1912] 1915, *The Elementary Forms of the Religious Life*, p. 414.
93 *Anthropos*, 1915, Vol. 9, p. 288.

6 The Boasians and the critique of evolutionism

1 See Douglas Cole, 1999, *Franz Boas: The Early Years, 1858–1906*.
2 Boas, 'The background of my early thinking' in George W. Stocking, Jr, 1974, *A Franz Boas Reader*. The following citations from Boas are taken from the same text.
3 See Erwin H. Ackerknecht, 1953, *Rudolf Virchow: Doctor, Statesman, Anthropologist*, and Klaus-Peter Koepping, 1983, *Adolf Bastian and the Psychic Unity of Mankind: The Foundations of Anthropology in Nineteenth Century Germany*.
4 Quoted in Ackerknecht, *Rudolf Virchow*, pp. 215–16.
5 Franz Boas, 1912, 'Changes in bodily form of descendants of immigrants'.

6   For Boas's relationship to German geography see Clyde Kluckhohn and Olaf
    Prufer, 1959, 'Influences during the formative years'; William Speth, 1978,
    'The anthropogeographic theory of Franz Boas'; and Cole, *Franz Boas*,
    Chapter 7.

7   Cited in Koepping, *Adolf Bastian*, p. 62.

8   See D. Cole, 1983, '"The value of a person lies in his *Herzenbildung*": Franz
    Boas' Baffin Island Letter-Diary, 1883–1884'.

9   Quoted in Cole, *Franz Boas*, pp. 121–2.

10 See Curtis Hinsley, 1981, *Savages and Scientists: The Smithsonian Institution
    and the Development of American Anthropology*, 1846–1910.

11 Franz Boas, 1887, 'The occurrence of similar inventions in areas widely apart'.
    Reprinted in George W. Stocking, Jr, 1974, *A Franz Boas Reader*, pp. 61–7.

12 A good account of the debate can be found in Hinsley, *Savages and Scientists*,
    pp. 98–100.

13 On Putnam, see Joan Mark, 1980, *Four Anthropologists*.

14 On Holmes, see Mark, *Four Anthropologists*.

15 In Stocking, *A Franz Boas Reader*, p. 60.

16 Ronald Rohner, 1969, *The Ethnography of Franz Boas* is a valuable guide to
    Boas's field expeditions.

17 Robert Lowie, 1947, 'Franz Boas', p. 311.

18 I. Goldman, 1980, 'Boas on the Kwakiut', pp. 335–6.

19 See his lecture 'The aims of ethnology', 1858, which he reprinted in his *Race,
    Language and Culture*, 1940, because 'it illustrates my early views regarding
    ethnological problems' (p. 626, note).

20 Franz Boas, 1889, 'First general report on the Indians of British Columbia',
    p. 825.

21 Boas, 'First general report on the Indians of British Columbia', p. 829.

22 Boas, 1890, 'Second general report on the Indians of British Columbia',
    pp. 604 and 609.

23 Franz Boas, 1897, 'The social organization and secret societies of the Kwakiut
    Indians', pp. 334–5.

24 Boas, 'The social organization and secret societies of the Kwakiutl Indians'
    p. 335.

25 Franz Boas, 1920, 'The social organization of the Kwakiutl'.

26 Paul Radin, 1958, 'Robert H. Lowie', p. 359.

27 Theodora Kroeber, 1970, *Alfred Kroeber*, p. 12.

28 Theodora Kroeber, *Kroeber*, p. 26.

29 Theodora Kroeber, *Kroeber*, p. 21.

30 See Peter J. Bowler, 1983, *The Eclipse of Darwinism*.

31 Robert Lowie, 1956, 'Reminiscences of anthropological currents in America
    half a century ago', pp. 1005–6.

32 Lowie, 'Reminiscences of anthropological currents', p. 1013.

33 Hinsley, *Savages and Scientists*, p. 283.

34 Franz Boas, 1904, 'The history of anthropology', reprinted in Stocking, *A Franz
    Boas Reader*.

35 Mark, *Four Anthropologists*, p. 48.

36 John Reed Swanton, 1904, 'The development of the clan system and of secret
    societies'; 1905, 'The social organization of American tribes'; and 1906, 'A
    reconstruction of the theory of social organization'.

37 Alfred Kroeber, 1909, 'Classificatory systems of relationship'.
38 F. G. Speck, 1915, 'The family hunting band as the basis of Algonkian social organization'.
39 Lowie, 'Reminiscences of anthropological currents', p. 995.
40 Alfred Kroeber, 1919, 'Zuni kin and clan', p. 49.
41 Kroeber, 'Zuni kin and clan', p. 187.
42 Kroeber, 'Zuni kin and clan', p. 49.
43 Franz Boas, 1910, 'Psychological problems in anthropology', reprinted in Stocking, *A Franz Boas Reader*.
44 A. Goldenweiser, 1910, 'Totemism, an analytical study'.
45 See especially Robert Lowie, 1914, 'Social organization'; 1915, 'Exogamy and the classificatory systems of relationship'; 1920, *Primitive Society*; and 1927, *The Origin of the State*.
46 Alfred Kroeber, 1920, Review of Lowie's *Primitive Society*, p. 380.
47 R. Jakobson, 1944, 'Franz Boas's approach to language', p. 194.
48 For a detailed account of this crisis, see George W. Stocking, Jr, 1968, *Race, Culture and Evolution*, Chapter 11.
49 Franz Boas, 1919, 'Scientists as spies'. Reprinted in Stocking, *A Franz Boas Reader*.
50 Mark, *Four Anthropologists*, pp. 161–2.
51 L. White, 1966, *The Social Organization of Ethnological Theory*.
52 Cited by Kluckhohn and Prufer, 'Influences during the formative years', p. 22.
53 Leslie White, 1949, *The Social Organization of Ethnological Theory*.
54 Marshall Sahlins, 1960, 'Evolution: specific and general'.
55 W. T. Divale and M. Harris, 1976, 'Population, warfare, and the male supremacist complex'.
56 J. H. Steward, 1936, 'The economic and social basis of primitive bands', and E. R. Service, 1962, *Primitive Social Organization: An Evolutionary Perspective*.
57 Marshall Sahlins, 1958, *Social Stratification in Polynesia*.
58 For an excellent review of this school and its successors see Benjamin S. Orlove, 1980, 'Ecological anthropology'. See also Alan Barnard, 1983, 'Contemporary hunter-gatherers: Current theoretical issues in ecology and social organization'.
59 Adam Kuper, 1999, *Culture: The Anthropologists' Account*, Chapter 5.

7 From Rivers to Radcliffe-Brown

1 Sandra Rouse, 1998, 'Expedition and institution: A. C. Haddon and anthropology at Cambridge', in Anita Herle and Sandra Rouse, *Cambridge and the Torres Strait*, p. 71.
2 The dedication of John Layard's *Stone Men of Malekula* (1942), reads: 'To the memory of Dr. W. H. Rivers who once told me that he would like to have inscribed on his tombstone the words, "he made ethnology a science"'.
3 C. S. Myers, 1923, 'The influence of the late W. H. Rivers on the development of psychology in Great Britain'.
4 Cited in A. H. Quiggin, 1942, *Haddon the Head-Hunter*, p. 97n.
5 Sandra Rouse, 1998, 'Expedition and institution: A. C. Haddon and anthropology at Cambridge', in Herle and Rouse, *Cambridge and the Torres Strait*. See also Quiggin, *Haddon the Head-Hunter*, and James Urry, 1982, 'From zoology to ethnology: A. C. Haddon's conversion to anthropology'.
6 Quiggin, *Haddon the Head-Hunter*, p. 77.

7   Quiggin, *Haddon the Head-Hunter*, p. 94.
8   Quiggin, *Haddon the Head-Hunter*, p. 115.
9   Anita Herle and Sandra Rouse (eds) 1998, *Cambridge and the Torres Strait: Centenary Essays on the 1898 Anthropological Expedition.*
10 Stanley A. Freed *et al.* 1988, 'Capitalist philanthropy and Russian revolutionaries: the Jesup North Pacific expedition'.
11 Rouse, 'Expedition and institution: A. C. Haddon and anthropology at Cambridge', p. 56.
12 Quiggin, *Haddon the Head-Hunter*, p. 97.
13 W. H. R. Rivers, 1910, 'The genealogical method of anthropological enquiry'.
14 W. H. R. Rivers, 1908, 'Genealogies, kinship, regulation of marriage, social organization', in *Sociology, Magic, and Religion of the Eastern Islanders*, Reports of the Cambridge Anthropological Expedition to the Torres Straits, Vol. 6, p. 144.
15 Rivers, 'Genealogies, kinship, regulation of marriage, social organization', p. 151.
16 Rivers, 'Genealogies, kinship, regulation of marriage, social organization', p. 141.
17 Rivers, 'Genealogies, kinship, regulation of marriage, social organization', p. 160.
18 Rivers, 'Genealogies, kinship, regulation of marriage, social organization', p. 177.
19 Rivers, 'Genealogies, kinship, regulation of marriage, social organization', p. 151.
20 W. H. R. Rivers, 1906, *The Todas*, p. 541.
21 Rivers, *The Todas*, pp. 509–10.
22 Rivers, *The Todas*, p. 541.
23 W. H. R. Rivers, 1907, 'On the origin of the classificatory system of relationships'.
24 W. H. R. Rivers, 1914, *Kinship and Social Organisation*.
25 Rivers, *Kinship and Social Organisation*, p. 95. For a valuable discussion of the Rivers–Kroeber debate see David Schneider's introduction to a reissue of Rivers's lectures: Schneider, 1968, 'Rivers and Kroeber in the study of kinship'.
26 Rivers, *Kinship and Social Organisation*, pp. 40 and 47.
27 Rivers, *Kinship and Social Organisation*, pp. 52–3.
28 Josef Köhler, [1897] 1975, *On the Prehistory of Marriage: Totems, Group Marriage, Mother Right*.
29 Köhler, *On the Prehistory of Marriage*, p. 144.
30 W. H. R. Rivers, 1911, 'The ethnological analysis of culture'.
31 Rivers mentioned Boas and his school only in passing.
32 F. Graebner, 1905, 'Kulturkreise und Kulturgeschichten in Ozeanien', and 1909, 'Die Melaanesische Bogenkultur und ihre Verwandten'. For a good English-language account of Graebner's work see Jurgen Zwernemann, 1983, *Culture History and African Anthropology: A Century of Research in Germany and Austria*.
33 Rivers, 'The ethnological analysis of culture', p. 359.
34 W. H. R. Rivers, 1914, *History of Melanesian Society*, Vol. 2, p. 4.
35 Elliot Smith has been blamed for converting Rivers to diffusionism, but Elliot Smith himself testified that Rivers made the shift independently of him. (See Warren R. Dawson, 1938, *Sir Grafton Elliot Smith*, p. 52.)
36 Quoted in Ernst Mayr, 1982, *The History of Biological Thought*, p. 547.
37 Rivers, *History of Melanesian Society*, Vol. 1, p. 1.
38 Slobodin, *Rivers*, pp. 40–3.
39 Nor was the emphasis in the title on 'society' accidental. 'Again, I have called the book a history of Melanesian society rather than of Melanesian culture,

because it is with social forms and functions in the narrower sense that I chiefly deal.' Slobodin, *Rivers*, pp. 7–8.

40 Rivers, *History of Melanesian Society*, Vol. 1, p. 3.
41 Rivers, *History of Melanesian Society*, Vol. 1, pp. 5 and 6.
42 Rivers, *History of Melanesian Society*, Vol. 2, p. 586.
43 A. R. Radcliffe-Brown, 1927, 'The regulation of marriage in Ambrym', p. 343.
44 A. R. Radcliffe-Brown, 1931, *The Social Organisation of Austalian Tribes*, note 5.
45 Rivers, *History of Melanesian Society*, Vol. 1, p. 5.
46 Rivers, *History of Melanesian Society*, Vol. 2, p. 76.
47 Rivers, *History of Melanesian Society*, Vol. 2, p. 65.
48 Rivers, *History of Melanesian Society*, Vol. 2, p. 52.
49 Rivers, *History of Melanesian Society*, Vol. 2, p. 292.
50 Cf. George W. Stocking, Jr, 1983, 'The ethnographer's magic: fieldwork in British anthropology from Tylor to Malinowski'.
51 On Radcliffe-Brown, see Adam Kuper, 1996, *Anthropologists and Anthropology: The Modern British School*, Chapter 2.
52 A. R. Radcliffe-Brown, 1914, 'Review of *The Family among the Australian Aborigines* by B. Malinowski', *Man* XIV, 16, pp. 31–2.
53 A. R. Radcliffe-Brown, 1913, 'Three tribes of Western Australia', pp. 193.
54 Radcliffe-Brown, 'Three tribes of Western Australia', pp. 190–1.
55 Radcliffe-Brown later elaborated the model, adding new types and sub-types, and his ideas have been the subject of much expert commentary. See especially John Barnes, 1967, *Inquest on the Murngin*, and Harold W. Scheffler, 1978, *Australian Kin Classification*.
56 See Radcliffe-Brown, 1935, 'Patrilineal and matrilineal succession', p. 289.
57 Adam Kuper, 1989, 'Radcliffe-Brown and Rivers: A correspondence'.
58 W. H. R. Rivers, 1914, 'Is Australian culture simple or complex?'
59 He later changed his mind on totemism. 'Australian totemism is a cosmological system by which the phenomena of nature are incorporated in the kinship organisation.' See A. R. Radcliffe-Brown, 1945, 'Religion and society'.
60 Rivers, *History of Melanesian Society*, Vol. 2, p. 89.
61 W. H. R. Rivers, 1915, 'Descent and ceremonial in Ambrym'.
62 See Jeremy MacClancy, 1986, 'Unconventional character and disciplinary convention: John Layard, Jungian and anthropologist'.
63 James Urry, 1985, 'W. E. Armstrong and social anthropology at Cambridge'. Armstrong never published his lectures, but the general argument appears as an appendix to his *Rossel Island* (1928).
64 T. T. Barnard, 1914, *The Regulation of Marriage in the New Hebrides*, Chapter 6. This chapter has been reprinted in G. De Meur (ed.), 1986, *New Trends in Mathematical Anthropology*.
65 Urry, 'W. E. Armstrong', p. 427 and 430, note 18.
66 Margaret Gardiner, 1984, *Footprints on Malekula*, pp. 45 and 47.
67 Bernard Deacon, 1927, 'The regulation of marriage in Ambrym', p. 327. Cf. H. W. Scheffler, 1970, 'Ambrym revisited: a preliminary report'.
68 Gardiner, *Footprints on Malekula*, p. 47.
69 Gardiner, *Footprints on Malekula*, p. 53.
70 Deacon, 'The regulation of marriage in Ambrym', p. 328.
71 Deacon, 'The regulation of marriage in Ambrym', p. 329.

72 A. R. Radcliffe-Brown, 1927, 'The regulation; of marriage in Ambrym', p. 345.
Cf. H. Scheffler, 1970, 'Ambrym revisited: a preliminary report'.
73 See Michael W. Young, 2004, *Malinowski: Odyssey of an Anthropologist*, especially Chapters 20 and 24, and Michael W. Young, 1979, *The Ethnography of Malinowski*.
74 B. Malinowski, 1927, *The Father in Primitive Psychology*.
75 B. Malinowski, 1930, 'Kinship', pp. 28 and 21.

8 Descent theory

1 Meyer Fortes, 1979, 'Preface' to L. Holy (ed.) *Segmentary Lineage Systems Reconsidered*. Fortes refers to E. W. Gifford, 1929, *Tongan Society*, but Gifford's essay (1926) 'Miwok lineages and the political unit in aboriginal California' is equally relevant.
2 M. Fortes and E. E. Evans-Pritchard, 1940, 'Introduction' to *African Political Systems*, p. 4.
3 Fortes and Evans-Pritchard, 'Introduction' to *African Political Systems*, pp. 6–7.
4 Fortes and Evans-Pritchard, 'Introduction' to *African Political Systems*, p. 11.
5 E. E. Evans Pritchard, 1940, *The Nuer*, p. 262.
6 Evans-Pritchard, *The Nuer*, p. 159.
7 Robertson Smith, 1885, *Kinship and Marriage in Early Arabia*, p. 56.
8 Evans-Pritchard, *The Nuer*, p. 205.
9 A. I. Richards, 1941, 'A problem of anthropological approach'.
10 Max Gluckman, 1945, 'Preface' to E. E. Evans-Pritchard, *Some Aspects of Marriage and Family among the Nuer*.
11 E. E. Evans-Pritchard, 1933–1935, 'The Nuer: tribe and clan', Part 3, pp. 86–7.
12 Evans-Pritchard, 'The Nuer: tribe and clan', p. 87.
13 Evans-Pritchard, *The Nuer*, p. 212.
14 E. E. Evans-Pritchard, 1945, *Some Aspects of Marriage and the Family among the Nuer*, p. 63.
15 E. E. Evans-Pritchard, 1951, *Kinship and Marriage among the Nuer*, p. 28.
16 M. Glickman, 1971, 'Kinship and credit among the Nuer', p. 309, note.
17 Evans-Pritchard, *Kinship and Marriage among the Nuer*, p. 47.
18 Evans-Pritchard, 'The Nuer: tribe and clan', Part 3, p. 76.
19 Evans-Pritchard, 'The Nuer: tribe and clan', Part 1, p. 28.
20 Evans-Pritchard, *The Nuer*, p. 195.
21 Evans-Pritchard, *The Nuer*, p. 203.
22 See L. Holy (ed.) 1979, *Segmentary Lineage Systems Reconsidered*, pp. 5–6.
23 Evans-Pritchard, *The Nuer*, pp. 202–3.
24 M. Fortes, 1945, 'An anthropologist's point of view'.
25 M. Fortes, 1945, *The Dynamics of Clanship among the Tallensi*; 1949, *The Web of Kinship among the Tallensi*.
26 Fortes, *Dynamics of Clanship among the Tallensi*, p. 63.
27 Fortes, *Dynamics of Clanship among the Tallensi*, p. 205.
28 Fortes, *Dynamics of Clanship among the Tallensi*, p. 203.
29 Fortes, *The Web of Kinship among the Tallensi*, p. 10.
30 M. Fortes, 1949, 'Time and social structure: An Ashanti case study'.
31 M. Fortes, 1953, 'The structure of unilineal descent groups', p. 34.
32 John Middleton and David Tait (eds), 1958, *Tribes Without Rulers*.

33 M. Gluckman, 1950, 'Kinship and marriage among the Lozi of Northern Rhodesia and the Zulu of Natal'.
34 Max Marwick, 1965, *Sorcery in its Social Setting*.
35 A. Southall, 1953, *Alur Society*.
36 E. R. Leach, 1961, *Pul Eliya*, p. 8.
37 E. R. Leach, 1962, 'On certain unconsidered aspects of double descent systems'.
38 Leach, *Pul Eliya*, p. 300.
39 Leach, *Pul Eliya*, p. 301.
40 Leach, *Pul Eliya*, p. 302.
41 Raymond Firth, 1963, 'Bilateral descent groups: an operational viewpoint'.
42 M. Meggitt, 1965, *The Lineage System of the Mae-Enga of New Guinea*.
43 J. A. Barnes, 1962, 'African models in the New Guinea Highlands'.
44 Barnes, 'African models in the New Guinea Highlands', p. 9.
45 Paula Brown, 1962, 'Non-agnates among the patrilineal Chimbu'.
46 L. Langness, 1964, 'Some problems in the conceptualization of Highlands social structures', p. 163.
47 M. Sahlins, 1965, 'On the ideology and composition of descent groups'.
48 Kaberry, 1967, 'The plasticity of New Guinea kinship'.
49 E. R. Leach, 1957, 'Aspects of bride wealth and marriage stability'. See the response by Fortes, 1959, 'Descent, filiation and affinity: a rejoinder to Dr Leach'.
50 See Claude Meillassoux [1975] 1981, *Maidens, Meals and Money*, and P.-P. Rey, 1975, 'The lineage mode of production' and (1979) 'Class contradiction in lineage societies'.

9 Towards the intellect

1 See Christopher Johnson, 2003, *Claude Lévi-Strauss: The Formative Years*, and David Pace, 1983, *Claude Lévi-Strauss: The Bearer of Ashes*.
2 Claude Lévi-Strauss [1955] 1976, *Tristes Tropiques*, p. 416.
3 Lévi-Strauss, *Tristes Tropiques*, p. 406.
4 Marcel Mauss, [1924] 1990, *The Gift*.
5 Didier Eribon [1988] 1991, *Conversations with Lévi-Strauss*, p. 41.
6 Eribon, *Conversations with Lévi-Strauss*, p. 43.
7 Marcel Granet, 1939, 'Catégories matrimoniales et relations de proximité dans la Chine ancienne'. See Eribon, *Conversations with Lévi-Strauss*, p. 99.
8 Claude Lévi-Strauss [1949] 1969, *The Elementary Structures of Kinship*, p. xxvii. This is from the preface to the second edition.
9 James George Frazer, 1918, *Folklore in the Old Testament*, Vol. 2, p. 97.
10 This question provides the heading for a section of the chapter in Frazer's book. See Frazer, *Folklore in the Old Testament*, p. 193.
11 Frazer, *Folklore in the Old Testament*, p. 198.
12 Frazer, *Folklore in the Old Testament*, p. 220.
13 Frazer, *Folklore in the Old Testament*, p. 220.
14 F. E. Richards, 1914, 'Cross-cousin marriage in South India'.
15 Frazer, *Folklore in the Old Testament*, pp. 220–1.
16 Frazer, *Folklore in the Old Testament*, p. 235.
17 Frazer, *Folklore in the Old Testament*, p. 240.
18 Frazer, *Folklore in the Old Testament*, pp. 245–6.

19 Frazer, *Folklore in the Old Testament*, p. 251.
20 T. C. Hodson, 1925, 'Notes on the marriage of cousins in India'.
21 R. Fortune, 1933, 'A note on some forms of kinship structure'.
22 Granet, 'Catégories matrimoniales et relations de proximité dans la Chine ancienne'.
23 For an introduction to the work of the Leiden school see P. E. de Josselin de Jong (ed.), 1977, *Structural Anthropology in the Netherlands*.
24 E. Durkheim and M. Mauss [1903] 1963, *Primitive Classification*.
25 J. P. B. de Josselin de Jong, 1935, *De Maleische archipel als ethnologisch studieveld*. This is available in English translation in P. E. de Josselin de Jong, *Structural Anthropology in the Netherlands*.
26 See P. E. de Josselin de Jong, 1984, *Unity in Diversity*, p. 2.
27 C. Lévi-Strauss [1949] 1969, *The Elementary Structures of Kinship*, p. 134.
28 Lévi-Strauss, *The Elementary Structures of Kinship*, p. 138.
29 Lévi-Strauss, *The Elementary Structures of Kinship*, p. 137.
30 Lévi-Strauss, *The Elementary Structures of Kinship*, p. 84.
31 Lévi-Strauss, *The Elementary Structures of Kinship*, p. 51.
32 Lévi-Strauss, *The Elementary Structures of Kinship*, p. 375.
33 Lévi-Strauss, *The Elementary Structures of Kinship*, p. 449.
34 This argument was first advanced by Lévi-Strauss in 1945, in an article 'Structural analysis in linguistics and in anthropology' that was published in English as Chapter 11 of his *Structural Anthropology* (1963).
35 Claude Lévi-Strauss, 1965, 'The future of kinship studies'.
36 E. R. Leach, 1951, 'The structural implications of matrilateral cross-cousin marriage', p. 89.
37 J. P. B. de Josselin de Jong, 1952, *Lévi-Strauss's Theory of Kinship and Marriage*.
38 Rodney Needham, 1962, *Structure and Sentiment*, p. 2.
39 The marriage choices of the Tswana of Southern Africa have been documented with a wealth of statistics by Isaac Schapera. Interestingly, Needham made the mistake of assuming that Tswana aristocrats married father's sister's daughters, or cross-cousins, while Schapera indicates clearly that their first choice should be marriage with a father's brother's daughter, and that this was in practice the most popular option. See Needham, *Structure and Sentiment*, p. 9. cf. Adam Kuper, 1975, 'Preferential marriage and polygyny among the Tswana'.
40 Claude Lévi-Strauss [1962] 1964, *Totemism*, translated by Rodney Needham.
41 Lévi-Strauss, *Elementary Structures of Kinship*, pp. xxxi and xxxii.
42 Louis Dumont, 1953, 'Dravidian kinship terminology'.
43 Reprinted in Louis Dumont, 1983, *Affinity as Value*, p. 70.
44 Dumont, in *Affinity as Value*, p. 171.
45 Rodney Needham, 1971, 'Remarks on the analysis of kinship and marriage'.
46 Lévi-Strauss, 'The future of kinship studies', p. 18.
47 Françoise Héritier, 1981, *L'exercise de la parenté*, p. 127. My translation.
48 Lévi-Strauss, *Totemism*, pp. 10–11.
49 Lévi-Strauss, *Totemism*, p. 101.
50 E. Durkheim and M. Mauss [1903] (1963), *Primitive Classification*.
51 Lévi-Strauss, *Totemism*, p. 89.
52 Eribon, *Conversations with Lévi-Strauss*, p. 163.
53 Claude Lévi-Strauss [1973] (1978), *Structural Anthropology 2*, pp. 28–9.

10 The return of the native

1 See, for example, the correspondence published in *Anthropology Today* 18 (3), June, 2002, pp. 23–5, under the heading 'Defining oneself, and being defined as, indigenous'.

2 Alan Barnard, 1992, *Hunters and Herders of Southern Africa: A Comparative Ethnography of the Khoisan Peoples*, p. 8.

3 See André Bétaille, 1998, 'The idea of indigenous people'.

4 Boutros Boutros-Ghali, 1994, 'Foreword' in Alexander Ewen (ed.) *Voice of Indigenous Peoples*, p. 9.

5 Boutros-Ghali, 'Foreword', pp. 9–13.

6 For a convenient review of the institutions and treaties in this field, see Florencia Roulet, 1999, *Human Rights and Indigenous Peoples*.

7 Various examples are reviewed in Alan Barnard, 1983, 'Contemporary hunter-gatherers: current theoretical issues in ecology and social organization', pp. 208–9.

8 Louis-Jacques Dorais, 1997, *Quaqtaq: Modernity and Identity in an Inuit Community*.

9 Henry Steward, 2002, 'Ethnonyms and images: Genesis of the "Inuit" and image manipulation. cf. Keiichi Omura, 2002, 'Construction of *Inuinnaqtun* (Real Inuit Way): Self-image and everyday practices in Inuit society'.

10 Boutros-Ghali, 'Foreword', p. 13.

11 See Martin Chanock, 2000, '"Culture" and human rights: orientalising, occidentalising, and authenticity'.

12 See, for example, Sam Gill, 1994, '"Mother Earth": an American myth', and Alice Kehoe, 1994, 'Primal Gaia: primitivists and plastic medicine men'.

13 Boutros-Ghali, 'Foreword', p. 13.

14 See Mark Nuttall, 1998, *Protecting the Arctic: Indigenous Peoples and Cultural Survival*.

15 Kirk Dombrowski, 2002, 'The praxis of indigenism and Alaska Native Timber Policies'.

16 See, e.g., Edwin Wilmsen (ed.) 1989, *We Are Here: Politics of Aboriginal Land Tenure*. Cf. on Australia L. R. Hiatt, 1996, *Arguments About Aborigines*, Chapter 2.

17 Hugh Brody, 2001, *The Other Side of Eden: Hunter–Gatherers, Farmers, and the Shaping of the World*, pp. 134–6.

18 Brody, *The Other Side of Eden*, p. 207.

19 Brody, *The Other Side of Eden*, 113–14.

20 Dean R. Snow, 1996, 'The first Americans and the differentiation of hunter-gatherer cultures', p. 131. See also Thomas D. Dillehay, *The Settlement of the Americas: A New Prehistory*, particularly Chapter 2.

21 Ronald J. Mason, 2000, 'Initial shield woodland'.

22 Donald Clark, 2000, 'Proto-Athapascan'.

23 Snow, 'The first Americans and the differentiation of hunter-gatherer cultures', p. 128.

24 José Mailhot, 1999, 'The Innu of Quebec and Labrador'.

25 See Colin Samson, 2003, *A Way of Life that does not Exist: Canada and the Extinguishment of the Innu* for an indigenist report, and see Larry Innes's review of the book (2004) for an excellent critique.

26 See Evelyn Plaice, 1990, *The Native Game: Settler Perception of Indian/Settler Relations in Central Labrador*, and Colin Sampson, 2001, 'Rights as the reward for simulating cultural sameness: the Innu in the Canadian colonial context'.
27 *The Times*, 22 April 2002.
28 George Silberbauer, 1965, *Bushman Survey Report*, p. 14.
29 The information used in this paragraph is drawn from James Suzman, 2002, 'Kalahari conundrums: relocation, resistance and internal support in the Central Kalahari, Botswana', pp. 1–2.
30 Robert K. Hitchcock, 2002, 'Botswana', p. 2.
31 Robert K. Hitchcock, 2002, '"We are the First People": land, natural resources, and identity in the Central Kalahari, Botswana', p. 18.
32 Suzman, 'Kalahari conundrums', p. 3.
33 Suzman, 'Kalahari conundrums', p. 4.
34 Cited in Henry Bredenkamp, 2001, 'Khoisan revivalism and the indigenous peoples issue in post-apartheid South Africa', p. 192.
35 See Robert Ross, 1976, *Adam Kok's Griquas*.
36 Linda Waldman, 2001, 'No rainbow bus for us: building nationalism in South Africa'.
37 Steven Robins, 2001, 'Whose "culture"? Whose "survival"?', p. 241.
38 William Ellis, 2001, 'Bushman identity: a land claim, and the three agendas', p. 9.
39 Steven Robins, 2001, 'NGOS, "Bushmen", and double vision: The ‡Khomani San land claim and the cultural politics of "community" and "development" in the Kalahari'.
40 Alan Barnard, 2003, '!Ke e: /xarra //ke – multiple origins and multiple meanings of the motto'.
41 Beth A. Conklin, 2002, 'Shamans versus pirates in the Amazonian treasure chest', pp. 1053–5.
42 James Suzman, 2003, 'Comment' on Adam Kuper, 'The return of the native', p. 399.

11 Conclusion

1 See, e.g. H. J. Claessen and P. Skalnik (eds) 1978, *The Early State*.
2 Paul Bahn and John Flenley, 2003, *The Enigmas of Easter Island*.
3 Robert Lowie, 1920, *Primitive Society*; 1924, *Primitive Religion*; and 1927, *The Origin of the State*.
4 See, e.g. Meyer Fortes, 1957, 'Malinowski and the study of kinship'.
5 Evie Plaice, 2003, comment on Adam Kuper, 'The return of the native', p. 397.
6 See Adam Kuper, 1999, *Culture: The Anthropologists' Account*.
7 'On fait de la science – et surtout de la sociologie – contre sa formation autant qu'avec sa formation. Et seule l'histoire peut nous débarraser de l'histoire.' Pierre Bourdieu, in his inaugural lecture at the Collège de France, *Leçon sur le leçon* (1982).

References

Ackerknecht, Erwin H. (1953) *Rudolf Virchow: Doctor, Statesman, Anthropologist*, Madison WI, University of Wisconsin Press.

Ackerman, Robert (1987) *J. G. Frazer*, Cambridge, Cambridge University Press.

Acton, J. F. E. (1907) *Historical Essays and Studies*, London, Macmillan.

Ankermann, B. (1905) 'Kulturkreise und Kulturschichten in Afrika', *Zeitschrift für Ethnologie*, 37, pp. 54ff.

Aristotle [350 BCE] (1931) *Politics*, translated by Benjamin Jowitt, Oxford, Clarendon Press.

Armstrong, W. E. (1928) *Rossel Island: An Ethnological Study*, Cambridge, Cambridge University Press.

Atiyah, P. S. (1979) *The Rise and Fall of Freedom of Contract*, Oxford, Clarendon Press.

Atkinson, J. J. (1903) *Primal Law*, London, Longman (bound with Andrew Lang, *Social Origins*).

Auel, Jean, (1980) *The Clan of the Cave Bear*, New York, Crown Publishers.

Bachofen, J. (1861) *Das Mutterrecht*, Basel, Schwabe.

Bahn, Paul and Flenley, John (2003) *The Enigmas of Easter Island*, New York, Oxford University Press.

Bailey, Anne M. and Llobera, Josep (eds) (1981) *The Asiatic Mode of Production: Science and Politics*, London, Routledge & Kegan Paul.

Balfour, H. *et al.* (1907) *Anthropological Essays Presented to Edward Burnett Tylor*, Oxford, Clarendon Press.

Barnard, Alan (1983) 'Contemporary hunter-gatherers: current theoretical issues in ecology and social organization', *Annual Review of Anthropology*, 12, pp. 193–214.

Barnard, Alan (1992) *Hunters and Herders of Southern Africa: A Comparative Ethnography of the Khoisan Peoples*, Cambridge, Cambridge University Press.

Barnard, T. T. (1924) 'The regulation of marriage in the New Hebrides', unpublished doctoral thesis, University of Cambridge.

Barnes, J. A. (1962) 'African models in the New Guinea Highlands', *Man*, 52, pp. 5–9.

Barnes, J. A. (1967) *Inquest on the Murngin*, London, Royal Anthropological Institute Occasional Papers No. 26.

Bayly, C. A. (1991) 'Maine and change in nineteenth century India', in Alan Diamond (ed.) *The Victorian Achievement of Henry Maine*, Cambridge, Cambridge University Press.

Beidelman, T. O. (1974) *W. Robertson Smith and the Sociological Study of Religion*, Chicago, University of Chicago Press.

Bétaille, André (1998) 'The idea of an indigenous people', *Current Anthropology*, 39, pp. 187–91.

Bieder, R. E. (1980) 'The Grand Order of the Iroquois: influences on Lewis Henry Morgan's ethnology', *Ethnohistory*, 27, 4, pp. 349–61.

Binford, Lewis (1989) 'Isolating the transition to cultural adaptations', in E. Trinkaus (ed.) *The Emergence of Modern Humans*, Cambridge, Cambridge University Press.

Black, John S. and Chrystal, George (1912) *The Life of William Robertson Smith*, London, Black.

Boas, Franz (1889) 'First general report on the Indians of British Columbia', *Report of the BAAS*, pp. 801–93.

Boas, Franz (1890) 'Second general report on the Indians of British Columbia', *Report of the BAAS*, pp. 562–715.

Boas, Franz (1897) 'The social organization and the secret societies of the Kwakiutl Indians', *Report of the US National Museum for 1895*, Washington, DC.

Boas, Franz (1920) 'The social organization of the Kwakiutl', *American Anthropologist*, 22, pp. 111–26.

Boas, Franz (1940) *Race, Language and Culture*, New York, Free Press.

Bourdieu, Pierre (1982) *Leçon sur le leçon*, Paris, Editions de Minuit.

Boutros-Ghali, Boutros, 1994, 'Foreword', in Alexander Ewen (ed.) *Voice of Indigenous Peoples*, Santa Fe, NM, for the Native American Council of New York City.

Bowler, Peter J. (1975) 'The changing meaning of "evolution"', *Journal of the History of Ideas*, xxxvi, pp. 95–114.

Bowler, Peter J. (1983) *The Eclipse of Darwinism. Anti-Darwinian Evolution Theories in the Decades Around 1900*, Baltimore, Johns Hopkins University Press.

Bredenkamp, Henry (2001) 'Khoisan revivalism and the indigenous peoples issue in post-apartheid South Africa', in Alan Barnard and Justin Kenrich (eds) *Africa's Indigenous Peoples*, Edinburgh, Centre of African Studies, University of Edinburgh.

Brody, Hugh (2001) *The Other Side of Eden: Hunter-Gatherers, Farmers, and the Shaping of the World*, London, Faber.

Brown, P. (1962) 'Non-agnates among the patrilineal Chimbu', *Journal of the Polynesian Society*, 71, pp. 57–69.

Browne, Janet (1995) *Charles Darwin: Voyaging*, London, Jonathan Cape.
Browne, Janet (2002) *Charles Darwin: The Power of Place*, London, Jonathan Cape.
Bunsen, C. C. J. (1854) *Outlines of the Philosophy of Universal History Applied to Language and Religion* (2 vols) London, Longman.
Burckhardt, F. and Smith, S. (eds) (1984) *The Correspondence of Charles Darwin, 1821–1836*, Volume 1, Cambridge, Cambridge University Press.
Burrow, J. W. (1966) *Evolution and Society: A Study in Victorian Social Theory*, Cambridge, Cambridge University Press.
Burrow, J. W. (1967) 'The uses of philology in Victorian England', in R. Robson (ed.) *Ideas and Institutions of Victorian Britain*, London, Bell.
Burrow, J. W. (1974) 'The "village community" and the uses of history in late nineteenth-century England', in N. McKendrick (ed.) *Historical Perspectives: Studies in English Thought and Society*, London, Europa.
Burrow, J. W. (1981) *A Liberal Descent: Victorian Historians and the English Past*, Cambridge, Cambridge University Press.
Campbell, G. (1852) *Modern India: A Sketch of the System of Civil Government*, London, John Murray.
Cave-Brown, J. (1857) *Indian Infanticide: Its Origin, Progress and Suppression*, London, W. H. Allen.
Chanock, Martin (2000) '"Culture" and human rights: orientalising, occidentalising, and authenticity', in Mahmood Mamdani (ed.) *Beyond Rights Talk and Culture*, Cape Town, David Philip.
Charbonnier, G. (1961) *Entretiens avec Claude Lévi-Strauss*, Paris, Plon.
Claessen, H. J. and Skalnik, P. (eds) (1978) *The Early State*, The Hague, Mouton.
Clark, Donald (2000) 'Proto-Athapascan', in Peter N. Peregrine and Melvin Ember (eds) *Encyclopedia of Prehistory*, vol. 2, *Arctic and Subarctic*, New York, Kluwer.
Cocks, R. C. J. (1988) *Sir Henry Maine: A Study in Victorian Jurisprudence*, Cambridge, Cambridge University Press.
Cole, Douglas (1983) '"The value of a person lies in his *Hertzenbildung*": Frank Boas' Baffin Island Letter-Diary, 1883–1884', in G. W. Stocking (ed.) *Observers Observed*, Madison, WI, University of Wisconsin Press.
Cole, Douglas (1999) *Franz Boas: The Early Years, 1858–1906*, Vancouver, British Columbia, Douglas and McIntyre.
Collini, S., Winch, D. and Burrow, J. (1984) *That Noble Science of Politics: A Century of Intellectual History*, Cambridge, Cambridge University Press.
Comte, Auguste (1983) edited by Gertrud Lenzer, *Auguste Comte and Positivism: The Essential Writings*, Somerset, NJ, Transaction Publishers.
Conklin, Beth A. (2002) 'Shamans versus pirates in the Amazonian treasure chest', *American Anthropologist*, 104, pp. 1050–61.
Corning, P. A. (1982) 'Durkheim and Spencer', *British Journal of Sociology*, 33, 3, pp. 359–82.

Darwin, Charles (1839) *Journal of Researches into the Geology and Natural History of the Countries visited by H. M. S. 'Beagle'*, London, Henry Colburn.

Darwin, Charles (1859) *The Origin of Species by Means of Natural Selection*, London, John Murray.

Darwin, Charles (1871) *The Descent of Man, and Selection in Relation to Sex*, London, John Murray.

Dawson, Warren R. (1938) *Sir Grafton Elliot Smith*, London, Cape.

Deacon, Bernard (1927) 'The regulation of marriage in Ambrym', *Journal of the Royal Anthropological Institute*, 57, pp. 325–42.

De Meur, G. (ed.) (1986) *New Trends in Mathematical Anthropology*, London, Routledge & Kegan Paul.

Desmond, Adrian and Moore, James (1991) *Darwin*, Harmondsworth, Penguin.

Dewey, Clive (1972) 'Images of the village community: a study in Anglo–Indian ideology', *Modern Asian Studies*, 6, 3, pp. 291–328.

Dewey, Clive (1991) 'The influence of Sir Henry Maine on agrarian policy in India', in Alan Diamond (ed.) *The Victorian Achievement of Henry Maine*, Cambridge, Cambridge University Press.

Diamond, Alan (ed.) (1991) *The Victorian Achievement of Sir Henry Maine: A Centennial Reappraisal*, Cambridge, Cambridge University Press.

Diderot, Denis (1773) *Supplément au Voyage de Bougainville*, Neuchatel, Switzerland, Imprimerie de la Societé typographique.

Dillehay, Thomas D. (2000) *The Settlement of the Americas: A New Prehistory*, New York, Basic Books.

Divale, W. T. and Harris, M. (1976) 'Population, warfare, and the male supremacist complex', *American Anthropologist*, 78, pp. 521–38.

Dombrowski, Kirk (2002) 'The praxis of indigenism and Alaska native timber politics', *American Anthropologist*, 104, pp. 1062–73.

Dorais, Louis-Jacques (1997) *Quaqtaq: Modernity and Identity in an Inuit Community*, Toronto, University of Toronto Press.

Downie, R. A. (1970) *Frazer and the Golden Bough*, London, Gollancz.

Dumont, L. (1953) 'The Dravidian kinship terminology as an expression of marriage', *Man*, 53, pp. 34–9.

Dumont, L. (1957) *Hierarchy and Marriage Alliance in South Indian Kinship*, Royal Anthropological Institute Occasional Paper no. 12, London, Royal Anthropological Institute.

Dumont, L. (1966) 'The "village community" from Munro to Maine', *Contributions to Indian Sociology*, ix, pp. 67–89.

Dumont, L. (1983) *Affinity as a Value: Marriage Alliance in South India with Comparative Essays on Australia*, Chicago, University of Chicago Press.

Durkheim, E. (1898) 'La prohibition de l'inceste et ses origines', *L'Année sociologique*, 1, pp. 1–79.

Durkheim, E. (1907) 'Lettres', *Revue néo-scolastique*, xiv, pp. 606–7, 612–14.

Durkheim, E. (1915) *The Division of Labour in Society*, London, Macmillan (original French edition, 1893).

Durkheim, E. (1915) *The Elementary Forms of the Religious Life*, London, Allen & Unwin (first French edition, 1912).

Durkheim, E. and Mauss, M. (1963) *Primitive Classification*, London, Cohen & West (original French publication, 1903).

Ellis, William (2001) 'Bushman identity: a land claim, and the three agendas', in Alan Barnard and Justin Kenrich (eds) *Africa's Indigenous Peoples*, Edinburgh, Centre of African Studies, University of Edinburgh.

Engels, Frederick (1972) *The Origin of the Family, Private Property and the State*, London, Lawrence & Wishart (originally published in German in 1884).

Evans-Pritchard, E. E. (1933–1935) 'The Nuer: tribe and clan', *Sudan Notes and Records*, Pt 1, 16, 1 pp. 1–53; Pt 2, 17, 1, pp. 51–7; Pt 3, 18, pp. 37–87.

Evans-Pritchard, E. E. (1940) *The Nuer: A Description of the Modes of Livelihood and Political Institutions of a Nilotic People*, Oxford, Clarendon Press.

Evans-Pritchard, E. E. (1940) *The Political System of the Anuak of the Anglo–Egyptian Sudan*, LSE Monograph No. 4, London, Lund.

Evans-Pritchard, E. E. (1945) *Some Aspects of Marriage and Family Among the Nuer*, Lusaka, Rhodes–Livingstone Institute, Paper no. 11.

Evans-Pritchard, E. E. (1951) *Kinship and Marriage among the Nuer*, Oxford, Clarendon Press.

Feaver, G. (1969) *From Status to Contract: A Biography of Sir Henry Maine 1822–1888*, London, Longman.

Ferguson, Adam (1767) *An Essay on the History of Civil Society*, Edinburgh, A. Millar and T. Cadell.

Firth, Raymond (1963) 'Bilateral descent groups: an operational viewpoint', in I. Schapera (ed.) *Studies in Kinship and Marriage*, Royal Anthropological Institute Occasional Paper no. 16, London, Royal Anthropological Institute.

Fison, Lorimer and Howitt, A. W. (1880) *Kamilaroi and Kurnai: Group-marriage and Relationship and Marriage by Elopement*, Melbourne, George Robinson.

Fitzroy, Robert (ed.) (1839) *Narrative of the Surveying Voyages of H.M.S. Adventure and Beagle Between the Years 1826 and 1836*, London, Henry Colburn.

Fortes, M. (1945) 'An anthropologist's point of view', in Rita Hinden (ed.) *Fabian Colonial Essays*, London, Allen & Unwin.

Fortes, M. (1945) *The Dynamics of Clanship Among the Tallensi*, Oxford, Oxford University Press.

Fortes, M. (1949) 'Time and social structure: an Ashanti case study', in M. Fortes (ed.) *Social Structure*, Oxford, Clarendon Press.

Fortes, M. (1949) *The Web of Kinship Among the Tallensi*, Oxford, Oxford University Press.

Fortes, M. (1953) 'The structure of unilineal descent groups', *American Anthropologist*, 55, 1, pp. 17–41.

Fortes, M. (1957) 'Malinowski and the study of kinship', in Raymond Firth (ed.) *Man and Culture: An Evaluation of the Work of Bronislaw Malinowski*, London: Routledge & Kegan Paul.

Fortes, M. (1959) 'Descent, filiation and affinity: a rejoinder to Dr Leach', *Man*, 59, pp. 193–7, 206–12.

Fortes, M. (1979) Preface to L. Holy (ed.) *Segmentary Lineage Systems Reconsidered*, Department of Social Anthropology, Queen's University, Belfast.

Fortes, M. and Evans-Pritchard, E. E. (eds) (1940) *African Political Systems*, Oxford, Oxford University Press.

Fortune, R. F. (1933) 'A note on some forms of kinship structure', *Oceania*, 4, pp. 1–9.

Frazer, J. G. (1887) *Totemism*, Edinburgh, Adam & Charles Black (reprinted in Frazer, 1910).

Frazer, J. G. (1890) *The Golden Bough: A Study in Comparative Religion*, London, Macmillan (2nd edition, 1900).

Frazer, J. G. (1894) 'William Robertson Smith', *The Fortnightly Review*, iv, pp. 800–7.

Frazer, J. G. (1899) 'The origin of totemism', *The Fortnightly Review*, pp. 71 (reprinted in Frazer, 1910).

Frazer, J. G. (1909) 'Howitt and Fison', *Folk-Lore*, 20, 2, pp. 144–80.

Frazer, J. G. (1910) *Totemism and Exogamy: a Treatise on Certain Early Forms of Superstition and Society* (4 vols), London, Macmillan.

Frazer, J. G. (1918) *Folklore in the Old Testament* (3 vols), London, Macmillan.

Freed, Stanley A., Freed, Ruth S. and Williamson, Laila (1998) 'Capitalist philanthropy and Russian revolutionaries: the Jesup North Pacific expedition (1897–1902)', *American Anthropologist*, 90, 7, pp. 7–24.

Freud, Sigmund (1918) *Totem and Taboo*, London, Hogarth Press (original German publication, 1913).

Fuller, L. (1967) *Legal Fictions*, Stanford, Stanford University Press.

Fustel de Coulanges, N.-D. (1864) *La Cité Antique: Étude sur le culte, droit, les institutions de la Grèce et de Rome*, Paris, Durand.

Gardiner, Margaret (1984) *Footprints on Malekula: A Memoir of Bernard Deacon*, Edinburgh, Salamander Press.

Gifford, E. W. (1926) 'Miwok lineages and the political unit in Aboriginal California', *American Anthropologist*, 28, pp. 389–401.

Gifford, E. W. (1929) *Tongan Society*, Honolulu, Bishop Museum Bulletin, no. 61.

Gill, Sam (1994) 'Mother earth: an American myth', in J. Clifton (ed.) *The Invented Indian: Cultural Fictions and Government Policies*, Somerset, NJ, Transaction Books.

Giraud-Teulon, A. (1867) *La mère chez certains peuples de l'antiquité*, Paris, Thorin.

Glickman, M. (1971) 'Kinship and credit among the Nuer', *Africa*, 41, 4, pp. 306–19.

Gluckman, Max (1950) 'Kinship and marriage among the Lozi of Northern Rhodesia and the Zulu of Natal', in A. R. Radcliffe-Brown and Daryll Forde (eds) *African Systems of Kinship and Marriage*, Oxford, Oxford University Press.

Goldenweiser, A. (1910) 'Totemism, an analytical study', *Journal of American Folklore*, xxiii, pp. 179–293.

Golding, William (1954) *The Lord of the Flies*, London, Faber & Faber.

Goldman, Irving (1980) 'Boas on the Kwakiutl: the ethnographic tradition', in Stanley Diamond (ed.) *Theory and Practice*, The Hague, Mouton.

Goldschmidt, Walter (ed.) (1959) *The Anthropology of Franz Boas*, Memoir no. 89 of the American Anthropological Association, Washington, D.C.

Graebner, F. (1905) 'Kulturkreise und Kulturgeschichten in Ozeanien', *Zeitschrift für Ethnologie*, 37, pp. 28–53.

Graebner, F. (1909) 'Die Melanesische Bogenkultur und ihre Verwandten', *Anthropos*, 4, pp. 726–80, 998–1032.

Granet, M. (1939) 'Categories matrimoniales et relations de proximité dans la Chine ancienne', *Annales sociologiques*, Series B, Vols 1–3.

Grey, G. (1841) *Journals of Two Expeditions of Discovery in North-Western Australia* (2 vols), London, Boone.

Grote, George (1851) (3rd edition) *History of Greece*, London, John Murray.

Gruber, Howard E. (1974) *Darwin on Man: A Psychological Study of Scientific Creativity*, New York, E. P. Dutton.

Haddon, A. C. (1904) Preface to *Reports of the Cambridge Anthropological Expedition to Torres Straits*, Vol. V, Cambridge, Cambridge University Press.

Haddon, A. C. and Rivers, W. H. R. (1904) 'Totemism', in *Reports of the Cambridge Anthropological Expedition to Torres Straits*, Vol. V, Cambridge, Cambridge University Press, pp. 151–93.

Hall, Edith (1989) *Inventing the Barbarian: Greek Self-definition through Tragedy*, New York: Oxford University Press.

Hall, Edith (1996) 'Commentary', *Aeschylus Persians*, Oxford, Aris & Phillips.

Hartog, François (1988) *The Mirror of Herodotus: The Representation of the Other in the Writing of History*, Berkeley, CA, University of California Press (first published in French, 1980).

Haven, Samuel F. (1856) 'Archaeology of the United States', *Smithsonian Contributions to Knowledge*, viii, pp. 1–168.

Hazelwood, Nick (2000) *Savage: The Life and Times of Jemmy Button*, London: Hodder & Stoughton.

Héritier, F. (1981) *L'exercice de la parenté*, Paris, Gallimard.

Herle, Anita and Rouse, Sandra (eds) (1998) *Cambridge and the Torres Strait: Centenary Essays on the 1898 Anthropological Expedition*, Cambridge, Cambridge University Press.

Herskovits, M. (1953) *Franz Boas: The Science of Man in the Making*, New York, Scribner.

Hiatt, L. R. (1996) *Arguments about Aborigines*, Cambridge, Cambridge University Press.

Hinsley, Curtis M., Jr (1981) *Savages and Scientists: The Smithsonian Institution and the Development of American Anthropology*, 1846–1910, Washington, DC, Smithsonian Institution Press.

Hitchcock, Robert K. (2002) *Botswana*, manuscript.

Hitchcock, Robert K. (2002) '"We are the first people": land, natural resources, and identity in the Central Kalahari, Botswana', manuscript.

Hobbes, Thomas (1651) *Leviathan*, London, Andrew Crooke.

Hodgen, Margaret T. (1964) *Early Anthropology in the Sixteenth and Seventeenth Centuries*, Philadelphia, PA, University of Pennsylvania Press.

Hodson, T. C. (1925) 'Notes on the marriage of cousins in India', *Man in India*, v, pp. 163–75.

Hopper, K. Theodore (1998) *The Mid-Victorian Generation: 1846–1886*, Oxford, Oxford University Press.

Hornblower, Simon (1991) *A Commentary on Thucydides Volume 1: Books I–III*, Oxford, Oxford University Press.

Hornblower, Simon (2004) 'Herodotus', in Adam Kuper and Jessica Kuper (eds) *The Social Science Encyclopedia*, 3rd edition, London: Routledge.

Howitt, A. W. and Fison, L. (1885) 'On the deme and the horde', *Journal of the Anthropological Institute*, 14, pp. 142–69.

Hudson, Winthrop S. (1965) *Religion in America*, New York, Scribner.

Humphreys, Sally (1983) *Family, Women and Death: Comparative Studies*, London, Routledge.

Innes, Larry (2004) Review of Colin Sampson, *A Way of Life That Does Not Exist*, *Anthropology and Education Quarterly*, Vol. 35, no. 4.

Jakobson, Roman (1944) 'Frank Boas' approach to language', *International Journal of American Linguistics*, 101, pp. 188–95.

Jhering, R. (1852–1864) *Geist des Römischen Rechts auf den Verschiedenen Stufen seiner Entwicklung* (4 vols), Leipzig.

Johnson, Christopher (2003) *Claude Lévi-Strauss: The Formative Years*, Cambridge, Cambridge University Press.

Johnson, Gordon (1991) 'India and Henry Maine', in Alan Diamond (ed.) *The Victorian Achievement of Henry Maine*, Cambridge, Cambridge University Press.

Jones, R. A. (1977) 'On understanding a sociological classic', *American Journal of Sociology*, 83, pp. 279–319.

Jones, R. A. (1981) 'Robertson Smith, Durkheim, and sacrifice: an historical context for *The Elementary Forms of the Religious Life*', *Journal of the History of the Behavioral Sciences*, 17, pp. 184–205.

Jones, R. A. (1985) 'Durkheim, totemism and the Intichiuma', *History of Sociology*, 5, 2, pp. 79–89.

Jones, R. A. (1986) 'Durkheim, Frazer and Smith: the role of analogies and exemplars in the development of Durkheim's theory of religion', *American Journal of Sociology*, 92, 3, pp. 596–624.

Jones, R. A. (1993). 'Durkheim and La Cité antique: An Essay on the Origins of Durkheim's Sociology of Religion', in S. P. Turner (ed.) *Émile Durkheim: Sociologist and Moralist*, London, Routledge.

Jones, W. R. (1971) 'The image of the barbarian in medieval Europe,' *Comparative Studies in History and Society*, 23, 4, pp. 376–407.

de Josselin de Jong, J. P. B. (1935) *De Maleische Archipel als Ethnologisch Studieveld*, Leiden, The Netherlands (a translation has been published in P. E. de Josselin de Jong (1977) *Structural Anthropology in the Netherlands*, The Hague, Martinus Nijhoff).

de Josselin de Jong, J. P. B. (1952) *Lévi-Strauss's Theory on Kinship and Marriage*, Leiden, Brill (reprinted in P. E. de Josselin de Jong (1977) *Structural Anthropology in the Netherlands*, The Hague, Martinus Nijhoff).

de Josselin de Jong, P. E. (ed.) (1977) *Structural Anthropology in the Netherlands*, The Hague, Martinus Nijhoff.

de Josselin de Jong, P. E. (ed.) (1984) *Unity in Diversity: Indonesia as a Field of Anthropological Study*, Dordrecht, Foris.

Kaberry, Phyllis (1967) 'The plasticity of New Guinea kinship', in M. Freedman (ed.) *Social Organization*, London, Cass.

Kantorowicz, H. (1937) 'Savigny and the historical school of law', *The Law Quarterly Review*, L111, pp. 330–43.

Karady, V. (ed.) (1969) *Marcel Mauss, Oeuvres:* Vol. 3, *Cohésion sociale et division de la sociologie*, Paris, Les Èditions de Minuit.

Karady, V. (ed.) (1975) *Emile Durkheim, Textes:* Vol. 2, *Religion, morale, anomie*; Vol. 3, *Functions sociales et institutions;* Paris, Les éditions de Minuit.

Karady, V. (1981) 'French ethnology and the Durkheimian breakthrough', *Journal of the Anthropological Society of Oxford*, xiii, 3, pp. 165–76.

Kehoe, Alice (1994) 'Primal Gaia: primitivists and plastic medicine men', in J. Cifton (ed.) *The Invented Indian: Cultural Fictions and Government Policies*, Somerset, NJ, Transaction Books.

Kemble, J. M. (1849) *The Saxons in England* (2 vols), London, Longman.

Keynes, R. D. (ed.) (1979) *The Beagle Record*, Cambridge: Cambridge University Press.

Keynes, R. D. (ed.) (1988) *Charles Darwin's Beagle Diary*, Cambridge, Cambridge University Press.

Klein, Richard (1989) *The Human Career: Human Biological and Cultural Origins*, Chicago, University of Chicago Press.

Kluckhohn, Clyde and Prufer, Olaf (1959) 'Influences during the formative years', in Walter Goldschmidt (ed.) *The Anthropology of Franz Boas*, Memoir no. 89 of the American Anthropological Association, Washington, DC, pp. 4–28.

Koepping, Klaus-Peter (1983) *Adolf Bastian and the Psychic Unity of Mankind: The Foundations of Anthropology in Nineteenth Century Germany*, St Lucia, University of Queensland Press.

Köhler, Josef (1975) *On the Prehistory of Marriage: Totems, Group Marriage, Mother Right*, Chicago, University of Chicago Press (first German edition, 1897).

Krader, Lawrence (1974) *The Ethnological Notebooks of Karl Marx*, Assen, Van Gorcum.

Krader, Lawrence (1975) *The Asiatic Mode of Production*, Assen, Van Gorcum.

Kroeber, Alfred (1909) 'Classificatory systems of relationship', *Journal of the Royal Anthropological Institute*, 39, pp. 77–84.

Kroeber, Alfred (1919) 'Zuni kin and clan', *Anthropological Papers of the American Museum of Natural History*, 18, pp. 39–205.

Kroeber, Alfred (1920) Review of Robert Lowie's *Primitive Society*, *American Anthropologist*, 22, pp. 377–81.

Kroeber, Theodora (1970) *Alfred Kroeber: A Personal Configuration*, Berkeley, CA, University of California Press.

Kuper, Adam (1975) 'Preferential marriage and polygyny among the Tswana', in Meyer Fortes and Sheila Patterson (eds) *Studies in African Social Anthropology*, London, Academic Press.

Kuper, Adam (1989) 'Radcliffe-Brown and Rivers: a correspondence', *Canberra Anthropology*, 11, 1, pp. 49–81.

Kuper, Adam (1994) *The Chosen Primate*, Cambridge, MA, Harvard University Press.

Kuper, Adam (1996) *Anthropology and Anthropologists: The Modern British School*, 3rd edition, London, Routledge.

Kuper, Adam (1999) *Culture: The Anthropologists' Account*, Cambridge, MA, Harvard University Press.

Kuper, Adam (2003) 'The return of the native', *Current Anthropology*, 44, 3, pp. 389–402.

Langham, Ian (1981) *The Building of British Social Anthropology: W. H. R. Rivers and his Cambridge Disciples in the Development of Kinship Studies, 1898–1931*, Dordrecht, D. Reidel.

Langness, L. L. (1964) 'Some problems in the conceptualization of Highlands social structures', *American Anthropologist*, 66, 3, Part 2, pp. 162–82.

Layard, John (1942) *Stone Men of Malekula*, London, Chatto & Windus.

Leach, E. R. (1951) 'The structural implications of matrilateral cross-cousin marriage', *Journal of the Royal Anthropological Institute*, 81, pp. 54–104.

Leach, E. R. (1954) *Political Systems of Highland Burma*, London, Athlone Press.

Leach, E. R. (1957) 'Aspects of bride wealth and marriage stability among the Kachin and Lakher', *Man*, 57, pp. 50–5.

Leach, E. R. (1961) *Pul Eliya*, Cambridge, Cambridge University Press.

Leach, E. R. (1961) *Rethinking Anthropology*, London, Athlone Press.

Leach, E. R. (1962) 'On certain unconsidered aspects of double descent systems', *Man*, 62, pp. 130–4.

Lee, Richard B. (1979) *The !Kung San: Men, Women, and Work in a Foraging Society*, Cambridge, Cambridge University Press.

Lee, Richard B. and Irven DeVore (eds) (1968) *Man the Hunter*, New York, Aldine.

Leopold, J. (1980) *Culture in Comparative and Evolutionary Perspective: E. B. Tylor and the Making of Primitive Culture*, Berlin, D. Reimer.

Le Play, Frédéric (1884) *L'Organisation de la famille, selon le vrai modèle signalé par l'histoire de toutes les races et de tous les temps*, Paris.

Letourneau, Charles (1888) *L'évolution du mariage et de la famille*, Paris, Delahaye et Lecrosnier.

Lévi-Strauss, Claude (1962) *Totemism*, London, Merlin Press (original French edition, 1962).

Lévi-Straus, Claude (1963) *Structural Anthropology*, Boston, Basic Books (original French edition, 1958).

Lévi-Strauss, Claude (1965) 'The future of kinship studies', *Proceedings of the Royal Anthropological Institute for 1965*, pp. 13–22.

Lévi-Strauss, Claude (1966) *The Savage Mind*, London, Weidenfeld & Nicolson (original French edition, 1962).

Lévi-Strauss, Claude (1969) *The Elementary Structures of Kinship*, Boston, Beacon Press (original French edition, 1949. The translation is based mainly on the second French edition, published in 1967).

Lévi-Strauss, Claude (1973) *Tristes tropiques*, London, Cape (original French edition, 1955).

Lévi-Strauss, Claude (1978) *Structural Anthropology 2*, Harmondworth, Penguin Books (original French edition, 1973).

Lévi-Strauss, Claude (1981) *The Naked Man*, London, Cape (original French edition, 1971).

Lévi-Strauss, Claude (1983) *Introduction to the Work of Marcel Mauss*, London, Routledge & Kegan Paul (original French publication, 1966).

Locke, John (1690) *Two Treatise of Civil Government*, London, Awnsham and Churchill.

Lovejoy, A. O. and Boas, G. (1935) *Primitivism and Related Ideas in Antiquity*, Baltimore, MD: Johns Hopkins University Press.

Lowie, Robert (1914) 'Social organization', *American Journal of Sociology*, 20, pp. 68–97.

Lowie, Robert (1915) 'Exogamy and the classificatory systems of relationships', *American Anthropologist*, 17, pp. 223–39.

Lowie, Robert (1920) *Primitive Society*, New York, Boni & Liveright.

Lowie, Robert (1924) *Primitive Religion*, New York, Boni & Liveright.

Lowie, Robert (1927) *The Origin of the State*, New York, Harcourt Brace.

Lowie, Robert (1947) 'Franz Boas', *Biographical Memoirs*, National Academy of Science, 25, pp. 303–22.

Lowie, Robert (1948) *Social Organization*, New York, Rinehart & Co.

Lowie, Robert (1956) 'Reminiscences of anthropological currents in America half a century ago', *American Anthropologist*, 58, pp. 955–1016.

Lubbock, J. (1865) *Prehistoric Times*, London, Williams & Norgate.

Lubbock, J. (1870) *The Origin of Civilization and the Primitive Condition of Man*, London, Longman.

Lukes, S. (1973) *Émile Durkheim: His Life and Work*, London, Allen Lane.

MacClancy, Jeremy (1986) 'Unconventional character and disciplinary convention: John Layard, Jungian and anthropologist', in G. W. Stocking (ed.) *Malinowski, Rivers, Benedict and Others: Essays on Culture and Personality, History of Anthropology*, Vol. 4, Madison, WI, University of Wisconsin Press.

McIlvaine, J. S. (1867) 'Malthusianism', *The Biblical Repertory and Princeton Review*, xxxix, pp. 103–28.

McIlvaine, J. S. (1923) 'The life and works of Lewis H. Morgan, LL.D.: an address at his funeral', *Rochester Historical Society Publication Fund*, Series 2, pp. 47–60.

McKelvey, Blake (1946) 'When science was on trial in Rochester: 1850–1890', *Rochester History*, VIII, 4, pp. 1–24.

McLennan, Donald (1885) *The Patriarchal Theory* ('based on the papers of the late John Ferguson McLennan'), London, Macmillan.

McLennan, J. M. (1865) *Primitive Marriage: an Inquiry into the Origin of the Form of Capture in Marriage Ceremonies*, Edinburgh, Black.

McLennan, J. M. (1868) 'Totemism', in *Chambers' Encyclopaedia*, London, Chambers.

McLennan, J. M. (1869–1870) 'The worship of animals and plants', *The Fortnightly Review*, 6, pp. 407–582; 7, pp. 194–216.

McLennan, J. M. (1876) *Studies in Ancient History*, London, Quaritch.

Mailhot, José (1999) 'The Innu of Quebec and Labrador', in Richard B. Lee and Richard Daly (eds) *The Cambridge Encyclopedia of Hunters and Gatherers*, Cambridge, Cambridge University Press.

Maine, Henry Sumner (1861) *Ancient Law*, London, John Murray.

Maine, Henry Sumner (1871) *Village Communities in the East and West*, London, John Murray.

Maine, Henry Sumner (1875) *Lectures on the Early History of Institutions*, London, John Murray.

Maine, Henry Sumner (1883) *Dissertations on Early Law and Custom*, London, John Murray.

Maine, Henry Sumner (1885) *Popular Government*, London, John Murray.

Malinowski, Bronislaw (1913) *The Family Among the Australian Aborigines*, London, University of London Press.

Malinowski, Bronislaw (1927) *The Father in Primitive Psychology*, London, Routledge & Kegan Paul.

Malinowski, Bronislaw (1929) *The Sexual Life of Savages*, London, Routledge & Kegan Paul.

Malinowski, Bronislaw (1930) 'Kinship', *Man*, 30, pp. 19–29.

Malinowski, Bronislaw (1935) *Coral Gardens and Their Magic*, London, Allen & Unwin.

Malthus, Thomas (1798) *An Essay on the Principle of Population*, London, Johnson.

Mannhardt, Wilhelm (1875) *Der Baumkultus der Germanen und ihrer Nachbarstämme*, Berlin, Borntröger.

Marett, R. R. (1936) *Tylor*, London, Chapman & Hall.

Marett, R. R. and Penniman, T. K. (eds) (1932) *Spencer's Scientific Correspondence with Sir J. G. Frazer*, Oxford, Clarendon Press.

Mark, Joan (1980) *Four Anthropologists: An American Science in its Early Years*, New York, Science History Publications.

Marwick M. (1965) *Sorcery in its Social Setting*, Manchester, Manchester University Press.

Mason, Ronald J. (2000) 'Initial shield woodland', in Peter N. Peregrine and Melvin Ember (eds) *Encyclopedia of Prehistory* Vol. 2, *Arctic and Subarctic*, New York, Kluwer.

Mauss, Marcel (1990) *The Gift: The Form and Reason for Exchange in Archaic Societies*, London: Routledge (original French publication, 1924).

Mayr, Ernst (1959) 'Agassiz, Darwin and evolution', *Harvard Library Bulletin*, xiii, 2, pp. 165–94.

Mayr, Ernst (1982) *The Growth of Biological Thought*, Cambridge, MA, Belknap Press.

Meek, Ronald L. (1975) *Social Science and the Ignoble Savage*, Cambridge, Cambridge University Press.

Meggitt, M. J. (1965) *The Lineage System of the Mae-Enga of New Guinea*, London, Oliver & Boyd.

Meillassoux, Claude (1981) *Maidens, Meal and Money. Capitalism and the Domestic Community*, Cambridge, Cambridge University Press (first French publication, 1975).

Meinhard, H. (1975) 'The patrilineal principle in early Teutonic kinship', in J. Beattie and R. Lienhardt (eds) *Studies in Social Anthropology*, Oxford, Clarendon Press.

Middleton, John and Tait, David (eds) (1958) *Tribes without Rulers*, London, Routledge & Kegan Paul.

Mill, James (1817) *The History of British India* (3 vols), London, Baldwin.

Mill, J. S. (1871) 'Mr Maine on village communities', *Fortnightly Review*, ix, pp. 543–56.

Momigliano, A. D. (1994) 'The ancient city of Fustel de Coulanges', in G. W. Bowersock and T. J. Cornell (eds) *A. D. Momigliano: Studies on Modern Scholarship*. (First published in Italian, 1970.)

Montaigne, Michel de (1943)*The Complete Works of Montaigne*, translated by Donald M. Frame, Stanford, CA, Stanford University Press (first published in French, 1588).

Montesquieu, Charles de Secondat, Baron de, 1914, *The Spirit of the Laws*, translated by Thomas Nugent, revised by J. V. Prichard, London, G. Bell & Sons (first French publication, 1748).

Moore, James R. (1979) *The Post-Darwinian Controversies: A Study of the Protestant Struggle to Come to Terms with Darwin in Great Britain and America 1870–1900*, Cambridge, Cambridge University Press.

Morgan, Lewis H. (1851) *League of the Ho-de-no sau nee, or Iroquois*, Rochester, NY, Sage & Bros.

Morgan, Lewis H. (1868) *The American Beaver and his Works*, Philadelphia, PA, J. Lippincott.

Morgan, Lewis H. (1868) 'A conjectural solution of the origin of the classificatory system of relationship', *Proceedings of the American Academy of Arts and Sciences*, vii, pp. 436–77.

Morgan, Lewis H. (1871) *Systems of Consanguinity and Affinity of the Human Family*, Smithsonian Contributions to Knowledge, 218, Washington, DC, Smithsonian Institute.

Morgan, Lewis H. (1877) *Ancient Society: Researches in the Lines of Human Progress from Savagery through Barbarism to Civilization*, New York, Holt.

Müller, Max (1861) *Lectures on the Science of Language*, London, Longman.

Mulvaney, D. J. and Calaby, J. H. (1984) *'So Much That is New': Baldwin Spencer, A Biography*, Melbourne, Melbourne University Press.

Murdock, G. P. (1949) *Social Structure*, New York, Macmillan.

Needham, Rodney (1962) *Structure and Sentiment*, Chicago, University of Chicago Press.

Needham, Rodney (1971) 'Introduction' and 'Remarks on the analysis of kinship and marriage' in Rodney Needham (ed.) *Rethinking Kinship and Marriage*, London, Tavistock, pp. xiii–cxvii, and 1–3.

Nuttall, Mark (1998) *Protecting the Arctic: Indigenous Peoples and Cultural Survival*, Amsterdam, Harwood.

Omura, Keiichi (2002) 'Construction of *Inuinnaqtun* (Real Inuit Way): self-image and everyday practices in Inuit society', in Henry Stewart, Alan Barnard and Keiichi Omura (eds) *Self-and-Other-Images of Hunter-Gatherers*, Osaka, Senri Ethnological Studies.

Orlove, Benjamin S. (1980) 'Ecological anthropology', *Annual Review of Anthropology*, 9, pp. 235–73.

Pace, David (1983) *Lévi-Strauss, The Bearer of Ashes*, London, Routledge & Kegan Paul.

Pagden, Anthony (1982) *The Fall of Natural Man: The American Indian and the Origins of Comparative Ethnology*, Cambridge, Cambridge University Press.

Pederson, H. (1959) *The Discovery of Language: Linguistic Science in the Nineteenth Century*, Bloomington, Indiana University Press.

Peel, J. D. Y. (1971) *Herbert Spencer: The Evolution of a Sociologist*, London, Heinemann.

Peel, J. D. Y. (ed.) (1972) *Herbert Spencer on Social Evolution*, Chicago, University of Chicago Press.

Plaice, Evelyn (1990) *The Native Game: Settler Perception of Indian/Settler Relations in Central Labrador*, St John's, Newfoundland, Institute of Social and Economic Research, Memorial University of Newfoundland.

Plaice, Evelyn (2003) Comment on Adam Kuper, 'The return of the native', *Current Anthropology*, 44, 3, pp. 396–7.

Quiggin, A. Hingston (1942) *Haddon the Head-Hunter*, Cambridge, Cambridge University Press.

Radcliffe-Brown, A. R. (1910) 'Marriage and descent in North Australia', *Man*, 32, pp. 55–7.

Radcliffe-Brown, A. R. (1912) 'Marriage and descent in North and Central Australia', *Man*, 64, pp. 123–4.

Radcliffe-Brown, A. R. (1913) 'Three tribes of Western Australia', *Journal of the Royal Anthropological Institute*, 43, pp. 143–94.

Ratcliffe-Brown, A. R. (1914) 'The definition of totemism', *Anthropos*, 9, 622–30.

Radcliffe-Brown, A. R. (1914) Review of *The Family among the Australian Aborigines* by B. Malinowski, *Man*, xiv, 16, pp. 31–2.

Radcliffe-Brown, A. R. (1918) 'Notes on the social organization of Australian tribes: Part I, *Journal of the Royal Anthropological Institute*, 48, pp. 222–53.

Radcliffe-Brown, A. R. (1923) 'Notes on the social organization of Australian tribes: Part II', *Journal of the Royal Anthropological Institute*, 53, pp. 424–47.

Radcliffe-Brown, A. R. (1927) 'The regulation of marriage in Ambrym', *Journal of the Royal Anthropological Institute*, 57, pp. 343–8.

Radcliffe-Brown, A. R. (1929) 'A further note on Ambrym', *Man*, 29, pp. 50–3.

Radcliffe-Brown, A. R. (1931) *The Social Organization of the Australian Tribes*, Sydney, Oceania Monographs no. 1; originally published in *Oceania*, 1, 1–4, pp. 34–63, 206–46, 322–41 and 426–56 (1930–1931).

Radcliffe-Brown, A. R. (1935) 'Patrilineal and matrilineal succession', *Iowa Law Review*, 20, 286–303.

Radcliffe-Brown, A. R. and Forde, D (eds) (1950) *African Systems of Kinship and Marriage*, London, Oxford University Press for the International African Institute.

Radin, Paul (1958) 'Robert H. Lowie: 1883–1957', *American Anthropologist*, 60, pp. 356–75.

Ratzel, F. (1885–1890) *Völkerkunde* (3 vols), Leipzig, Bibliographisches Institut.

Resek, Carl (1960) *Lewis Henry Morgan: American Scholar*, Chicago, University of Chicago Press.

Rey, Pierre-Philippe (1975) 'The lineage mode of production', *Critique of Anthropology*, 3, pp. 27–9.

Rey, Pierre-Philippe (1979) 'Class contradiction in lineage societies', *Critique of Anthropology*, 4, pp. 41–60.

Richards, A. I. (1941) 'A problem of anthropological approach', *Bantu Studies*, 15, 1, pp. 45–52.

Richards, F. J. (1914) 'Cross-cousin marriage in South India', *Man*, xiv, pp. 194–8.

Rivers, W. H. R. (1904) 'Kinship' and 'The regulation of marriage', in *Reports of the Cambridge Anthropological Expedition to Torres Straits*, Vol. V, Cambridge, Cambridge University Press.

Rivers, W. H. R. (1906) *The Todas*, London, Macmillan.

Rivers, W. H. R. (1907) 'On the origin of the classificatory system of relationships', Balfour *et al.*, *Anthropological Essays Presented to Edward Burnett Tylor*, Oxford, Clarendon Press.

Rivers, W. H. R. (1908) 'Genealogies, kinship, regulation of marriage, social organization', in *Sociology, Magic, and Religion of the Eastern Islanders*, Reports of the Cambridge Anthropological Expedition to the Torres Straits, Cambridge, Cambridge University Press.

Rivers, W. H. R. (1910) 'The genealogical method of anthropological inquiry', *Sociological Review*, 3, pp. 1–12.

Rivers, W. H. R. (1911) 'The ethnological analysis of culture', presidential address to Section H of the British Association for the Advancement of Science' *Nature*, 87, pp. 356–60.

Rivers, W. H. R. (1914) 'Is Australian culture simple or complex?', *Reports of the British Association for the Advancement of Science.*

Rivers, W. H. R. (1914) *Kinship and Social Organization*, London, Constable.

Rivers, W. H. R. (1914) *The History of Melanesian Society* (2 vols), Cambridge, Cambridge University Press.

Rivers, W. H. R. (1915) 'Descent and ceremonial in Ambrym', *Journal of the Royal Anthropological Institute*, 45, pp. 229–33.

Rivers, W. H. R. (1924) *Social Organization* (ed. W. J. Perry), London, Kegan Paul.

Rivière, Peter (1970) Introduction to *Primitive Marriage* by John McLennan, Chicago, University of Chicago Press.

Robertson, William [1777] (1820) *The History of the Discovery and Settlement of America*, London, J. Haddon.

Robertson Smith, W. (1880) 'Animal worship and the animal tribes among the Arabs and in the Old Testament', *The Journal of Philology*, 9, pp. 75–100.

Robertson Smith, W. (1885) *Kinship and Marriage in Early Arabia*, Cambridge, Cambridge University Press.

Robertson Smith, W. (1889) *Lectures on the Religion of the Semites*, Edinburgh, A. & C. Black.

Robins, Steven (2001) 'NGOs, "Bushmen", and double vision: the ‡Khomani San land claim and the cultural politics of "community" and "development" in the Kalahari', *Journal of Southern African Studies*, 27, pp. 833–53.

Robins, Steven (2001) 'Whose "culture"? Whose "survival"?', in Alan Barnard and Justin Kenrich (eds) *Africa's Indigenous Peoples*, Edinburgh, Centre of African Studies, University of Edinburgh.

Rohner, Ronald P. (ed.) (1969) *The Ethnography of Franz Boas*, Chicago, University of Chicago Press.

Ross, Robert (1976) *Adam Kok's Griquas*, Cambridge, Cambridge University Press.

Roulet, Florence (1999) *Human Rights and Indigenous Peoples*, Copenhagen, International Workgroup for Indigenous Affairs, Document 92.

Rouse, Sandra (1998) 'Expedition and institution: A. C. Haddon and anthropology at Cambridge', in Anita Herle and Sandra Rouse (eds) *Cambridge and the Torres Strait: Centenary Essays on the 1898 Anthropological Expedition*, Cambridge, Cambridge University Press.

Sahlins, Marshall (1958) *Social Stratification in Polynesia*, Ann Arbor, MI, University of Michigan Press.

Sahlins, Marshall (1960) 'Evolution: specific and general' in Marshall Sahlins and Elman R. Service (eds) *Evolution and Culture*, Ann Arbor, MI, University of Michigan Press.

Sahlins, Marshall (1965) 'On the ideology and composition of descent groups', *Man*, 65, pp. 104–7.

Sahlins, Marshall (1968) *Tribesmen*, Englewood Cliffs, NJ, Prentice-Hall.

Sahlins, Marshall (1972) *Stone Age Economics*, Chicago, Aldine.

Samson, Colin (2001) 'Rights as the reward for simulating cultural sameness: The Innu in the Canadian colonial context', in Jane K. Cowan, Marie-Bénédicte Dembour, and Richard A. Wilson (eds) *Culture and Rights: Anthropological Perspectives*, Cambridge, Cambridge University Press.

Samson, Colin (2003) *A Way of Life That Does Not Exist: Canada and the Extinguishment of the Innu*, London, Verso.

Savigny, F. K. (1834–1835) *Die Geschichte des Römischen Rechts in Mittelalter* (7 vols), Heidelberg, Mohr.

Scheffler, Harold W. (1970) 'Ambrym revisited: a preliminary report', *Southwestern Journal of Anthropology*, 26, pp. 52–65.

Scheffler, Harold W. (1978) *Australian Kin Classification*, Cambridge, Cambridge University Press.

Schneider, David M. (1968) 'Rivers and Kroeber in the study of kinship', in W. H. R. Rivers, *Kinship and Social Organization*, London School of Economics Monographs on Social Anthropology, London, Athlone Press, pp. 7–16.

Service, Elman R. (1962) *Primitive Social Organization: An Evolutionary Perspective*, New York, Random House.

Service, Elman R. (1966) *The Hunters*, Englewood Cliffs, NJ, Prentice-Hall.

Silberbauer, George (1965) *Bushman Survey Report*, Gaberones, Bechualand Government.

Slobodin, Richard (1978) *W. H. R. Rivers*, New York, Columbia University Press.

Smith, M. (1985) 'Four Germans jurists', *Political Science Quarterly*, x, 4, pp. 664–92.

Snow, Dean R. (1996) 'The first Americans and the differentiation of hunter-gatherer cultures', in Bruce Trigger and Wilcomb E. Washburn (eds) *The Cambridge History of the Native Peoples of the Americas*, Vol. 1, Cambridge, Cambridge University Press.

Southall, A. (1953) *Alur Society: A Study in Processes and Types of Domination*, Cambridge, Heffers.

Speck, F. G. (1915) 'The family hunting band as the basis of Algonkian social organization', *American Anthropologist*, 17, pp. 289–305.

Speck, F. G. (1915) *Family Hunting and Social Life of Various Algonkian Bands of the Ottawa Valley*, Ottawa, Geological Survey, Canada, Memoir 70, no. 8, Anthropological series.

Spencer, Baldwin (1928) *Wanderings in Wild Australia*, 2 vols, London, Macmillan.

Spencer, Baldwin and Gillen, F. J. (1904) *The Northern Tribes of Central Australia*, London, Macmillan.

Speth, William W. (1978) 'The anthropogeographic theory of Franz Boas', *Anthropos*, 73, pp. 1–31.

Srinivas, M. N. (1975) 'The Indian village: myth and reality', in J. Beattie and R. Lienhardt (eds) *Studies in Social Anthropology*, Oxford, Clarendon Press.

Stanton, William (1960) *The Leopard's Spots: Scientific Attitudes toward Race in America 1815–1859*, Chicago, University of Chicago Press.

Starobinski, Jean (1993) 'The word *civilisation*' in *Blessings in Disguise: Or the Morality of Evil*, Cambridge MA, Harvard University Press.

Stein, Peter (1980) *Legal Evolution: The Story of an Idea*, Cambridge, Cambridge University Press.

Stern, Bernard J. (ed.) (1930) 'Selections from the letters of Lorimer Fison and A. W. Howitt to Lewis Henry Morgan', *American Anthropologist*, 32, pp. 257–453.

Stern, Bernard J. (1931) *Lewis Henry Morgan: Social Evolutionist*, Chicago, University of Chicago Press.

Steward, Julian H. (1936) 'The economic and social basis of primitive bands', in Robert Lowie (ed.) *Essays in Anthropology Presented to A. L. Kroeber*, Berkeley, CA, University of California Press.

Steward, Julian H. (1955) *Theory of Culture Change*, Urbana, IL, University of Illinois Press.

Stewart, Henry (2000) 'Ethnonyms and images: genesis of the "Inuit" and image manipulation', in Henry Stewart, Alan Barnard and Keiichi Omura (eds) *Self-and-Other-Images of Hunter-Gatherers*, Osaka, Senri Ethnological Studies.

Stocking, George W., Jr (1968) *Race, Culture, and Evolution: Essays in the History of Anthropology*, New York, The Free Press.

Stocking, George W., Jr (ed.) (1974) *A Franz Boas Reader: The Shaping of American Anthropology, 1883–1911*, Chicago, University of Chicago Press.

Stocking, George W., Jr (1983) 'The ethnographer's magic: fieldwork in British anthropology from Tylor to Malinowski', in G. Stocking (ed.) *Observers Observed: Essays in Ethnographic Fieldwork*, Madison, WI, University of Wisconsin Press.

Stocking, George W., Jr (1987) *Victorian Anthropology*, New York, The Free Press.

Stocking, George W., Jr (1995) *After Tylor: British Social Anthopology 1888–1951*, Madison, WI, Wisconsin University Press.

Stokes, E. (1959) *The English Utilitarians and India*, Oxford, Clarendon Press.

Stokes, W. (1892) *Life and Speeches of Sir Henry Maine*, London, John Murray.

Suzman, James (2003) 'Kalahari conundrums: relocation, resistance and international support in the Central Kalahari Botswana, *Before Farming* 2002/3_4 (12) pp. 1–10 (Internet journal, www.waspjournals.com).

Suzman, James (2003) Comment on Adam Kuper, 'The return of the native', *Current Anthropology*, 44, 3, pp. 399–400.

Swanton, John R. (1904) 'The development of the clan system and of secret societies among the Northwestern tribes', *American Anthropologist*, 6, pp. 477–85.

Swanton, John R. (1905) 'The social organization of American tribes', *American Anthropologist*, 7, pp. 663–73.

Swanton, John R. (1906) 'A reconstruction of the theory of social organization', B. Laufer (ed.) *Anthropological Papers Written in Honor of Franz Boas*, New York, Stechert, pp. 166–78.

Thucydides [431 BCE] (1954) *History of the Peloponnesian War*, Harmondsworth, Penguin Books.

Trautmann, Thomas R. (1987) *Lewis Henry Morgan and the Invention of Kinship*, Berkeley, CA, University of California Press.

Tylor, E. B. (1865) *Researches into the Early History of Mankind and the Development of Civilization*, London, John Murray.
Tylor, E. B. (1866) 'The religion of savages', *The Fortnightly Review*, 6, pp. 71–86.
Tylor, E. B. (1871) *Primitive Culture* (2 vols.) London, John Murray.
Tylor, E. B. (1881) Obituary of McLennan, *The Academy*, xx, pp. 9–10.
Tylor, E. B. (1889) 'On a method of investigating the development of institutions; applied to laws of marriage and descent', *Journal of the Anthropological Institute*, 18, pp. 245–72.
Tylor, E. B. (1899) 'Remarks on totemism, with especial reference to some modern theories respecting it', *Journal of the Anthropological Institute* (ns) 1, pp. 138–48.
Urry, James (1982) 'From zoology to ethnology: A. C. Haddon's conversion to anthropology', *Canberra Anthropology*, 5, 2, pp. 58–85.
Urry, James (1985) 'W. E. Armstrong and social anthropology at Cambridge, 1922–1926', *Man*, 20, pp. 412–33.
Vinogradoff, P. (1892) *Villainage in England*, Oxford, Clarendon Press.
Vinogradoff, P. (1904) *The Teaching of Sir Henry Maine*, London, Frowde.
Vogt, W. P. (1976) 'The use of studying primitives: a note on the Durkheimians, 1890–1940', *History and Theory*, 15, pp. 33–44.
Waldman, Linda (2001) 'No rainbow bus for us: building nationalism in South Africa', in Alan Barnard and Justin Kenrich (eds) *Africa's Indigenous Peoples*, Edinburgh, Centre of African Studies, University of Edinburgh.
Warner, W. L. (1937) *A Black Civilization: A Study of an Australian Tribe*, New York, Harper.
Wellhausen, Julius (1885) *Prolegomena to the History of Israel*, Edinburgh, Black (first German edition, 1883).
Westermarck, Edward (1891) *The History of Human Marriage*, London, Macmillan.
Westermarck, Edward (1927) *Memories of My Life*, London, Allen & Unwin.
White, Leslie A. (ed.) (1937) *Extracts from the European Travel Journal of Lewis Henry Morgan*, Rochester Historical Society Publications, XVI, pp. 219–389.
White, Leslie A. (1957) 'How Morgan came to write systems of consanguinity and affinity', *Papers of the Michigan Academy of Sciences, Arts, and Letters*, xlii, pp. 257–68.
White, Leslie A. (1959) *The Evolution of Culture*, New York, McGraw-Hill.
White, Leslie A. (1964) Introduction to *Ancient Society* by Lewis Henry Morgan, Cambridge, MA, Harvard University Press.
White, Leslie A. (1966) *The Social Organization of Ethnological Theory*, Houston, Rice University Studies, no. 52.
Wikman, K. Rob V. (ed.) (1940) *Letters from Edward B. Tylor and Alfred Russel Wallace to Edward Westermarck*, Proceedings, Åbo Akademi, Åbo, Finland.

Wilmsen, Edwin (1989) *Land Filled with Flies: A Political Economy of the Kalahari*, Chicago, University of Chicago Press.

Wilmsen, Edwin (ed.) (1989) *We are Here: Politics of Aboriginal Land Tenure*, Berkeley, CA, University of California Press.

Wilson, R. J. (ed.) (1967) *Darwin and the American Intellectuals*, Homewood, IL, Dorsey Press.

Wintroub, Michael (1998) 'Civilizing the savage and making a king: the royal entry festival of Henri II (Rouen 1550)', *Sixteenth Century Journal*, 29, 465–94.

Wolf, Eric (1966) *Peasants*, Englewood Cliffs, NJ, Prentice-Hall.

Wouden, F. A. E. van (1968) *Types of Social Structure in Eastern Indonesia*, The Hague, Martinus Nijhoff (first Dutch publication, 1935).

Young, Michael W. (ed.) (1979) *The Ethnography of Malinowski*, London, Routledge & Kegan Paul.

Young, Michael W. (2004) *Malinowski: Odyssey of an Anthropologist, 1884–1920*, New Haven, CT, Yale University Press.

Zwernemann, Jurgen (1983) *Culture History and African Anthropology: A Century of Research in Germany and Austria*, Uppsala, Uppsala Studies in Cultural Anthropology, no. 6.

Index

Acton, Lord 49
Aeschylus 22
Agassiz, Louis 60, 61, 72, 120
agnates 44, 52
Algonkian Indians 129
Amazonian Indians 9, 12, 204; see
   also Brazilian Indians
American Indians 7, 29, 35, 63–5,
   67–8, 70, 86, 128, 129; see
   also Algonkian; Iroquois;
   Kwakiutl; Zuni
Ambrym 144, 152–7; Deacon on
   154–7
animism 84–5, 86, 103
anti-globalisation movement xii,
   218
Aquinas, Thomas 26, 223
Aristotle 71; on barbarians 22; on
   politics 22, 25.
Armstrong, W.E. 153, 156, 159
Aryan see Indo–European
Ashanti 173–4
Athens, ancient 20–2, 62
Atkinson, J.J. 105–6
Auel, Jean 112
Austin, J. 40, 46, 47
Australian aborigines 7, 9, 76–7,
   86, 93, 204; Durkheim on 109,
   110–11; family among 104–5;
   kinship and marriage 93–7,
   102, 140, 144–7, 148–51, 182,
   83; Malinowski on 104–5, 149,
   157; and Melanesia 152,
   155–6; Radcliffe-Brown on

144–5, 148–51; and Rivers
   146–7; totemism among 93–7,
   99–101
Aztecs 76, 77

Bachofen, J. 3, 54, 55, 98
Baffin Island (formerly Baffin
   Land) 118
Bandelier, A. 77, 80
barbarian 18, 73, 75, 76, 79, 223;
   Aristotle on 22; Greeks and
   20–2; and language 25, 26;
   Montaigne on 23–4; Romans
   and 24–5, 26; and tyranny
   21–2
Barnard, Alan 9
Barnard, T.T. 153, 154, 156
Barnes, John 176–7, 178
Bateson, William 143
Bastian, Adolf 116–17, 118, 119,
   127, 128
Benedict, Ruth 115
Bentham, Jeremy 40, 42–3, 45–6,
   47, 48
Binford, L. 6
Boas, Franz 10, 103, 163, 181,
   198, 219, 221–2; assessed 132;
   on Baffin Island 118; biography
   115–21, 131–2; at Columbia
   university 120, 125–31, 135,
   147, 157; field methods 120–2;
   and Jesup expedition 137; on
   Kwakiutl 120–5; and Morgan
   115, 121–2, 124, 127, 128,

Related titles from Routledge

Anthropology and Anthropologists

The Modern British School (3rd edition)

Adam Kuper

> Its great merit is that it not only describes all major developments in method, theory and controversy; it also gives much biographical information about the persons responsible for those developments ... Kuper writes lucidly, economically, and occasionally with refreshing irreverence.
>
> *British Book News*

On its first publication in 1973 Adam Kuper's entertaining history of half a century of British social anthropology provoked strong reactions. But his often irreverent account soon established itself as one of *the* introductions to anthropology.

Since the second revised edition was published in 1983, important developments have occurred within British and European anthropology. This third enlarged and updated edition responds to these fresh currents. Adam Kuper takes the story up to the present day, and a new final chapter traces the emergence of a modern European social anthropology in contrast with the developments in American cultural Anthropology over the last two decades.

Anthropology and Anthropologists provides a critical historical account of modern British social anthropology: it describes the careers of the major theorists, their ideas and their contributions in the context of the intellectual and institutional environments in which they worked. It is essential reading for all students of social anthropology; it will also appeal to lay readers with an interest in the field.

Adam Kuper is Professor of Anthropology at Brunel University. He has taught at universities in Uganda, Britain, Sweden, Holland and the United States, and was the founding chairman of the European Association of Social Anthropologists. He is the author of a number of books on the history of anthropology and on African ethnography, including *The Invention of Primitive Society* (1988) and *The Chosen Primate* (1994).

Pbk: 0–415–11895–6

Available at all good bookshops
For ordering and further information please visit: www.routledge.com

Related titles from Routledge

Anthropology

The Basics

Peter Metcalf

The ultimate guide for the student encountering anthropology for the first time, *Anthropology: The Basics* explains and explores anthropological concepts and themes in a highly readable and easy to follow manner.

Making large, complex topics both accessible and enjoyable, Peter Metcalf argues that the issues anthropology deals with are all around us – in magazines, newspapers and on television. Engaging and immensely interesting, he tackles questions such as:

- What is anthropology?
- How can we distinguish cultural differences from physical ones?
- What is culture, anyway?
- How do anthropologists study culture?
- What are the key theories and approaches used today?
- How has the discipline changed over time?

A strong addition to this established and successful series, this exciting text presents students with an overview of the fundamental principles of anthropology, and also provides a useful guide for anyone wanting to learn more about a fascinating subject.

Hbk: 0–415–33119–6   Pbk: 0–415–33120–X

Available at all good bookshops
For ordering and further information please visit www.routledge.com

Arguing with Anthropology

An Introduction to Critical Theories of the Gift

Karen Sykes

It is something of a stroke of genius to make gift exchange the guiding thread of an introductory book ... Sykes introduces many of the most important debates that dominate anthropology today. As that rare book that accessibly introduces students to the discipline without talking down to them, I think this book will be widely used.

Joel Robbins, University of California San Diego

Arguing with Anthropology is a fresh and original guide to key elements in anthropology, which teaches the ability to think, write and argue critically. Through an exploration of the classic 'question of the gift', which functions in anthropology as a definitive example of the entire human experience, it provides a fascinating study course in anthropological methods, aims, knowledge and understanding. The book's unique approach takes gift-theory – the science of obligation and reciprocity – as the paradigm for a virtual enquiry which explores how the anthropological discipline has evolved historically, how it is applied in practice and how it can be argued with critically. By giving clear examples of real events and dilemmas, and asking students to participate in arguments about the form and nature of enquiry, it offers working practice of dealing with the obstacles and choices involved in anthropological study.

- From an experienced teacher whose methods are tried and tested
- Comprehensive and fun course for intermediate-level students
- Clearly defines the functions of anthropology, and its key theories and arguments
- Effectively teaches core study skills for exam success and progressive learning
- Draws on a rich variety of Pacific and global ethnography

Karen Sykes is a Senior Lecturer in Anthropology at the University of Manchester, where she teaches a popular introductory course in anthropology. She received her doctorate from Princeton University in 1995 and has conducted research in Melanesia since 1990.

Hbk: 0–415–25443–4   Pbk: 0–415–25444–2

Available at all good bookshops
For ordering and further information please visit: www.routledge.com